Tantra Goddess

D1418180

Tantra Goddess

A Memoir of Sexual Awakening

Caroline Muir

Monkfish Book Publishing Company

Rhinebeck, NY

Printed in the United States of America.
Book and cover design by Joe Tantillo.
Cover Photography: Monique Feil
www.moniquefeil.com

Monkfish Book Publishing Company
22 East Market Street, Suite 304
Rhinebeck, New York 12572
www.monkfishpublishing.com
USA 845-876-4861

ISBN 978-0-9823246-8-4

Library of Congress Cataloging-in-Publication Data:
Muir, Caroline.
Tantra goddess : a memoir of sexual awakening / Caroline Muir.
    p. cm.
ISBN 978-0-9823246-8-4 (pbk. : alk. paper)
1. Muir, Caroline--Sexual behavior. 2. Tantrism. I. Title.
BF1623.S4M82 2011
306.7092--dc23
[B]
                                        2011037910
Disclaimer:
Tantra Goddess is a personal memoir into intimacy during my years as a pioneer of tantrically-based sexual healing practices and learning the joys of sacred sexual love. Any reference to mind altering substances or to the inclusion of more than one sexual partner, is in no way required or recommended for the practice of Tantra Yoga. Our School and Institute are clearly against any use of alcohol or intoxicating substances during sexual healing classes and trainings.

This book is dedicated to my greatest teacher:

Acknowledgements

I wish to express my heartfelt gratitude to Will Block, my sweetheart and partner, for his patience and support during the five years of recapitulation of my life and loves. His loving acceptance of Charles Muir and our friendship as well as the work we have birthed has given me the courage to bring this book to you.

Deep gratitude to Suzanne Sherman, my patient and skilled writing consultant, editor, and dedicated friend for achieving the impossible out of what I sent her in the years I was learning how to use my Mac. She taught me that God is in the details, among many other things.

And last but never least, my gratitude and enduring love to Charles Muir, beloved friend for all time, who was the central character of this memoir until I discovered that the central character was really me.

Always, in all ways,

Caroline Muir

A Note from the Author

I have always wanted to be where the most love is. *Tantra Goddess* is a memoir of how far I have traveled, how deeply I have looked, and how willing I have been to risk all for the truth that dwells within my own heart. Many whom I write about have opted to remain themselves…others have requested their names be changed…and still others have spoken to me from the other side of this life. I hope I have heard their heavenly whispers accurately.

The beloved is, for me, the divine lover who languishes radiantly in the core of my heart. There is also a quality of belovedness that manifests as a feeling and a way of caring for another. Join me as we reach toward the beloved through love-in-action.

As the beloved takes form for you, remember that courage and perseverance are the hallmarks of a pioneer. Conscious sexual loving, practiced as an art form, is not for the faint of heart, but for the kings and queens and poets of love. Your body is an instrument for loving. Fine-tuning your instrument warms you for the symphony of harmonies that you play with another. Falling in love becomes a rising into love, an ever-ascending spiral of refinement of that which is sacred. Each moment calls us into an awareness of how well we live the true nature of love.

Each of you will have your own perception of what a goddess is or how she looks or even the language she speaks. I perceive goddess as the divine in woman. That is the birthright of every female, just as it is the birthright of every male to embody the presence of God in the light that he emanates from within. That presence does not negate our humanness, our frailties, or our desires and attachments. Goddess as feminine energy is awakening in our culture and in the hearts and souls of those who wish to maintain balance. I practice living in Tantric union with myself, and the life around me, weaving an expanded awareness into the practical necessities of life.

This blending or weaving of our masculine and feminine energies manifests in our sexuality in how we express love through the physical. I jumped at the opportunity to live within the sanctity of marriage and into an expanded version of union, hoping to dissolve the old paradigm of lying, cheating, and "having affairs." I dared to explore the realms of truth in sacred union with my beloved. Cultural myths teach us how to be men and women. Divine wisdom teaches us how to weave the masculine into the feminine and the feminine into the masculine. Perhaps this is the age of truth spoken of by mystics and sages.

Pleasure is a rite of passage into the realms of spirit, but only when it is joined to every cell of your being. Sexuality is by itself a biological necessity in which desire for satisfaction is the goal. Tantra comes alive when I surrender to the mystery by way of mastery.

My passion is to share with you what is possible when you love yourself as much as you want another to love you. Impeccable integrity is a minefield of traps, luring the gods or goddesses to continue. The way to freedom is marked by the feeling in your belly joined to your heart and joined to your mind keenly focused on your innate intelligence.

Sexual pioneering may not be nearly as wild or wanton as you would hope mine has been. Notice your own agenda, belief systems, opinions, proclivities, and judgments as you journey with me through these pages. I believe that spiritual/sexual education is the next frontier in human sexuality. Healing the feminine as mightily as she loves is the passion I now share with you. May her wisdom soar beyond the comfort of her silence.

The All-American Dream

The horizon line beckoned as I drove the open highway from New York City to Colorado, my hair flying in the wind and my spirit soaring. With a couple of duffel bags stuffed with jeans and flannel shirts and my cat in a carrier in the back seat, I was freedom bound, headed for whatever was calling me. If I needed other clothes, I'd buy them later. My box of jewelry-making tools and supplies was tucked in the back in case I decided to try to make some money at it. A thermos of coffee would get me over the first state line, and from there it would be adrenalin and snacks I'd buy when I stopped for gas. I would drive until the night seemed too long and I had to pull over to get some sleep, then I'd pitch my tent at a KOA, dwarfed by monstrous camping trailers, and curl up in my sleeping bag, my kitty purring beside me. The next morning I would be back in my Jeep for the last leg of the journey to my brother's doorstep.

"I can see why you'd want to leave New York," Johnny had said when I called to say I needed a place to stay for a while, "but why would you leave your family?" Didn't I have everything I wanted? A husband with a good career, an adorable five-year-old daughter, a two-story house in the suburbs? What had happened to the life and the city that had thrilled me? All I could say was New York was poisoning me. I had to go.

Twelve years earlier Arnie and I had rented an upstairs flat in the Bronx, the instant his army duty was done. Pelham Parkway was worlds away from the Kansas prairies of my childhood, with our flat that shared a fenced yard with a row of identical brownstones lining both sides of the street. I loved everything about our neighborhood—the bakeries, the delis, the Italian markets, the hair salons everywhere. "Hey, Wonder Bread," our friend Ed Yaconetti would say to me as I lifted another fresh pastry out of a pink box. "Ever have a cannoli back there in Kansas?" This love affair with opening a waxed paper envelope filled with a chocolate éclair or chocolate chip cannoli drove me not only into the bakeries but into the offices of diet doctors in Manhattan, a very "in" thing to do in 1963.

Every day I rode the subway to Manhattan to my job as a secretary at New York Life Insurance on 39th and Park Avenue, two blocks from Grand Central Station. After work I picked up fresh loaves of bread for nineteen cents and wedges of Parmesan and spicy Italian sausage to make Arnie's favorite dinners—his mama's good Italian sauce over every kind of pasta. Arnie's career in advertising was taking off, and at night we'd share stories about our workdays in the big city.

I was in love with my life, our friends, our Saturday evenings with the Yaconettis for an Italian dinner that Marie or I prepared while our husbands talked and laughed about the pros and cons of everything. We stayed up late playing cards or board games and having a zany, hilarious time. Life with Arnie in the Bronx was a hundred times better than anywhere in the playgrounds of my childhood.

Until November 22, 1963, that is. After President Kennedy was shot, people seemed more serious on the subways. The whole world seemed a different place. Culture seemed to be changing around us, and sex suddenly became a bigger part of our lives, with Arnie asking me to go with him to sex shops on Times Square and sit with him in half-empty theaters watching porn films. I tried to be interested, looking around the dusty, sleazy shops as he pointed out this and that and sitting through movies that seemed endless. *Playboy* arrived in the mail every month, and I pored over the slick pictures of buxom women with him and dressed up for the Playboy Club some Saturday nights to have drinks and look at the Bunnies, their oversized bosoms pushed into a daunting cleavage. I didn't like how women were objectified, and I liked it even less when Arnie and his friends called out from our car window, "Hey, look at *that!*"

every time a shapely woman walked by. But Arnie was my husband and I wanted to be a good wife, so I didn't say a word.

When Arnie and I had married two years earlier I was a virgin, and I was still a virgin a week after our wedding. Maybe it was because of all the douching—a friend of my mother's had undertaken my education in "feminine hygiene" and I was so well douched every day that I had none of the natural fluids that might have made penetration possible. And maybe it was Arnie's inexperience at stimulating me and my discomfort at being naked with a man. We had petted heavily during our year of dating, but never naked. Now I slept in pink curlers and baby doll pajamas and made sure the room was completely dark when we climbed into bed. (I had to be in a dark room for the next several years every time we had sex.) When we finally stumbled onto a jar of good ol' Vaseline, I said goodbye to my virginity. It hurt, it was bloody, and it was disappointing, but I was officially Arnie's wife and a member of the world of women and wives at last.

Around us, friends were getting pregnant and having babies, but try as I might, I was not. I had no idea what having children really meant to me, but Arnie was certain he wanted them—four daughters, to be exact—and I wanted whatever he wanted. We tried everything we knew. Once I even stood on my head after intercourse to help the sperm find their way.

It was around this time I ventured outside my marriage. There seemed to be opportunities everywhere! I flirted with my handsome, married boss and heated up afternoons in his office making out pressed up against the mahogany paneling, impaled by an erection that never saw the light of day. On my lunch hour one day I met one of his clients, the CEO of a thread manufacturing company, at a midtown hotel, trading my cotton briefs for something black and lacy at a department store nearby. His desire for me was fulfilled before I even unwrapped our sandwiches. So much for another attempt at this thrilling thing called sex. But I kept on with the kissing and fondling and many times released my pent-up sexual energy in the ladies' room on the 42nd floor, perched precariously on the commode with my legs in the air. I wondered if any other secretaries did this, too.

Later, after I left that job, I told Arnie about these escapades. He was shattered to think I would break our vow of monogamy so casually. "You don't even like sex that much!" But that was exactly why my indiscretions never seemed a big deal to me, because I didn't like sex that much. The sexiest we got was counting how many clitoral contractions I could have during orgasm. We had read that women can have several clitoral contractions during orgasm, and this interested us. Every chance Arnie got he would find his way between my legs to give me orgasms with his mouth and try to increase my number of contractions. "Just lie back and let me taste you," he would say. Not a problem! I was happy to receive Arnie pleasuring me, and I liked that he seemed to love doing it. But oh, if only sex could be over after my orgasm! When it came to intercourse I could only pretend to like it, and I was never interested in oral sex with him. Anything having to do with his penis caused me to numb out and disappear inside, and at twenty years old, I was too naïve to wonder why.

On New Year's Eve 1964, sex was hot and heavy after celebrations at the Yaconettis' house, and just before dawn I woke with a terrible shock. Fiery pain shot through my insides. "Holy shit, Arnie!" I moaned, doubling over. "I think I need an ambulance." My gynecologist met us at White Plains Hospital. Two hours later I was in emergency surgery to save my life.

The next morning I lay in a hospital bed with a painful ache in my belly. I was black and blue above and below a wide ribbon of gauze wrapped around my abdomen, up to my waist and down to my knees. What the hell had happened?

Dr. Carey finally came in, and he gently explained. A cyst the size of a large grapefruit had ruptured and was spilling poison into my bloodstream. I had lost a significant amount of blood internally. "But you'll be as good as new when the incision heals," he assured me, "minus one ovary. We had to take it out along with the cyst around it."

I'd lost an ovary? The night before, intercourse had been fast and hard. I was still trying to get pregnant, and my only association with that now was debilitating pain. My kind doctor was suddenly my hero; he helped women. Arnie was the perpetrator; he caused me pain. How could I make sense of all this?

Two years later I was hospitalized again, this time to find out that my fallopian tubes had been deformed before birth. More surgeries. We'd been married eight years when a second ovarian cyst was discovered and another surgery resulted in a complete hysterectomy. I was twenty-six years old. It was the end of my menstrual flow.

"Like a cigarette?" Dr. Carey said, offering me a Marlboro as I took a seat in his office. He lit my cigarette and then gave me the news that he'd decided to remove my uterus while I was "under" since it was clear I wouldn't be able to get pregnant anyway. I inhaled deeply to block the torrent of tears. "You can always adopt," he said.

What now? I felt lost without a purpose as a wife. Arnie agreed with the doctor: we could adopt. I wasn't so sure. How would I know how to mother when I couldn't even carry a baby in my own body? There was no one to talk with about it. My mother had stopped being a mother so long ago she wouldn't have any idea what to suggest. My Aunt Helen was busy raising her four children and whenever we talked about it, all she did was encourage me to follow my husband's lead.

With no one to hear me and no idea what else to do, after a year of discussions I decided to say yes to adoption. I would give notice at work, and we would move from our brownstone in the Bronx to a house in New Rochelle that my grandfather Nank would buy us so we could start our family in the suburbs. Arnie would commute to the city and be home with us all weekend.

Fifteen months later and three days after we moved into the four-bedroom split level in New Rochelle, the American Dream was realized: Our baby was here. We hurried to the agency when the call came, nervous and excited, and when Robin Lee was placed in my arms and I saw her blue eyes for the first time, it was love at first sight. We signed the papers and took our daughter home.

But why did Robin Lee cry so much and so loud for so long? I did everything Dr. Spock advised—her formula was warm to my wrist, her room was perfectly appointed, Mommy and Daddy loved her so much. Through the long days at home alone with her I smoked pack after pack of cigarettes, worried there was nothing I could do to console my baby. Granted, I was her third mother in the first eighteen days of her life, but she had it all now, didn't she? While Arnie was in the city, juiced by the creative atmosphere at the advertising agency, I was home all day with her, washing diapers and folding and putting them away. In the afternoons I settled her into her English pram and took her for long walks. I kept the house spotless, watched afternoon soaps while she napped, prepared hot dinners, and entertained our friends on weekends. Our Christmas party had a list of seventy-five to one hundred guests, and invitations went out just after Thanksgiving and before the round of Christmas cards went out. I worked for days on the appetizers—bacon-wrapped Chinese savories and cheesy puff pastries, foie gras–topped poppy seed crackers, and melty Brie en croûte. We rented glassware, dishware, and silverware, and we served martinis and Champagne on silver trays that Arnie's ad-men pals in their striped ties and three-piece suits passed around the crowd. I loved these gala affairs; entertaining seemed to come naturally to me.

I was in the groove of my life. Who cared that my Scotch and waters had become Scotch on the rocks, that my 5:00 p.m. cocktail hour gradually started earlier and earlier? When Arnie rented a studio apartment in the city so he could stay there Monday through Thursday to work on a screenplay he was writing, I was happy for him. He came home for long weekends to play with his daughter, play golf, watch sports, and have sex with me on Saturdays. Robin was the center of our universe, all we could talk about—what she was learning, when and where she would start preschool.

And then Musak turned to music, orange linen golf slacks became tattered tie-dyed jeans, the *Village Voice* replaced the *New York Times*, and sex on Saturdays became sex five times a day. Arnie's teenaged nephew, Steven, came to live with us.

Steven was seven years younger than I was, only a child when I was a senior in high school and invited to his house for dinner sometimes by his parents, Jill and Frank. I'd met Jill and Frank at the school football games, when I was head cheerleader and their eldest son was the leading tight end. When they introduced me to Jill's twenty-three-year-old brother, Arnie, he fell in love with me as quickly as they had. But time had passed, and now Arnie and I had our own child. Steven was a high school dropout, dropping acid and smoking pot. Frank and Jill thought we could help him shape up and find his way in society.

Steven's adoration for us was clear right away. What I didn't know was that I had been the object of his sexual fantasies for years. I could tell he was undressing me with his eyes, and I flirted back, letting him know I liked that look he gave me. I needed something new in my life, something to take the edge off.

One morning, while Robin napped, I slipped into the room where Steven slept. He opened his eyes as I was undressing. In moments, I ravished this boy-man, who then ravished me. Afterward, we lay together close in each other's arms. "I know it doesn't make sense, Steven," I whispered, "but I don't feel like I've done anything wrong."

"How can love be wrong?" Steven said. "I've loved you since the first day you walked into our house."

With this tender, passionate lover, a "nanny" for my child, and a great helper around the house, life in the suburbs improved overnight. And Arnie was ready for some improvements, too. He joined me in trading our "straight life" for bong hits and perfectly rolled joints as we let Steven usher us into the New Age. We listened to Dylan, the Beatles, the Rolling Stones, Judy Collins, and Joan Baez on a record player that had only known Sinatra, Nat King Cole, and Big Band. Steven baby-sat so Arnie and I could go to our first rock concert—Sly and the Family Stone—at the Fillmore in the East Village. That night, smoking grass right there in our seats, connecting with the masses of rock fans, we feared we looked terribly straight, but nobody seemed to mind our off-the-rack polyester. It was all about doing your own thing.

The times they were a-changin'.

For the rest of the year, my love affair with Steven stayed undercover, but it woke a sleeping sexual giant in me. Steven's soft voice and gentle manner, his loving focus on me, his availability, and his desire to spend all of his time with me fed a new fire inside. I *did* like sex after all! In fact, I couldn't get enough of it. The part of me that had questioned my identity as a woman since losing my ability to give birth gave way to a sense of belonging. I never felt like a Playboy Bunny with Steven. He wanted to caress *my* lovely breasts, not look at slick pictures of naked women. He wanted to make love with *me*, not ask me to watch two women making love in some porn film I could see over his shoulder while he took his pleasure with me. I was his porn film just being myself, playing out the role of wife and mother. We rode bicycles in Central Park and marched for peace in DC with Arnie. We got high on life, on marijuana, on each other. We roamed Greenwich Village, met Arnie after work and rode the Staten Island Ferry just for the view of New York City at night. We took Robin on daytime excursions and held her while she napped, breathlessly gazing at her sweet face. We played Dylan and the Beatles while preparing Arnie's favorite pastas on Friday nights and we never missed a beat in our integrity to show up with our love for him.

Reports to the family in Florida, meanwhile, were that Steven was adjusting well to family life in New York and he would soon have a direction for his life. He was in good hands. Truth was, it was Arnie and I who were in good hands, as Steven brought to us the unfolding wave of expanded consciousness sweeping the country and the world.

Finally, a year after he had come, Steven boarded a plane to return home to Florida. We said a tearful goodbye at the Kennedy Airport and I drove home, sad to face a cavernous house.

When Arnie came home that weekend, we sat in our matching TV chairs with a clean ashtray and fresh packs of Marlboros at our side, and I told him we needed to talk. He leaned back and lit a cigarette, classic ad-man style. "What's up?"

My mouth was dry. "Arnie," I said, "you might have noticed I've been more distant from you than usual."

He shrugged. Maybe he hadn't noticed.

"I've been having an affair."

"Who?" he said, without taking his eyes off me.

"Steven."

He jumped up and practically ran to our guest bathroom, slamming the door shut before vomiting up the news into the black commode. I stayed in my chair, squirming, wondering what could possibly happen next. I had no idea what I wanted. I just knew I couldn't go on with this secret any longer. When Arnie came back, he sat down, lit another cigarette, and inhaled deeply. "I've had an affair myself."

"*You* had an affair?"

"A photo rep at work. We even snuck into the house one night when you were away."

I was horrified, amazed, and impressed all at once. "Did the neighbors see you?"

He shook his head. "She stayed on the floor of the car until we got into the garage."

We howled with laughter at that and rolled a joint, smoking and laughing and sharing our secrets. This was the friend I'd needed. I felt genuinely happy for Arnie, happy our affairs had brought us so much joy. And I was freed from guilt, which was a huge relief. But we knew we needed something to help our marriage if we were going to stay together and personally thrive.

That's when Dr. Thelma came into our lives.

We started seeing Dr. Thelma, first separately and then together. Dr. Thelma was a marriage and family psychotherapist in White Plains. At her suggestion I joined one of her therapy groups, and it was there I had my first awakening. Dr. Thelma asked each woman in the group to ask the woman beside her to identify herself. Easy. The woman seated to my left faced me. "Who are you?" she asked, her brown eyes looking boldly into mine. "I'm Kern," I smiled, using my childhood nickname to introduce myself. She glanced at Dr. Thelma, who nodded for her to go on. She looked at me again and repeated it: "Who are you?" "I'm Arnie's wife," I said, still smiling. She came back a third time. "Who are you?" I was starting to squirm. What was this game anyway? "I'm Robin's mother," I said, knowing that my success with answers was over. She asked yet another time. "Who are you?" At that point I shattered, dissolving into tears. "I don't know! I don't know! I don't know!"

I quit Dr. Thelma after that meeting. I was tired of her tough-love ways of banging at the locked doors of me. This was my second bad experience with psychotherapy—a cold, clinical Freudian psychiatrist I'd seen when Arnie and I were first married wouldn't stop trying to get me to say "penis" and was fascinated by what I've always called "rocking my legs." Robin was about to enter kindergarten, giving me even more time to wonder what I was doing with my life, but I enrolled in some classes at Westchester Community College. I signed up for a yoga class and jewelry-making and devoted myself to flirting with my hippie jewelry teacher. These were comfortable protections, easy distractions. On Arnie's weekends home he continued to devote himself to his daughter with the kind of adoration I wanted from him. I felt invisible to them except when it came to fulfilling their needs for food and comfort.

At Christmas that year we visited Johnny and his new wife, Cherrie, in Colorado. It was 1972, and Cherrie was pregnant with their first child. I was excited for Johnny. We were each other's lifeline to family, and he and Arnie were like brothers. Johnny had visited us in New York a few times when he was on leave from the army and, later, when he was in college. We confided in each other about our confusion and sadness about our mother, who had long suffered from mental illness, and about Dad and his wives and our stepsisters, and how we felt about what they expected of us. The truth was always easy to share with Johnny. I was the older sister, and in some ways, I suppose, a replacement for the lost parts of our mom.

After we visited Johnny and Cherrie that Christmas, on the way home, we stopped in Chicago for a friend's New Year's Eve party. There, I met a man who would instantly shake up my world and lead me to this day, driving west to start a new life.

"This is my brother Eddie," our friend Lee had said, and Eddie and I shook hands.

Eddie returned my smile with all the information I needed.

I endured the evening, my thoughts a zillion miles away as I sat close to Arnie while he made everyone laugh. Eddie hugged me goodnight in the wee hours of the morning, his eyes gazing longingly into mine. He whispered, "I'm meeting a friend in April to sail from England to Spain in his forty-five-foot ketch. There's plenty of room for you, Kern. Come with me!"

All the way home and for weeks after that, all I could think about was Eddie's invitation. We talked often by phone after I put Robin to bed when Arnie was away at his studio in Manhattan, and I trembled uncontrollably as we spoke, which worried me. Why was I so affected by this man? I was a responsible mom, a loving wife. Eddie was single with little to tie him down besides an apartment in Chicago he'd give up to go to Europe. I had to join him. I had to know life wasn't passing me by. I had to grab this brass ring. The adrenalin was intoxicating.

One Saturday night after Arnie had read Robin her bedtime story and turned out her light, I joined him on the couch. I had already decided to tell him as plainly as I could that I'd been invited to go on a sailing trip with Eddie and his friend.

"I need to go on this adventure, Arnie."

"And what does that mean?"

"I need a break for a while. And I need a break from mothering for a while, too."

Arnie frowned. "Are you seeing someone?"

I told him I wanted to sail from England to Spain with Eddie. I would leave in early March and return in early July. "I want to taste parts of life I have missed before it's too late, Arnie. Can you understand that?"

"And who is Eddie?"

I reminded him.

Arnie nodded, probably remembering my silence on the long drive back to New York after that New Year's Eve, my fading interest in serving him his favorite dinners on his weekends home. He sighed a long sigh. "Are you in love with this guy?"

"I don't know, Arnie, but something big is happening. I haven't stopped thinking about him since we met. This is the chance of a lifetime to learn more about myself, an opportunity I may never have again." Eddie and I planned to travel through England, Wales, and Scotland, then sail from southern England to the northern coast of Spain before I returned home.

"You've been talking to this guy, making plans?" Arnie was surprised, but curious. "What about Robin Lee? What about us?"

"I suppose you could call it a leave of absence," I said. "We can look at it all when I'm home in three months."

I reminded him that I'd gotten engaged in my senior year of high school and had married him just after my eighteenth birthday, and he surprised me then, with the greatest possible show of true love. "Do what you need to do, Kernie. I may be your husband, but I'm also your friend."

I flung my arms around his neck and held him close, loving him more in that moment than ever before.

After that, though, the tension between us was thick. We slept on the farthest edges of our king-sized bed, and every day I had to steel myself against what I would miss, or I may never have gone. I couldn't bear thinking of Robin wondering why I wasn't there to send her off to school in the mornings after brushing out her long, tangled hair. Why I couldn't cook dinner for her, or read to her, or talk to her about her friends in preschool. To distract myself, I spent hours on the phone with Eddie, making lists of travel arrangements I needed to make, filling and re-filling my duffel bags with "cute outfits for Europe," and going through the motions of mothering and housekeeping with my mind thousands of miles away. Arnie changed his schedule to be home more nights while I was gone, and we began training a part-time nanny to pick up Robin from school, watch her in the afternoons, and cook dinner for them.

At last the morning of my departure came. I packed Robin's lunch and saw her off to school, then sat with my bags, waiting for the taxi that would take me to Kennedy Airport. I felt heavy and exhilarated. It was a major crossroads, choosing the unknown and unpredictable over everything familiar. It also meant I was now a carrier of the great scarlet letter "A," for abandonment. My mother had carried that letter, and look how well I survived. I assumed those I was leaving would survive just as well. How could I create harm with this choice?

Springtime in Paris may be romantic, but England in April is nothing but bloody cold. Right away, I had to buy wool clothing and rain gear, as Eddie and I traveled through England, Scotland, and Wales. We stayed in quaint bed-and-breakfast inns and made love while gazing out the windows at a life so different and so far away from New York or Chicago. I had hoped for something sensational with Eddie, something like the passion I had enjoyed with Steven or even the comfort and sense of family I felt with Arnie, but Eddie had far less experience with relational love than I had, and sex was disappointing. It didn't matter much, though. I had other things on my mind. Adventure was the fuel that drove me as we got ready to sail the open sea. And London! The pubs and the people, the British Museum, Piccadilly, the double-decker buses, the birdman in Wellington Park—all of it gave me a joyous sense of aliveness as we geared up to meet the boat in Falmouth, on the southern coast.

On June 1, we set sail on the *Seawatch*, Captain Chuck's forty-five-foot vessel. We had trained hard in the art of sailing, traveling through inlets and around the harbors near Falmouth, admiring the southern English countryside and learning from Captain Chuck how essential it was that we wear life vests, take orders, and pay attention at all times. In less than two hours we were outside of predictable waters surrounding the Port of Falmouth and on our way. In three nights and four days we would be across the Bay of Biscay. Then we would dock for a few weeks in Santander, Spain, and go on to sail the northern coast of Spain into warmer weather south toward Portugal.

From the start, the waters were rough. The boat rocked hard and the swells rose high around us, sending poor Eddie below deck to his bunk, severely seasick. It looked like it was going to be up to Captain Chuck and me to get us through. "Kern," Captain Chuck said to me that first night, "you and I are going to have to split Ed's watch. Can you do it?"

Eddie's watch was six hours on, six hours off. I would have to take the wheel while Captain Chuck slept. I knew I had no option but to say yes. Our lives depended on my answer. "Sure, Chuck," I said, as confidently as I could. "I can do it."

That night, when the moon was high in the sky, Captain Chuck set the compass for our destination. My job was to watch those degrees on the compass, hold the wheel on course, and line the tall mast with a particular star. "Do a good job," the captain said, bidding me goodnight before heading down to his bunk.

Enough adrenalin pumped through me to sail us to China as I sat alone that night, the icy wind whipping my face and threatening to send my wool cap and goose-down hood flying. I was too thrilled to be frightened as I kept an eye on the compass, the water, the sky, and the sails. The world seemed huge and amazing. The next two nights were the same, thrilling and mind-blowing. My two overstuffed duffle bags of "cute outfits for Europe" sat zippered in the hull, leaving me little space to lie down during my precious few hours of sleep time. But that was nothing compared to what went on for poor Eddie, who never left his bunk while

Captain Chuck and I traded off guiding the *Seawatch* to our destination.

When the Port of Santander came into view, ecstasy surged through every cell of my being, my legs sprawled over the bow and encircling the carved Nordic sea goddess. I had helped guide us to safety. I had done it. I was more than a wife and mother. I was courageous. I helped save lives. I could be counted on.

And I had to start a new life.

When we got back to the States, Eddie planned to move to Aspen, Colorado. I would move to Colorado, too, with Robin, and live in the mountains near Johnny and his family. I'd see Eddie in Aspen now and then and do everything I could to find out what more there was to this life besides living in a container that wasn't my size. I wanted to discover my potential, and I could only do that by moving forward, sails set on the brightest star in the sky. That had been my epiphany during my second night at sea.

I rehearsed my words: "Arnie, I have to get out of New York. I know you have no desire to live in the wild, and I'm burnt out on city life. I have loved New York with you, but I need to be free." When that didn't sound right, I tried, "I can be a better friend living closer to nature than I can a wife living in this container that's too small for me," and "I am questioning my ability to stay sane if I have to remain a housewife and mother."

But back in New York I discovered it was easier to rehearse the truth than to confront someone I truly loved. My resolve quickly faded. Robin was bubbling over with stories about school and summer plans, and Arnie was as attentive to me as he'd been when we were first together. He seemed confident things would return to normal. It was easier to sail a forty-five-foot boat all night, responsible for three lives, than it was to tell Arnie I had to go.

Then one day, I hit bottom. A cop flashed his lights in my rear view mirror during rush hour as I drove home to New Rochelle. I didn't understand at first that he wanted me to pull over, so I turned onto the East River Drive ramp. Traffic stopped in both directions as the police car somehow wound through it to pull me over. I was doomed. I had read about cops who harassed, even raped, innocent women like me, women who had done nothing more than make a wrong turn. Certainly this cop would rape me in the dark tunnel just ahead. I locked the car door and sat trembling as he approached. He banged on the driver's side window. "Open the window, lady." I let him knock a few more times. Finally, I rolled the window down just enough to reach out and smash my burning cigarette into his cheek. As he reeled in pain, I jumped out of the car and ran through the slowed traffic, begging drivers to help me. But this was New York. No one paid attention.

After the officer apprehended me and calmed me down, he wrote out two twenty-five-dollar tickets. By then he seemed okay to me, and I apologized for the big burn mark on his cheek. We talked for a few minutes about our kids at home, and I realized this cop was just a man, someone's dad. I felt terrible. I knew at that moment I had to leave New York. The city was turning me into someone even I didn't want to know.

That night I told Arnie I would always be grateful for our nearly twelve years together. In many ways, we'd grown up together, sitting in our matching armchairs as America the Beautiful changed in front of our eyes on the TV screen. We'd watched combat in Vietnam, race riots on city streets, civil rights marches through the South, Martin Luther King's "I Have a Dream" speech in front of thousands. We'd ridden the end of the Kennedy Era into the Sexual Revolution, seen the first man walk on the moon, had almost gone to Woodstock—too much traffic made us turn back for home, a decision we regretted later. We'd entertained friends, gotten high at rock concerts, never missed a New York Rangers or Giants game, adopted our daughter, and created a beautiful home for our family. I appreciated all of it.

Arnie said he understood. He'd expected this. But when I said I want-ed to take Robin with me, he roared. "You will *not* take my daughter from this house!"

It was clear there would be no debate. My throat burned as I agreed to grant him full custody. I knew Robin would be in good hands with her father. He was stable. He adored her. He always had her best interests in mind. We would work out the visits.

Three weeks later the Jeep was packed, and Arnie and Robin stood on the doorstep as I forced myself to make this ride toward my rising star.

I would break up my own family with only vague hopes of a better future halfway across the continent. Arnie's eyes were cold. With one hand holding firmly onto our daughter's shoulder, I revved the engine. Part of me wanted to run back and hug them both, to reassure them—reassure myself—but I couldn't. I had to make this departure as smooth and light as I could, for Robin's sake, for all of us. It was heartbreaking, but there was no turning back.

Chapter Two

On My Way

It was dusk when I pulled into the driveway of Johnny's chalet high in the mountains west of Denver, among boulders and wildflowers. Butterflies fluttered in my belly as I saw my brother and his wife moving about through the living room window: I was really here.

Johnny and Cherrie welcomed me warmly and made me feel at home right away, leading me into the nursery, where I would sleep in a single bed near my six-month-old godson and nephew Josh's crib. He had grown so much since my visit just after he was born in February. We peered into the crib together, whispering so as not to wake the littlest angel of the family. "I'm so glad you're here," Cherrie said, squeezing my hand.

Johnny owned a gallery, The Hands of Man, in the nearby town of Evergreen, showcasing the work of local artists in ceramics, silver, and stone. Artists were a big part of this community, along with hippies, cowboys, young families, and old timers who liked to live the simpler life in the Colorado Rockies. I expected to fit right in.

During the day I helped Cherrie at home while Johnny ran the gallery. In a few months, I would work in the gallery two days a week making silver jewelry at the workbench Johnny also used and waiting on the occasional tourist or customer who came to shop. It smelled woodsy and earthy in there, with the cedar shelves and burning piñon pine in the pot-bellied stove. At night, Johnny cooked our hometown favorites—fried chicken and mashed potatoes, hamburgers or steak on the barbecue. We stayed up late getting high on homegrown and laughing until our sides split, listening to the Moody Blues. As teenagers and through our twenties we had lived in our own little worlds, and it felt good to share some old favorites as we made new memories. Cherrie and baby Josh cuddled close to the tremendous love between brother and sister. On weekends, Johnny and I hiked in the mountains and he listened to my musings, never trying to fix anything, just listening or offering to help in any way. I loved him for his unconditional acceptance of me as I tried to make sense of this freedom I had chosen.

With Johnny's help, before long I found a one-room log cabin to rent on Turkey Creek Road in Conifer, fifteen minutes from his house. I didn't have much with me, but Johnny and Cherrie scrounged up a futon from their old apartment in Denver, pulled some cookware out of storage, and unpacked some chipped pottery that hadn't sold in the gallery. I sewed gingham curtains for my country cabin and wove soft cowhide into pillows for the funky old couch. I had a great time perusing yard sales for treasures, and embroidering or sewing what needed my touch. Winter would be cold, and I had a cord of wood delivered for my big moss rock fireplace. When that was stacked neatly outside and covered with a tarp, I stood back and surveyed it all. Living like this for the winter would feed my pioneering soul.

As soon as I was settled in, I took a job waitressing at the Little Bear, a tavern in Evergreen popular with the cowboys and hippies, who somehow got along harmoniously. I spoke by phone every few weeks with Eddie, who was creating his new life five hours away in Aspen, until he told me (on my thirtieth birthday) that it wasn't time for him to be in a relationship. This was my first big rejection in my single life, but I got over it pretty quickly. Eddie and sailing to Spain had been a bridge. I was ready to fall in love with *my* life now, and I had the cutest little log cabin this side of the Mississippi.

I had almost forgotten what autumn turning to winter can do to your spirit when you stand under the big night sky and breathe in the scent of pine and wood fires in the crisp Colorado air. These were the mountains of my childhood, the getaway I had loved as a child, sitting beside clear, rushing streams while my father or Nank fished and I counted leaves sailing by on their way to somewhere. From this good place, New York seemed never to have existed.

It was in my blood, this thirst for adventure. I come from a long line of pioneers. My great-grandparents left Scotland in the 1890s with their three boys—one of them my grandfather Nank—to travel west by covered wagon in search of everything America might be. They settled near Ames, Iowa. Fifty years later, as soon as World War II ended, my parents settled on the Missouri side of State Line, with their baby girl, Carolyn, as my birth name was spelled. Three years later their second child, Johnny, was born, completing the picture: a handsome Irishman for a dad with piercing blue eyes and black wavy hair, a beautiful young mother with almond-shaped eyes and a radiant smile, two cars parked in the driveway, a manicured lawn out front, weekends golfing and sunning at the country club. Acres and acres of cornfields surrounded our house and I romped there with my brother and our dog, running down the rows and dropping into their shade to watch clouds pass by. Sometimes I played in our yard, swinging on a tree swing or climbing the apple tree for the view of "forever"—anywhere else, the horizon line, and all its possibilities. From the outside, everything at home looked great, but I knew better. My father had a hot temper, and he and my mom fought so loud sometimes I dreamed of leaving home and taking Johnny with me. One night, I decided it was time to take action. While our parents raged in their bedroom down the hall, I scooped up Johnny in my arms and held him tight. "Let's call the police." He looked at me with wet eyes as I dialed "O" on our telephone.

"Now, little girl," the woman at the other end of the line said to me, "you can't be bothering us with family squabbles."

I hung up. *Squabbles?* "Okay, Johnny. That's it. Tomorrow we'll run away to Nank and Nanny's." I was sure I could remember the way to our grandparents' house.

That night I made piles of "supplies"—dresses, clean underwear, clothes for Johnny, my new pink Easter hat—and we went to sleep in our beds. When we woke up, the house was still quiet. I emptied a box of Cheerios into a paper bag while Johnny pulled the Radio Flyer wagon around the front. "Get in," I said, and Johnny obeyed, legs tucked under as I surrounded him with our supplies. We walked for blocks, stopping at a church to use the bathroom. The wagon flipped once on a turn, muddying the folded clothes, but I piled them back in. I felt heroic. I was Johnny's angel! I was saving our lives!

Our grandparents' housekeeper, Minnie, answered the door when we finally reached our destination. "Well, look who's here!" she cried, looking us over. "Oh dear. Your grandparents is out. When they gets back they'll see as to what to do." She ushered us inside and gave us cookies and milk.

Our parents picked us up that night. They scolded us in front of our grandparents and warned me never to do that again. They were especially angry that I'd called the police. (The police had phoned them and tattled on me. And I'd thought they were supposed to protect me!) It would be years before I would leave my family again for a chance at something better.

When I was twelve, my family splintered and would never pick up the pieces. My mother had a nervous breakdown and overnight was living in a hospital for the mentally ill. The asylum was in Kansas City, a drive from our home in Prairie Village, one of the many suburban communities that had sprouted up on the prairies after the war. She stayed for a few months in an old brick building with bars on the windows, where they sedated her and gave her shock therapy to try and cure her. Both Johnny and I missed her terribly. When she did come home, she slept most of the day and night, but besides that, she didn't seem too different. Then one day not too long after, they packed her up again and sent her even farther away, to Menninger's Clinic for the Mentally Ill, in Topeka.

To take care of things at home while Dad was away all day at his dry cleaning plant in Kansas City, he hired a housekeeper. I didn't care—I was out most of the time, losing myself in my social life. I lived for dances, parties, and spending nights as often as I could with my best girlfriends, Gerri and Nash.

When my mother was finally released from Menninger's, she tried to step back into her role as wife and mother, but she couldn't. She had been diagnosed as manic depressive and schizophrenic, Dad said, and her doctor and her father, Grandpa Nank, had advised him to file for divorce and take full custody of the kids. Before I knew what was happening, Mom was back at Menninger's, Dad had sold our house (goodbye, beloved apple tree!), and Johnny and I moved in with Nank and Nanny, leaving Dad free to live closer to work in Kansas City. He would see us on weekends.

I loved my grandparents, especially Nank. When we were younger our parents would send us to their house for weekends, and on hot summer nights I'd share Nank's bed by the window. He slept upstairs and Nanny had her own rooms downstairs. I'd fall asleep beside him listening to the songs of the crickets after watching him snore softly beside me for a time. I loved his funny old face and wisps of gray hair pulled out as if they were trying to look sleek and long. On walks along Brush Creek he told me stories about growing up on a farm in Iowa. I was his "little daisy," and I loved watching his eyes go soft when he called me that. He was my first big taste of real love, always assuring me with his gentle warmth, "Little daisy of mine, you can never make me mad enough to not love you." Oh, there were times I tried to prove him wrong, but nothing I did ever shook him.

Not long after Johnny and I moved in with Nank and Nanny, Nanny went into the hospital and never came home again. Gin bottles were found hidden all over the house, which explained Nanny's "funny moods." Mom escaped from Menninger's a few days after the funeral and hitchhiked the 250 miles home to Prairie Village. Nank didn't have the heart to send her back, and he moved her into the room Nanny had recently vacated.

All of us somehow managed our various assignments for survival. There we were, the four of us, a splintered family living in separate rooms in a big house no one could really call home. Nank stayed in his wing, Mom, Johnny, and I used the other three rooms, and no one saw each other much. Mom slept a lot, and when she was awake she roamed the house in her nightgown, mumbling words no one could understand. Twice that year, Johnny found Mom bleeding in bed after attempts to slash her wrists.

For years I had worshipped my mother. For Johnny she was a skirt to hide behind when Dad raged at her, at me, at the world. For me, she was comfort when Dad lost his temper over a simple thing like reaching into the cookie jar after dinner. "Fatso!" he would yell, whacking me across the head with the back of his hand and sending me to my room to sob my heart out. Mom would come in after a while with a plate of those cookies and a glass of cold milk. Dad took his temper out on Johnny now and then, but I was older, and sassier, and a girl, and he had a thing for girls. Once, reeking of Scotch, he took a hairbrush to my legs and buttocks, slapping me over and over until my tender skin was bloody. I wailed inside each time the bristles hit, but I never made a sound. My mother stayed out of it, never shouted at him to stop and leave me alone, and I didn't really care. I assumed I must have been bad to deserve this, and no one needed to see it.

Before she got sick, Mom kept house, threw parties, and volunteered as a Cub Scout mom and Girl Scout mom. She met Dad at the country club on weekends and visited with girlfriends while I swam or practiced with the water ballet team. We went to church with Nank and Nanny, and now and then with Dad, too, and I sang in the choir, tears running down my cheeks sometimes from the beauty of the songs as the organ music lifted up my spirit to meet God.

Since she'd been in the hospital, I didn't know how to talk to Mom. Johnny was the good boy, keeping an eye on her when he came home from school, while I did everything I could to stay away. Nash and Gerri were the world to me. We threw water balloons at passing cars, drove too fast in the family car I "stole" when Nank was sleeping, spray-painted the word "F U C K" on the elegant statuary around town, and prized our star piece of contraband, a sign that read "DO NOT STEAL THIS SIGN." My diet consisted of jumbo packs of Hydrox cookies dipped in milk, Campbell's Tomato Soup, and Hormel chili supplemented by trips to Winstead's Drive-In for double cheeseburgers in Gerri's '57 Chevy. I had a charge account with the local cab company and the local drug store and soda fountain, and everything was "neat" and "swell." My older friends had driver's licenses, and the 3.2 beer sold in Kansas flowed freely at the basement den parties where "Kernie and the gang" hung out. Nash and I were wannabe beatniks, and we read Henry Miller and Anaïs Nin while soul-searching our way through ninth and tenth grades. Nash asked questions about morality, politics, and philosophy, opening my mind to questioning authority and to expanded ways of thinking. She planned to quit high school early and travel the world. I wanted to do it, too.

But my family had other ideas for me. The summer before my junior year my dad remarried and decided his kids needed more supervision. He would send me to a boarding school he'd heard about in Fort Lauderdale, and Johnny would go to a military academy.

I was outraged. Leave my friends? Johnny? The love between us surpasses all understanding; we were everything to one another.

Boarding school. I felt ostracized, barred from my past. Miss Harrington, the dorm mother, a stern spinster who lived in an apartment at the entrance to the one-story house where twenty other girls shared rooms, was now my authority figure. I instantly hated her. It was the job of teenage girls to give the dorm mother a hard time, and I was good at my job. But I was determined to make this boarding school thing work.

A friendly person by nature, I jumped in to my new life with abandon. I listened to the chatty girls, gathering data. Just where would I fit in? My roommate, Adrianne, was okay, blonde and tall and about as lost as I was, having just arrived from Michigan. Adrianne and I staked out our personal territory, hung our old school banners over our beds, and began the process of adjusting to an environment that was hardly terrible, given that the Fort Lauderdale beaches were our backyard on the weekends. We wore Bermuda shorts to classes, walking in our saddle shoes the short distance to the local soda shop, school dining room, and classrooms. The air was humid and heavy, and it made my curly hair frizz, but Adrienne helped me style it into something cute. I tried to make friends with the day students who lived off campus with their parents, hoping I would be invited for overnights on the weekends, but it didn't happen often.

Before the first semester ended, I began to notice some good things about being new. I had a clean slate here at Pine Crest Prep. No one had parents who didn't think I was a good influence on their daughter (no supervision at home, you know!). No one knew my mother's story. I had friends, I dated boys, and I joined the cheerleading team. For my sixteenth birthday, Nank gave me a Chevy Impala convertible, which kicked off as much fun as I knew how to have and still make it to graduation. I flirted relentlessly with the tall basketball players and had a crush on most of the cute guys on the football team, but for the most part, I found boys disappointing. I loved making out with them and vying for their attention, but I was terrified of their penises and had no interest in sex. I vowed to remain a virgin until I married.

By Christmas, Dad was getting another divorce and moving to Fort Lauderdale to live with his new girlfriend, Marty—his ex-wife's friend— two miles from me. Her two daughters were day students at my school, which is how Dad had heard of Pine Crest Prep in the first place. I thought it was strange he didn't ask me to come and live with them, but he didn't, and I decided it was best this way. I had more freedom. Before I knew it, Dad and Marty were off to Las Vegas to get married, and suddenly I had inherited two stepsisters. ("I'm a *cocksman*," Dad had once boasted. "The women love me." "What's a cocksman?" I had asked.) News came from home that Nank had remarried, too, a blue-haired woman named Elizabeth who I was sure was after his money, and he moved Mom into an apartment near his house. Gerri and Nash visited from Kansas that Christmas, bringing me a taste of home, until Gerri surprised me speechless by falling in love with my roommate and running away with her not too long after that. I had never even heard of a lesbian, and here my best friend turned out to be one! Was everybody nuts or what?

Senior year was a new story. Johnny hated military school and Dad let him join me at Pine Crest. I had been voted captain of the Pantherettes, my cheerleading team, and my popularity would help Johnny be accepted. We would tolerate the occasional weekend visits to Dad's new life and be pleasant enough to his stepdaughters when we ran into them at school.

Football fans came to our school games, and two of them were Jill and Frank, a couple of the friendliest people I had ever met. Jill and Frank never missed a game, and they were interested in me—a girl whose father lived nearby and kept her at boarding school. They invited me home for Italian dinners, laughed at the way I pronounced "Parm-ee-ze-an," and begged me to come live with them. They would have taken Johnny, too, a fact we both loved, but Dad would never have allowed that. He showed his true colors when he asked, "Who are these guineas you two are friends with?" (I later learned that "guinea" was derogatory slang for Italians, and I seethed inside that I had a dad who was so lame.)

Sometime around my birthday, Jill told me about her brother, Arnie. He was in the service and he would be staying with them for a couple of weeks over Christmas. "You have to meet him," Jill told me. "He's going to love you as much as we do."

And they were right. Arnie loved me right away, and I was intrigued by him. Arnie was older than the other boys I knew—twenty-three! Almost a real *man*. I loved talking with him. I thought he was the most intelligent, gentle, and sophisticated person I'd ever met. And he never lost his cool, even with my dad. When Dad said, "I would never let my daughter get serious about a skinny wop from New York," Arnie just gave Dad a respectful smile and said, "Jack, your daughter is in good hands with this skinny New York wop," and he swept me out the door, my hand in his.

Life at Jill and Frank's house was warm and full of family love and laughter. I spent more time there when Arnie was in town, visiting with his family, eating as a group around a big table, laughing, cuddling, and talking late into the night. Before he went back to the army base in South Carolina we went on a few dates, dressing up and going to see Ella Fitzgerald at a Miami hotel, a gift from cousin Joe. Our next date took us to a Miami nightclub to hear Lenny Bruce, the raunchiest comedian of the day. I blushed through the show, which amused Arnie. No matter how I tried to hide it, I was a Kansas girl at heart.

When Arnie left, I missed him badly. We lived for the letters we wrote to one another and for the occasional long-distance phone call. Over spring break, Arnie proposed. I said yes in a heartbeat. I was *wanted!* I was *adored!* For the rest of the school year I proudly sported my diamond engagement ring, to the envy of the other girls.

After my high-school graduation, Johnny and I moved into our mother's apartment back in Kansas. As soon as I could, I would leave there forever. She was zoned out, smoked a lot, and didn't do much to help me get ready for my wedding, although she did perk up to go with me to buy our dresses (mine was ice blue with a long train and lots of pearls and lace, hers was a mocha cream silk and lace). Arnie's mother filled my hope chest with embroidered aprons, linen tablecloths and napkins, and monogrammed towels from Portugal, and Nank planned to walk me down the aisle. Dad wasn't invited to the wedding, a revolutionary act for me. But how could I invite him? When I told him Arnie and I were engaged, he said, "You'll never get into a country club married to that wop."

Arnie's family became mine as soon as we married, and when we visited them every year in Florida, I would take off alone to visit my father. I wanted to believe I had a connection to my family, too, even if it meant putting up with my dad showing me off at his country club and sitting through his third and fourth martini while he and Marty argued over the smallest things, and he criticized everything and everyone in sight. I didn't like his macho style or how I felt with him or his comments about me—he liked to say, "You're just a girl, you'll never amount to anything," as his eyes lowered to stare at my breasts—but I was determined to keep up the illusion as long as I could.

Now Arnie, Robin, and I were family, and that was *not* an illusion. But I was leaving them. I wasn't going to get my father on the phone and tell him what I was doing. He would claim to have been right all along, and he wouldn't have been right about anything. I didn't want his or anyone else's comments to mar the fragile foundation of my choice. My stability was essential as I pioneered the new landscape of my life.

Winter came hard and cold in the Rockies, but I loved the snow and the adventure of driving through it to work at the Little Bear. Live music rocked the tavern nights and weekends, and tips were good. For added income I pulled out my jewelry-making tools, bought some more silver and supplies, and started up a business I called Every Cloud Has a Silver Lining. Back in New York, jewelry-making had been a good time-filler. Now it would be part of my livelihood. A cook at the Little Bear built me a workbench using wood from old, abandoned sheds in fields nearby. That bench was the focal point of my living room, next to the big rock fireplace where fires roared all winter as I created hundreds of hollow silver beads for necklaces out of sterling, then set uneven rounds of turquoise stones for the pendants, belt buckles, and earrings. I fit right in with the locals and became one of Johnny's favorite artists at his gallery.

Every mountain girl needs a dog, and it was time for me to get mine. I chose the pick of the litter, a Golden Retriever puppy I named Jeremiah Johnson, and we became inseparable right away. Any loneliness that crept in vanished when Jeremiah and I stepped outside under that starry sky. Some afternoons before work I'd jump into the Jeep with Jeremiah and drop by Johnny's for a visit. He and Cherrie were supportive of me and my choices, and they never wavered in their love for Arnie and Robin. These were unusual times.

And every Sunday, I called "home." Arnie and I talked long and deeply, like the friends we had always been. "Robin misses you a lot, Kernie, and I miss you, too, my blue-eyed Kansas girl," he would say. "But I get that you have to do this." I felt incredibly fortunate to have a husband so supportive of me. But eventually it was time to make agreements over visiting rights and put the divorce papers through with lawyers we hired. Our uncontested divorce would be finalized in about a year.

One bitter cold January day, two tall cowboys walked through the swinging saloon doors at the Little Bear. "Who is that?" I asked another waitress, as the doors swung shut behind them and the men looked around for a seat.

"Rick and Victor," she said. "They come in from time to time."

I hung back to get a good look. The men wore Stetsons perfectly perched on their heads, topping weathered faces. They looked like real cowboys to me.

I maneuvered my way into getting their table, introduced myself, and asked for their orders. Rick's emerald eyes sparkled when he looked at me, and chatting with them was easy. I accepted Victor's invitation to join them for a drink at the end of my shift.

Before we finished our second pitcher these cowboys invited me to join them on a road trip to Aspen the next day. They sold Western-style belt buckles for a living, twenty dollars apiece, and the bars in Aspen in January were good business. I was in. I traded shifts with another waitress before I left the tavern to go pack. The next morning I was back in Evergreen to meet up with my new companions.

I climbed into the front seat of Victor's pickup, settling in between two men who smelled like hangovers needing a shower. I was quite the contrast in my sunshine-yellow down vest, clean Levi's, and flannel shirt, my braids tied with yellow velvet ribbons. It would be a grand adventure.

Rick and Victor were friendly cowboys, good men with big hearts, but when it came to money, these two really lived on the edge. As we drove out of town in Victor's camper pickup I realized that my new friends not only had a nearly empty gas tank, but they had no gas money. Victor said, "We're pretty embarrassed, ma'am, but we wonder if it might be possible to borrow twenty dollars from you to git us to Aspen. We'll pay you back, no problem."

"It's true, Miss Kernie. We are terribly sorry, but we're not gonna make it too far on no gasoline," Rick said. I pulled out a twenty and we were on our way.

About an hour down the road, another twenty bought more Coors, and the men entertained me without pause for the six hours over the Continental Divide and into the quaint ski village of Aspen. All day I wondered which one I would sleep with, Rick or Victor. Rick was the cuter of the two, and he was charming in that effortless way of mountain men. I thought it would probably be Rick.

It's freezing in late January at 8,000 feet, and the long, winding road into Aspen was terrifying and exciting with two singing cowboys in an old pickup with questionable brakes and no heater. What joy it was to see the glow of lights through a window at the Hotel Jerome and a big parking place for our rig at the side entrance.

The moment we entered, the real fun began. Out of the men's sacks came the leather rolls filled with brass belt buckles stamped with bucking broncos, horseshoes, pine trees, and "COORS." In no time, these guys had sold enough belt buckles to the men at the bar to pay for the evening. I was ready for a hot buttered rum. After my drink I took a walk while they worked a few more bars, and we met up again in an hour for some elk and venison with "taters" and beer. They handed me a couple of bills to repay me for the help getting there and stashed rolls of bills in their wallets. It had been a good night. After dinner they taught me to play pool. We played darts, partied some more around town, and they sold more belt buckles. Around 3:00 a.m. it was time to find the old pickup and get some sleep.

It was clear by now that I would be sleeping with Rick. We climbed under his down sleeping bag, and by morning, I was his gal.

For a week we traveled the Colorado interstates and highways, getting to know each other in ways that only come with the intimacy of traveling. Rick opened up, telling stories of growing up on a ranch in southern Colorado. He and his father had hunted in high country, and he'd hauled elk and venison out of the hunting camp and back to the butcher in Durango. He'd been in Vietnam, was wounded at nineteen, and sent home with a Purple Heart. His stories tore my heart open. Since he'd been back home, he and Victor had traveled together, like Butch Cassidy and the Sundance Kid, selling belt buckles, making some kind of living. I vowed then to love Rick into wellness, to do my part for the war effort and help him heal his wounds.

In this land of cowboys, Rick was the sweetest man around. When he wasn't selling belt buckles with Victor in bars from one end of the state to the other, he spent nights with me. He rode in rodeos, carried a can of Skoal chewing tobacco in his right hip pocket, lined up three pairs of cowboy boots in my closet below his western shirts with their various horse and horseshoe designs, and wore fitted boot-cut Levis. Sometimes he'd fill the freezer with elk and venison steaks from his hunting trips in the high country with his dad, then cook up meat-and-potato dinners that tasted like sweet home on the range. And sex was great with this cowboy. He knew about pleasuring me in some of my favorite ways before riding his cowgirl into the open country of abandoned passion. He was quiet much of the time, but he was easy to be with, so I didn't care.

That summer we took a month-long mule pack trip into the mountains together. I quit my job at the tavern in late spring, gave up my cabin, and Rick and I moved in with his folks on their ranch near Durango to get ready for our trip. It would be the next big adventure in the life of this young pioneer.

Rick's folks were old-fashioned farmers, the kind who don't say much and get a lot done. They went to bed at 8:30 so they could rise before dawn to start the routine all over again. Fried eggs, bacon, and potatoes were eaten before sunrise, and then Rick fell into step with his dad, who was happy to have his strong young son around to help with chores. We baled hay and rode and worked with the horses that would come with us on the trip. I learned to knit scarves with Rick's mom in front of the daytime soaps, and every day I sketched the shapes of clouds, studied their forms, and worked in my jewelry studio, which we set up in the junk shed near the hay barn. The old pot-bellied stove in there kept me cozy and warm while I worked. But sales were slow at best in that area, and we had to make do with what we had, which wasn't much in terms of money but was a lot in quality of life. We filled our gas tank from the supply on the ranch, ate elk and venison with those yummy fried "taters" Rick's mom cooked each night, scraped up enough cash to take in a drive-in movie, eat popcorn, and have hot sex in the privacy of our pickup in the parking lot. At night, while lightning storms lit up the western sky, we made love quietly in Rick's childhood bedroom in this farmhouse on the mesa while his folks slept only feet away in the next room. Sometimes, for more privacy, we spent the night on haystacks in the barn with our little family of dogs—Rick's two Australian Shepherds and Jeremiah Johnson. It was peaceful out in this simple farmhouse under a big Colorado sky with my man, my dog, and my chance to experience more of life.

In early July we packed huge leather saddlebags with cans of beans, tuna, milk, Spam, and other basic survival food, dog food, cartons of Marlboros and cans of Skoal, and a supply of marijuana buds. Fishing lures, lines, and poles went in, too, along with rain gear and changes of denim and flannel. We would follow an old Spanish trail along the Continental Divide at an average altitude of 12,000 feet and stay out for about a month. It was wilderness wilder than any I'd ever known, but Rick knew the area like some kids know their backyards. I trusted my guide completely.

Rain came the week we headed out, unseasonable rain, strange in July. But it didn't stop us. Rain or shine, we were going.

Those first days with the well-grazed mules were tough on Rick, who had the responsibility of tying the gear onto the animals every morning and re-tying it throughout the day when it slipped out of balance. The dogs chased rabbits as we rode trails so steep I was sure one of our round-bellied mules would slip and roll down the mountain with our gear tied to her back. But we all were making it just fine. Rick led the animals, and I pulled up the rear.

Lightning storms were frightening events. You could feel them coming—your hair would stand up on your arms. When a lightning storm approached, you had to tie up the horses and mules and take cover crouched against an embankment and away from tall trees. Rick said more people died in those mountains being struck by lightning than are killed driving the highways.

Rick taught me all about mountain life as we camped by crystal clear mountain lakes, catching trout and frying them up within minutes out of the icy water. The flesh was succulent and the pinkest I'd ever seen. Even the boxed mashed potato flakes tasted like pure heaven when they were drenched in butter, and the instant biscuits from a mix melted in our mouths in seconds flat. We watched herds of elk cross the green velvet meadows, humbled by their majesty and their number. Wildflowers peeked out of the undergrowth in the pine forests, and every night we warmed our fingers and toes in front of a roaring campfire. Many times I was sure we were lost, but Rick always found the disappearing trail and led us through the wilderness until we finally dropped low enough in altitude to follow the railroad tracks into the old mining town of Silverton.

In Silverton, a nineteenth-century mining town, I felt on top of the world. Tourists seeing us ride into town might have taken us for real prospectors as we rode in pulling our mule train, dusty and covered with the proof of having lived in the wilderness for thirty days. We tied up our horses and mules to the wooden rails lining the unpaved road and walked into town with our dogs. Rick had an old girlfriend in Silverton, and we visited her and rested for a few days, until Rick's dad could come to collect us with his horse trailer. We loaded the horses and mules into his trailer and climbed into the pickup, eager for our familiar roof and *real* bed.

Back at Rick's family ranch, it was time to consider our next move. I had no plans besides creating more jewelry to sell at local craft fairs and galleries for food and gas money. Rick had an idea: let's take the top off your jeep and drive to New York to see your daughter, then see what's around the bend. What a grand idea! Four days later, windblown and sunburned, we pulled into the driveway of the older house further in the country where Arnie had moved with Robin after selling our New Rochelle house. My old life was completely gone except for the people who inhabited it and some familiar furniture.

Robin squealed when she saw us pull up in the jeep, three dogs barking in the rear, and she ran into my open arms. Arnie welcomed us warmly, giving Rick a warm handshake. When we had a few private moments, Arnie admitted to me that Robin often woke during the night crying for her mother. It broke my heart to hear it, but I didn't know what to say. I knew Arnie had climbed his own mountains: packing up a life that had split wide open, selling the house, finding a simple place in the country to live. He was writing and working freelance so he could be home with our daughter and serve as both mother and father to her. I ached hearing all of this, yet I praised him, as did Rick, for the good man he so obviously was. We regaled him with stories of our high-country adventures, and somehow his heart opened to Rick, who from then on he called "brother." I swore to him and to all who would listen that our friendship would remain with us for life.

Robin was another story. Right away, Robin and Rick were inseparable. With me, though, Robin was cautious. She hung back. In later years I would learn that the scarlet letter had left its mark, as it had on me, although I wasn't willing to admit it.

All the way home to Colorado, I blamed myself for failing as a wife and mother. I hadn't kept up my part of the commitment. It was a hard reality to take. Another reality I couldn't avoid was that I had to find work. Victor asked us to go with him to his uncle's uranium mines in Gateway. "You oughta join me up there for a while. He needs a few hands," he told Rick.

We were clearly "on the run," though from what I'm not sure. All I knew was that adventure and travelin' that lonesome highway were leading us where we needed to go and feeding this pioneer girl's spirit. As long as we had a destination, we were happy. I sold my Jeep for a pickup, waved goodbye to Rick's folks, packed up what I'd take with me, and we were on our way to the Colorado-Utah border and the little town of Gateway, population 52.

Fish for dinner caught fresh from the Dolores River and wild aspara-
gus picked on the riverbanks was appealing for a while, but after eight
months, living in a plain two-bedroom farmhouse with Victor and his
girlfriend got old. And mining was taking its toll on Rick. Hard physical labor in a mineshaft a mile down into the earth for minimal pay was
anything but a cowboy's dream. It was time for something new.

For years Rick had thought about becoming a farrier, making a living
shoeing horses and being free to go where he wanted. It was a perfect job
for a cowboy, and it sounded like a fine idea to me. Rick found a farrier
school in El Paso, had a friend there we could stay with, and we moved
again, squeaking by on savings until he got his license and could get some
paid work. When farrier school ended we were just about flat broke, my
divorce was finalized, and the settlement check on its way would buy us
a ticket out of there. We begged the managers of a bank in south Texas to
cash my out-of-state check, then drove the dying pickup to a used car lot
and bought a shiny new truck complete with a camper trailer. California
would be the next stop, and this camper would be our traveling home.

Arnie lived in Woodland Hills outside Los Angeles now, in a spacious
suburban house, and Robin was much happier there. There were other
kids in the neighborhood, and the swimming pool entertained her day in
and out. We visited them on our way north, promising to come back to
visit often. We wanted someplace rugged and green, a place with a lot of
horse ranches and great big skies.

The Northern California coast along Highway One is famous for its
expanses of rolling hills dotted with grazing cows, stunning rocky shores,
and empty beaches. Dairy farms and ranches, private estates, and rural
dream houses fill the area, and we chose this area for our destination,
parking the trailer in a campground near Point Reyes State Park, about
thirty miles north of San Francisco. There was lot of money in Marin
County, and we expected a thriving business. The campground had good
showers, laundry facilities, and corrals for the horses we would bring out
soon from Colorado. The sleepy little town of Point Reyes Station, with
its bookstores, galleries, and bakery where the locals hung out was just
minutes away, and it offered some balance to the life of solitude I led.
Mostly I sought the peace of the windswept beaches and hiking trails

through the sloping hills and redwood forests and along the serene waterways of Tomales Bay. We had enough money to feed the horses and dogs and enough for our ground chuck and potatoes stew, and somehow we always scraped together enough change for gas, Skoal and Marlboros, and homegrown, which was pretty cheap back then.

Rick would need a horseshoeing rig to get started; our fifteen-foot "home" hauled from El Paso just wasn't going to do it. He found a used produce trailer, hung a sign on the side—"Garvan's Horseshoeing Service"—and he was ready for business. I set up my jewelry-making tools and sat down with a lot of new ideas. I would sell what I made at local craft fairs, and there seemed to be a lot of them in the Bay Area.

Rick's country ways were adorable to me. He was polite, gentle, helpful, kind, and always ready to lend a helping hand to anyone who asked. We made love every morning or night, after his efforts to earn his living. We didn't talk much, it just wasn't Rick's style, and for a while I didn't mind, but after a time I began to miss having friends to talk with. I found classes in Hatha yoga in town and stayed up late reading books about metaphysics and past-life regression. Rick wasn't interested in any of it, and I had to keep my thoughts to myself. I'd always known our styles were different, but they were beginning to scrape against each other a bit—the sweet, simple cowboy and this Kansas girl turned New York wife, turned suburban mom, turned jeweler and mountain woman, turned California soul searcher. Our quarters started feeling cramped, and sometimes I'd lose my patience. Climbing over Rick in the middle of the night to get to our tiny toilet, I once stepped into a smelly tobacco can that had been ripening for months. "Can't you keep your goddamn spittoon outside?" I'd cried, pounding on him, and he wrestled me down and tickled me until I collapsed in laughter and love.

A year into life on the California coast, we decided it was time for a change. Jet Spencer, a friend of Rick's from Durango, lived in Ojai, an hour north of Los Angeles. Jet was an artist with a crowded art studio, but he had floor space for a couple of friends until we found our own next home, and our dogs wouldn't be a problem. Work seemed promising in Ojai. The inland winters would be shorter, which could mean more work for Rick, and Arnie and Robin would be much closer. Rick drove the horses in the horse trailer all the way back to Durango to his folks' ranch, and I packed everything up and got ready for the move.

I hadn't been in touch much with Grandpa Nank since I'd left Arnie and headed west; in fact, I had been silent for several years. How could I explain to him what I was doing? Johnny told me Nank was living in a nursing home in Kansas and not doing too well. He was ninety-two. As soon as Rick got back from Colorado and we were settled into our room in Ojai, I used the last of our savings to fly to Kansas City for a long-overdue visit to my beloved Nank before it was too late.

⸙

As the cab from the airport in Kansas City turned up the drive to my roadside motel, I felt my stomach tighten as I tried to rehearse what I would tell Nank I was doing. I had to have a better story for him than the truth. How would this self-made man, this farmer's son who graduated college and became a veterinarian in 1908, feel about his "daisy" sleeping on a mattress on the floor in her boyfriend's friend's back room, living off meager earnings from her jewelry sold at craft fairs and his paltry earnings shoeing horses? Nank had bought me a beautiful four-bedroom home in New Rochelle and set me up for the good life with my husband so we could adopt our first child before I turned thirty. What in the world could I say?

But as soon as I got to the nursing home, I knew there was no need to worry. While I was so busy living my life, Nank had grown old and senile. I had expected to sit with him and hold his hand, to kiss his face and tell him I loved him, to thank him for loving me more than anyone in my young life.

He didn't recognize me.

"Nank, it's me!" I cried, sitting in the chair they'd put beside him for our visit. "It's Carolyn … your little daisy. Don't you remember me?" He looked ancient and lost.

"You don't recognize anyone, do you, Dr. Graham," the nurse said, straightening his collar and stepping back to look at us both. She saw this all the time, didn't she? I noticed a small card extending from the end of a plastic stick at the center of a wilting bouquet of spring flowers. I tugged it free and read, "Love from Mary"—my mother. She knew her dad was here. Did she care? Did she visit him? I had no idea what anything meant to her anymore. I had tried to reach my mother over the past few years and she had never answered or returned my calls. I just wanted was to make sure she was all right in her little apartment alone. I looked at the second bouquet, the fresh one. The card tucked into that bouquet read, "I love you, Elizabeth."

"His wife comes here every week," the nurse told me. I gave her a weak smile. Maybe I should call Elizabeth. Or maybe there was no one to call.

Guilt nearly sickened me as I held Nank's gnarled hand and asked him to forgive me, certain that any moment he would break into a smile and we would talk, like old times. I reminded him of how Johnny and I used to salt his coffee at breakfast when we stayed there, biting our tongues to keep from laughing. "Mmmmm, delicious," he'd always say. He taught us to play gin rummy and canasta and let us win and collect our candies and shiny quarters. I told him all about that, too.

He fell asleep while I talked, mouth open, drool snaking its way down his roadmap face.

After that first visit to Nank I nearly ran the mile back to my motel room to get my bearings. My grief seemed boundless. I cried and cried, and then I rallied and put myself back together. This was why I'd come, wasn't it? To see Nank. I splashed cold water on my face, brushed my hair into place, and headed back out.

For the next three days I was at that nursing home, getting to know the people who made up Nank's new family, all of them overflowing with warmth and good will. When it was time to say goodbye, my chest felt horribly tight as I kissed his craggy face. I sobbed all the way back to the motel, walking the shoulder of the highway as cars sped past. I had felt like this my first night at boarding school, but that was a different kind of loneliness. There was no end in sight with this one. I crawled into the flimsy bed and prayed for sleep.

In the morning I flew back to California and Rick picked me up at the airport in LA. We barely spoke all the way back to Jet's house an hour north. I hated to think of what was ahead of me. The jewelry business just wasn't cutting it, and Rick had smashed his thumb horseshoeing and couldn't work until it was healed. There would be applications to fill out for a waitressing job at Carrow's and other coffee shops in town. Raines, the local department store, wasn't hiring.

A week later, I came home tired and discouraged after a day of filling out job applications. "Your brother called," Jet said. "He said he's been trying to reach you. You better call him right away."

Johnny? Was everything all right? I grabbed my purse and headed out to find a payphone for some privacy.

"Are you sitting down?" Johnny's voice on the other end of the phone line sounded strangely comforting.

"I'm in a phone booth, I can't sit down. Are you all right?"

"Nank died. I got the news yesterday and flew to Kansas City last night. The service was this morning. I haven't been able to reach you."

"Oh, my God!" The tears came fast.

I told Johnny I felt I had helped Nank die. I had whispered to him that he could head for the light, that I was okay, Johnny was okay, he was okay. Johnny waited a few minutes while I cried. "I need to tell you something else," he said. "I met with a bank trustee and the attorney handling Nank's affairs."

I clutched the telephone cord to my chest and tried harder to listen.

"We both inherited a sizable trust fund."

"Sizable?"

"Enough to support us for the rest of our lives if we live modestly," he said.

I gasped. "I applied at Carrow's yesterday! The waitresses have to wear short skirts and knee-high black boots. I don't have to work there! Thank you, Nank."

After we hung up I sat down on the grass outside the phone booth for a long time. Nank was still watching over me, my guardian angel. (*"You can always count on me, my little daisy. I will never let you down."*) He had given me many gifts, taught me to value integrity and kindness, showed me love. And now he had left me set for life. Because of his gift I would be able to choose work that had real meaning to me.

I had once believed with all my heart that I would be a good mother. But I knew now that day-to-day parenting was not a bigger life purpose for me, and I was in the process of trying to forgive myself for not showing up for my daughter the way she needed. Could my disappointment in myself as a mother propel me toward a greater good, something beyond adventure and wandering? What was I here to offer that is greater than being a good mother? I wanted to give back to life as much or more than I felt I had received.

That day, sitting by the phone booth, I had no idea of the role destiny would play or had already played in my choices. All I knew was that opportunity lay at my feet and I was ready to start walking.

Chapter Three

The Power of Connection

While we waited for my funds to come through, Rick and I rented a small house by a dry creek bed in the poorer section of the Ojai Valley. Paint peeled off the clapboard sides and we had no furnishings besides a secondhand bed and a black and white TV. The abandoned garden surrounding the house survived somehow in the dry, caked soil. But I vowed to make this place our home for as long as we needed it. I had no idea how much money the trust fund would generate, and I was careful not to overextend myself in this flush of expansiveness. A few cans of fresh paint and some good yard sale furniture would get us off to a good start and the scent of sweet orange blossoms was everywhere.

But one night we pulled back the bed covers to find four scorpions resting on the bed sheets. I screamed and ran outside. How would I endure this? We slept in the truck that night.

The next day Rick got a call to shoe some horses at a nearby ranch and I went along for the ride; anything to get out of our private ghetto. We drove our rig—a white Ford pickup pulling a tall corrugated aluminum trailer that still bore the word "PRODUCE" in faint lettering—up a winding road, and passed through the gate to the Levines's five-acre ranch. We passed corrals, tack rooms, and a barn before pulling to a stop in front of an older ranch house situated under the oak trees. Madeleine

Levine approached as I climbed out of the truck, her arms outstretched to greet me.

"You're here!" she said, giving me and then Rick a generous hug. Along with glistening white teeth and a perpetual smile, she wore a low-cut T-shirt, contoured riding pants, and knee-high riding boots. She waved for us to follow her. ""Come meet Barry. He'll love you, Kernie. He *loves* company. Rick and I will work on my horses."

Rick and I glanced at each other and followed her into the funky house then into a bedroom, where I was met by a pair of blue eyes so intense they shook me to the core. His face, crowned by a head of medium brown curls threaded with silver, made my knees tremble. His look was so bold and forthright I felt naked under his gaze.

Barry Levine was a successful Hollywood screenwriter who lived most of his life from bed. He weighed over four hundred pounds and could barely walk to the bathroom or to the car to drive into Hollywood for meetings with the heads of all the major studios. But that didn't hold him back. He was creative, productive, and very interested in women. He motioned for me to stay while Madeleine took Rick to the stable to begin their day of grooming and shoeing her magnificent Arabians.

I looked around the room. There was a large sunken bathtub encircled by windows nearby, and the accoutrements of bed life surrounded him: pillows of various sizes, a water-filled carafe, a tray of vitamins, a breakfast plate with remnants of an English muffin. "Would you take my tray to the kitchen?" Barry said.

It was as if I were ordered by royalty to perform the task. "Of course I will," I said, feeling his gaze as I walked from the room. When I returned from my errand, Barry nodded toward a worn easy chair across from him. "Have a seat," he said. "I want to connect with those eyes." His commands were clear and benevolent.

No one had ever asked to "connect" with my eyes before. I wasn't sure I even knew what he meant by "connect." I sat down. Barry looked into me more deeply than anyone had ever looked into me, more deeply than I had even looked into myself. I felt vulnerable in front of the most astounding sight I had ever seen.

Barry lay belly down on his king-sized bed clad in a cornflower blue velour caftan. He supported himself on his elbows, a telephone nestled in the crook of his arm. His flesh took up half the bed. "So where did you get this name? Kernie. That is your name, right?"

I told him my brother hadn't been able to say "Carolyn" when we were kids, and Kernie became a nickname that stuck. "You can call me Kern," I said, feeling strangely familiar already with this mammoth being before me.

He smiled, focusing his sharp intensity on me. "Kern. Do you have any idea how absolutely adorable you are? When I saw you jump out of that pickup, my first thought was how can I spend time with her? Kern, let me ask you. Does this horseshoeing cowboy speak to your heart? Are you happy?"

I felt exposed under that direct gaze of his. With nowhere to hide I came pouring out. I told my new confidant how sad I was not to be able to reach inside of Rick and contact the person in there. I shared my grief about my grandfather's death and told him the news of my inheritance.

"How wonderful!" Barry cried. "An heiress just walked into my bedroom! How does it feel to go from rags to riches?" He asked me why I was settling for a sweet, sexy, yet-to-incarnate cowboy like Rick. I jumped to Rick's defense, though even as I spoke of what a good man he was, tears burned my eyes. I could see it coming: I was going to have to make another change very soon.

Rick had been an "I'll save you" relationship and the fulfillment of this Kansas girl's dream of the all-American cowboy. It felt so natural to just love him. He had survived Vietnam and was my way of serving the cause. He was my partner in rebellion—rebellion against my dad, rebellion at the confined though expansive container of a life I had created with Arnie. Was I so unprepared? Was I truly just a rebellious, lost and lonely teenager acting out unexpected behavior?

Rick was also a man I loved sharing my sexuality with. I felt safe with Rick in many ways. Life with him had been a grand adventure. But my romantic fantasies of loving a cowboy had failed to include the realities of living with an emotionally damaged Vietnam vet. I had thought he would rehabilitate simply by our being together, or that my love for him could cure anything, but it was proving to be a long and arduous return for this wounded cowboy.

We talked about my situation and what possibilities there might be for better living conditions than having scorpions for bedmates. Barry was a problem solver, and we were soon creating solutions for me. These solutions would require me to become more responsible and more accountable. I was ready for it.

Barry explained why a fifty-four-year-old man his size welcomed visitors in his sunny bedroom. Barry craved complete presence by anyone within his range. Two years earlier he had undergone intestinal bypass surgery and he was still recovering from the new and radical surgery. He had weighed 600 pounds when he went in for the surgery, which involved removing most of his intestinal tract. Barely digested food went straight to the colon, where it was eliminated many times throughout the day and night. He was proud to weigh only 450 pounds now, but the dozens of trips to the bathroom were exhausting and much of the nutrients from the food he ate were never absorbed due to the removal of his intestines.

Barry was part of the in-club in Hollywood, and well-known producers and directors were often on the other end of his phone line. He had achieved enormous success with several hit films that decade, and he continued to sell his screenplays. Barry was commanding and clear. He wasted no time on small talk. He quickly gathered the information he needed to identify me—I was thirty-four and divorced with a daughter living with her dad. Rick and I had recently moved to Ojai from the North Coast, where I practiced Hatha yoga and dabbled in self-taught massage, metaphysics, and past-life regression. I offered to show him a few of the stretches from my yoga practice. I was very flexible, and he was delighted to see my movements. It was an extreme contrast to him, as he could barely even walk to the bathroom or to the large tub near his bed.

From his bed—his throne—Barry watched life on his ranch through a large picture window. He needed and wanted to be informed of everything, and he was thoroughly entertained by Madeleine's prowess with her Arabians. She would ride by his window on her favorite black stallion, spectacular in her riding pants and leather boots, her lovely breasts bouncing in a thin tee-shirt. As she passed she would call out a greeting to

"Barr." Soon we were twinkling sensual magnetism to one another, and I had to admit I felt turned on. When we said goodbye, the Levines invited me to come back and visit anytime.

The next morning, our phone rang. The Levines wanted to know if we had a portable TV they could borrow. Their television had broken and Barry needed a TV as soon as possible. Rick had to return that day to finish shoeing Madeleine's horses, so we put our 24-inch TV in the trailer along with Rick's anvil, dozens of pairs of horseshoes, mallets, nails, an acetylene torch for heating steel, and other tools of the trade. I rode in the trailer to make sure the TV reached its destination safely.

"It's not color!" Barry wailed, when he saw what we had brought him.

But we were still saving the day for Barry, as watching TV helped him relax and kept him tuned into shows that were important for his work. He and Madeleine were grateful for our generosity and assured us Barry's TV would be working again soon.

Barry and I talked through another afternoon, and at the end of it he told Madeleine I wanted to relocate. "Why don't you move in here?" she said. "We have a small cottage here you could rent."

That night I told Rick my plans. I explained it was time for us to take some space and for him to get his financial life together. I could not sleep in a house with scorpions, and I wanted more. I wanted someone to help me buy my own vehicle, help me invest my new money, and show me some family love. I invited Rick to spend one night a week with me in my new cottage and be my lover, but I wanted to live apart.

Rick was in a spin. "You just met them!"

"I know."

It had only been a week since we'd met the Levines. But what choice did I have? I couldn't do the adventurous existence of hand-to-mouth survival anymore.

After all those months in a trailer and then in the rental on the dry creek bed, the cottage was a relief with its relative comforts. I spent the days cleaning and setting up my house, planting flowers out front, and running errands in town for Barry or Madeleine. Madeleine came into Barry's room in the evenings and brought dinner to us on trays. I liked giving nurturing and healing touch and she asked me to sit with Barry as often as I wanted and massage him. "He needs touch more than anything," she had said. I massaged Barry's huge expanse of back, neck, legs, and feet, and enjoyed flirtatious play with this amazing creature draped in velvet caftans. As I massaged Barry, he drifted in and out of lazy naps and moaned with delight. Sometimes Madeleine would come in and sit in the easy chair across from the bed, playing her guitar and capturing my heart as she sang haunting love songs she and Barry had written about their love for each other. Between songs, she told me stories of her career as a singer/songwriter, playing with Kenny Loggins and appearing on the Smothers Brothers show. She told me how she had met Barry and how he had seduced her. Madeleine came from a Mafia-connected family, and Barry was a New York Jew who had started his career in New York City clubs, where he discovered a famous comedy act in the 1960s. In Hollywood he rose fast to the top, but he was unhappy there and he ate his way to this immense weight, stopping only when he realized the threat it was to his life. With Madeleine's support he had agreed to the radical surgery that could save his life from the ravages of obesity.

The Levines were different from anyone I had known. They were vibrant and loving. I loved talking with Barry and laughing at his stories. His wit earned him millions before it was all used up keeping him alive. But besides his great creative wit, Barry and Madeleine were dedicated to emotional authenticity and to speaking their minds; you never had to wonder how they felt. I needed that and found it easier to do it myself with their support and modeling. They knew that emotional health meant physical health, and both were top priority. Their nutritionist taught me how to eat to maximize my health and energy. In a year, I cleansed a lifetime of pizza and cheeseburgers and lost the last of my baby fat.

In the beginning I was in denial of the sexual attraction between Barry and me. I couldn't imagine how sex could fit into this unfolding new relationship. But I was melted butter under his gaze. Barry had confided to me that Madeleine was not terribly interested in sex, and he needed pleasure—he wanted passion. He was also distressed that because of the size of his belly he couldn't even reach his penis to pleasure himself. My compassionate heart responded. Three years before I would meet Charles

Muir and eight years before I would hear of Tantra or sexual healing, I offered to assist Barry with his dilemma and surprised myself with my own sexual healing: Here was a penis so unthreatening I began healing my confusing fear of them. A vulnerable penis belonging to a vulnerable man was nothing to be afraid of.

Barry insisted that his fiery Italian wife would not want to know what we did. Even if she did know, she would not want to be told. I knew she loved Barry, but their differences were obvious, too. Madeleine was always outdoors—repairing buildings, grooming or riding her horses, or playing music in her studio. She stopped in throughout the day to confer with Barry or bring him lunch. Sometimes she picked up her guitar and sang for us. I loved their connection and creativity, loved being part of their daily concerns and commitments. I wanted to help in any way I could, even if it meant taking care of Barry's needs and fantasies without sharing it with his wife. We talked constantly about sex, and when he asked me one day to touch my own "pussy" while he watched, I shyly agreed. The curtains were drawn and we told Madeleine through the window, "Barry's napping."

Being with Barry was my first experience with a man who talked me into orgasm, looking deeply into my eyes as I pleasured myself in the easy chair across from his bed. I would then massage his back and he would roll over so I could lift his small member out of its nest and place it into my mouth. In just a few seconds he would squeal and orgasm, thanking me over and over as I wiped and powdered him like a baby on a changing table. After reapplying the Noxzema to his always-sore anus, I covered him with one of his velvet caftans and he rested. I was then free to help with chores, work outside with Madeleine, or write in my journal in the quiet, cool solitude of my rustic cabin.

Barry had told me of the many Hollywood beauties he had dated and that he had always "scored." He was successful, which appealed to any actress, but he also knew how to connect with the heart and soul of a woman. I understood now that for Barry scoring meant he got to see and touch and taste a woman while being pleasured himself. Intercourse was not in his repertoire.

Barry's meetings at the Hollywood studios were frequent, and I became his driver. I would haul Barry, lunch, and anything else he might need in my new Dodge van, where he would lie in the back on a big futon with Indian print bedspreads draped all around for the full-day excursions into Los Angeles. We laughed and talked, Barry entertaining me the whole way. We stopped on the coast so Barry could breathe in the scent of the sea with all the van windows open wide, and we'd visit his favorite seafood drive-in and feast on calamari and fries or fish and chips. He never left the van for these picnics, as walking was the most difficult thing in his life and he needed to save his energy for the meetings in Hollywood. When we were ready to head "back to the ranch," we'd call Madeleine, who would tell us what to pick up for dinner.

One day, a woman named Mira came to visit the ranch, and she fell in love with our zany, creative family. Mira was a burnt-out fashion designer whom the Levines knew, and she was ready to leave Los Angeles and live a quieter life. We offered her the empty bedroom in the old ranch house, just around the corner and a few steps down from the Levines' suite. The family was growing.

Mira quickly fell into step as our helper in service to all of the family needs. She tie-dyed the fabric we used for Barry's caftans and made colorful wall hangings and slipcovers. She never accepted Barry's invitations to relieve him of his sexual tension, but she loved him and waited on him in every other way. I adored Mira as I adored Madeleine and Barry.

Evenings now saw the four of us getting high, telling stories, and listening to Madeleine play guitar. Recreational excursions into altered states of consciousness were a regular part of our lives. Barry and Madeleine were quasi-hippies, like Mira and me, and we took our share of mescaline and LSD, loving the magic of our times together. Barry didn't believe in alcohol or cigarettes, and we had to sneak them, a small thrill, as if we were kids hiding our pranks from Big Daddy. I used a lot of mouthwash and mints to cover my smoking habit.

In stolen moments, Barry and I played with our sexuality in our precious but limited way, always watching to make sure we didn't get caught. That was a big part of the excitement. And we escaped being caught in the nick of time more than once. I don't remember much about my own sexual satisfaction with Barry, but my heart was full and I felt needed and loved beyond measure. He only penetrated me once in those two years, proudly, with his few inches of love and a heart full of vulnerability. Somehow he miraculously heaved himself on top of me and thrust six times before falling over in post-orgasmic bliss.

One of the great gifts of my time with Barry was that I began to understand that sexuality expressed along with genuine love is essential for me. It is what makes me tick—it is how I expose my vulnerability and experience my totality. With Barry, I thought of myself as a healer. I knew the power of love, and I knew how to transmit my love through my hands, eyes, and body. I also learned how to *receive* love through my eyes. This was our primary foreplay—our eyes did most of the kissing, fondling, and caressing that prepares most people for sex. I was pioneering sexual loving before I had a clue that this was my spiritual work.

And what a relief it was to discover I could choose another family after having left my own. I felt nourished, integral, and I was aware for the first time of my freedom, even the freedom to create more family. The Levines and Mira welcomed my daughter on visits and graciously entertained Johnny, Rick, and Arnie, and even my dad and his wife, Marty, when they came once to visit. For the Levines it was enough just knowing they were my kin and my duty to them was paramount to all.

In 1977, two years after I'd moved to the Levines' ranch, I decided it was time to find out if Rick and I had anything worth salvaging. We visited, and our passion for each other was magnetic. I asked Rick to live with me at the Levines', with Madeleine and Barry's blessings. Within months I bought a house, a typical suburban house with a swimming pool, just a short walk into the town of Ojai. We moved in. When Rick asked me to marry him, I said yes. His emotional wounding from Vietnam and from his early childhood concerned me, but I didn't want to think about it. I wanted a life of ease, and that seemed possible with Rick now that I knew more about loving, communicating, and relating in a successful way. I believed in the healing power of love and trusted that Rick would get all he needed with my love and greater commitment. The future was filled with magnificent dreams.

Chapter Four

Angel Sister Lover Friend

I was married again, and this time I wasn't going to do everything my husband's way. I wasn't having the burgers and beer of our last round. I insisted that Rick eat salads, sprouts, fresh vegetable juices, and nuts and seeds. While Rick looked for work, I went to yoga classes, took long bike rides and hikes into the surrounding hills, visited the Theosophical Library to immerse myself in the metaphysical and mystical, and kept up my commitment to a healthy way of life. We got a second Golden Retriever and named him Jake, and both dogs stayed home with Rick while I drove into Los Angeles to give massages in clients' homes, mostly people in the film industry. I hauled my table up many long staircases into grand mansions to help and heal the movers and shakers of LA. I don't know how these people found me, but they did and they kept asking me back.

Back at home, Rick couldn't seem to find a fit for himself. This time, I wasn't feeling the struggle of going along with him—I was feeling the strain of supporting him. When Robin was a pre-teen visiting us in Ojai, the two of them would get along as I always had wanted to with her—talking, laughing, swimming in the pool, hanging out like friends. I would clean up after them, feed them, and be the parental adult, a role I did not like. Resentment grew as I once again assumed the role of caretaker, structure- and rule-maker, with what felt like a family of two children rather than two adults and one child.

We were growing more restless and irritated. One day Rick bounded into the living room, where I sat curled in a chair, reading. His eyes were bright, the way they looked when he had a good idea. "Kern, I was thinking," he said, dropping into the chair next to mine. "Let's drive to Carmel Valley and see Jet." He kissed me. "It'll be good for us. We haven't seen him since he moved."

I considered it for a minute. Why not? Jet managed a few galleries in Carmel that featured handmade arts and crafts. Maybe seeing him again would inspire Rick to get something more going on here at home. "Let's go," I said.

In love with spontaneity, we threw some things in a bag as the dogs jumped into the back of the pickup, sensing as they always did that we were going somewhere and it might be real fun for them. We drove the five hours north, arriving at Jet's after dinner. We got acquainted with his new place and settled into our futon in the art studio. It was cold with the electric heater, but we made our own heat. The vacation was off to a good start.

In the morning Jet gave us a tour of his studio, showed us his recent paintings, and made us a pot of coffee to take out to the porch. "So there's a party tonight," Jet said, settling back in his chair, his big legs stretched out straight before him. "This woman named Gigi."

Rick grinned. "Uh huh."

"Her thirtieth birthday. Come with me. You'll love her."

Rick winked at me. "Why not?"

I agreed. A party in Carmel Valley sounded like fun.

That night we went to Gigi's house. I was entranced by her the moment I saw her standing at the buffet table, her curves draped in apricot yoga pants and an apricot cashmere sweater. Her silky long hair swung about her face as she turned to greet us. "Jet!" she cried, opening her arms to greet him. Jet hugged her and then introduced us. "Meet my pals from down south."

She took my hand in both of hers. "Good to meet you."

"Happy birthday," I said. Her face seemed familiar, but I couldn't imagine why.

We followed Gigi through the crowded rooms, clearly not the only people wowed by this woman who sparked the air around her. Even her husband seemed shadowed by her radiance. Gigi led us into the back garden. "Take a look around," she called out, turning to greet more friends. We were offered a joint by some people taking in the sunset on the patio. Jet joined them, leaving me and Rick to explore the winding paths of Gigi's garden. It was wonderfully wild with climbing roses and blooming purple irises everywhere.

All I could think of was Gigi. What a smile! And hadn't I heard her voice a thousand times before? I had become interested in past lives and I thought we might have known each other in an earlier incarnation. I was determined to get to the bottom of it.

At the end of the evening Gigi and I agreed that we wanted more time to get to know each other. She invited us to dinner the following night. I didn't even check with Rick, who was beside me as I confirmed, with sparkling eyes, "We'll be there, Gigi. Let me know what I can bring."

For years I had fantasized about being intimate with a woman, and Gigi was exactly the kind of woman who attracted me. Levine had tantalized me with stories of women loving one another, and it was my favorite fantasy in my own sexual pleasuring. But I was too shy to pursue fulfillment of my fantasy, and no woman had ever approached me.

The fragrance of bread baking and a fire blazing in the woodstove welcomed us the following evening as we entered Gigi's home and were swept into the arms of the divine mother within her. She served us a delicious meal and then we took seats by the wood-burning stove while the men visited at the other end of the room. Gigi's son, Mitch, was twelve, a gorgeous young male image of her. I told Gigi she reminded me of my mother. "I know this sounds strange, but you *smell* like my mother, Gigi," I laughed. I told her about a cream my mother wore, from a cosmetics company that an old friend of hers had founded.

Gigi sat up straight. "My aunt founded a cosmetics company!"

"This was a long time ago. I think my mother started wearing that cream when my dad was in the army and they lived in Carlisle."

"My mother lived in Carlisle! My dad was stationed there."

Chills ran up my spine.

"What's your mother's name?" Gigi asked.

"Mary Graham Cusack."

"I can't believe this! I know that name."

It was too late to call Gigi's mother and tell her she had met her old friend's daughter, but she would call her first thing the next morning and then call me. "She always wondered what happened to your mom after the war. She is going to be so excited."

As Rick and I drove in silence to Jet's house that night, I could feel something shifting in me. A missing part of me was falling into place. No one had a context for what was occurring between Gigi and me. I was about to see my own beauty reflected back through the recognition of it in Gigi's eyes. I was about to discover that my sexuality was mine, to be shared as I wished with whomever I wished. I was about to be reborn into a more faceted version of who I thought I was.

The next morning, Gigi called. "Wait 'til you hear this, Kern. Our moms were best friends in that apartment complex during the war. My mother babysat you when your parents went out or your mom had to run to the store. She gave your mom her first jar of that cream around the time you were born. Mom wants us to come over *immediately*."

Gigi picked me up at Jet's house and Rick stayed behind while we drove to her mother's house in Carmel for this remarkable reunion. Her mother beamed as she opened the door and swept me into her arms. She plucked a cotton ball from deep inside her abundant cleavage: there it was, my mother's smell. She said, "You loved to pull these from my bra when I held you in my arms. You always knew where to look for that good smell, sweet Carolyn."

I inhaled the familiar, soulful scent of my mother.

We sat together talking and Gigi and I learned that we are the third generation in both of our families to become friends through accidental meetings. Our grandparents had met each other while traveling with a group to Greece, and back home in Kansas and Ohio they had continued their friendship. Our fathers ended up in the same platoon in the army, their wives had become close friends, and now Gigi and I had met. It was destiny.

A week after our return to Ojai, I turned around and drove back to Carmel Valley to fall into Gigi's arms. Her husband was out of town, and

Mitch was staying with his grandparents. Through the day we walked hand in hand along the streets of Carmel, stopping into boutiques to browse and buy trinkets that pleased us. We tried on cute hats that framed our faces and delighted in each other as we left the store wearing them. We bought flannel nighties to warm us as we talked late into the night. We played with our passion, exploring each other sexually. We lacked the expertise to express our passion, but we met each other full of desire, certain that there was room in both of our marriages for the truth of this aliveness to express itself.

Who would start the lovemaking? What would we do? I wished I had paid attention to exactly what those men did when they placed their soft lips upon my goddess button of passion. Should I lick softly or with more pressure, faster or slower, up and down or sideways with circles? How would I get a breath of air or keep my neck from cramping? Did she like it? Should I be looking at her? How could I ask her for directions with my mouth buried in her yoni? And if she did come, should I keep on going? We were total novices with 100-horsepower passion fueling us as we curled up close, content to be together this way. When we picked up Mitch on Sunday we both wore big Cheshire-cat grins.

After a few perfect days with Gigi and Mitch, I went home. I felt lost, alone, and confused in Ojai. We called each other every day. We admitted that we felt constricted with our men and expansive with one another. We felt completely seen by each other, something we did not feel in our marriages. What did this mean? What trouble had we started? Our identities were heterosexual, yet we loved each other in a way I had never known with anyone.

Gigi and I were the sisters we both had always wanted. We also were each the child our parents couldn't figure out, the one who caused the big stir in the family. Gigi had gotten pregnant with Mitch when she was in high school. I had married at eighteen. We had disappointed our parents, never going to college and fitting into their picture of the perfect daughter, the *only* daughter. But here, with each other, we found the un-conditional love we needed.

I began traveling often between Ojai and Carmel. Rick saw me dizzy with excitement whenever I spoke with Gigi on the phone or packed a suitcase to go and see her, and he never said a word. He must have felt threatened and sad, but I think he didn't want to interfere with my happiness. And I didn't want to talk about it. I didn't know where my relationship with Gigi was going any more than I knew what to do with this man I loved and had married but wasn't sure was right for me.

In Carmel Gigi and I spent endless hours curled up with cups of tea talking about our marriages, our fantasies, our sexual histories, our longings, and our passions until we finally had to admit we would rather be free to be with each other—or anyone else, for that matter—than living the lives we were living. We encouraged each other to make whatever changes were needed to claim our sovereignty as autonomous women.

Within months after our meeting, Gigi told her husband she wanted a separation and eventually they divorced. I remained unresolved about what to do with Rick. Our primary challenges were how to bridge our extreme differences and his financial frustrations. Meanwhile, Gigi and Mitch kept the home fires burning and counted the days until my next visit. I loved seeing her come in from the garden on a sunny morning carrying baskets overflowing with vegetables and herbs. She fed us meals Mitch and I agreed were the best anywhere. Gigi took book-binding orders at her shop in town, and in her art studio at home she created sculptures, paintings, weavings, beadwork, everything beautiful, creative, and inspiring.

At the end of the year, after a year and a half of marriage, Rick and I decided to separate. He would move to Los Angeles to study acting, and we could visit each other. Jeremiah would go with him, as he had become Rick's dog, and I would keep Jake. There was no urgency about divorce. Gigi and I considered living together, but decided not to. I didn't want to leave Ojai and I didn't want to put any more distance between Rick and me or to move farther away from Robin. I felt empowered now that I claimed my love for this woman and opened to love and friendship on new levels. I stood taller and walked with more grace. I was melting sweet butter in every cell of my being at even the thought of my angel sister lover friend.

I had never been so happy and so much in love, and neither had Gigi. We relaxed into self-acceptance, understanding that love is all that's accurate, not labels for our sexuality. Gigi was very visible in her small community, yet she wasn't afraid to flaunt her sexy love for me in public. We were as much in love with life as with each other, and our passion seemed to enhance our appeal to men, who flocked to her door after her husband left, to see her or to see us both if I was visiting. We had lovers, and every so often, feeling tentative and daring, continued our own sexual explorations together. We were ripe with life as we tasted the forbidden-yet-so-available nectar of our juicy, loving friendship and we drank from the strength of that friendship during the waves of uncertainty that come with divorce and readjustment to autonomy.

In Ojai, the four-bedroom house with the pool felt too big sometimes without Rick, but I had to stay open to possibility. Gigi's life was full. We saw each other less as the months went on, talking by phone about life and our dreams and who we were dating, if there was someone that especially interested us. She would eventually settle on her next husband and move away from Carmel, and I would fall in love again and again and again. I would learn many years later that Gigi had saved all of the cards and letters we wrote to one another in that first, passion-filled year we knew each other. On her dressing table she would keep a porcelain figurine of a woman set into a padded burgundy velvet box, a gift I gave her soon after we met. That figurine is a symbol that says my heart is always at home on your hearth. That feeling goes with us wherever we are.

Carmel Valley, it turned out, had more delicious surprises in store for me. One evening, during a visit to Gigi, a friend named Mackie and I attended a yoga class that Charles Muir taught at the Carmel Women's Club. I had taken yoga classes before, and I knew every teacher had a different style. Charles' style interested me because of his focus on our chakras (energy centers), on deep slow breathing, and on a quiet mind. His instruction was clear, and his hypnotic voice was positive and empowering. "As you exhale, send your love to your stiff or aching back," he would say. "Remember to bring your busy mind back to following your breath as you inhale, expanding your lungs and filling them with the prana in the air, sometimes seen as an angel in the air." In my inner vision I saw angels flying up my nostrils along with my breath and felt love in my heart before exhaling the breath into my aching back. By the end of the two-hour class I was light-hearted, grounded, and eager to pay my ten dollars.

Charles said good night to each of us as we left, finding our way to our cars in the chilly night air. I thanked him, smiling into his startlingly blue eyes. As Mackie and I walked to the car, she said with a knowing twinkle in her eye, "I thought you'd like Charles." She told me he was offering a weeklong yoga retreat in February at a spa in Mexico and she was planning to go. "Come and room with me," she said. What an idea! Why not go? It was a dream of mine to spend a week at a yoga retreat. I wanted more of what I had just experienced. I needed this kind of soul expansion. "Count me in," I said.

Chapter Five

Kundalini, Here I Come

Rio Caliente Spa is tucked into the Sonora Mountains of central Mexico about an hour's drive from the airport in Guadalajara. At its source is a volcanic river, making its way downstream through wild high desert once inhabited by the Quichol Indians. The spa was built in the early '60s at the source of the hot river as a retreat for people who wanted to soak in its healing waters. People primarily came down from the cold New York and New England winters to "take the waters," as Charles did, in 1968, when a yoga teacher of his in New York City first introduced him to Rio Caliente. Some years later it was a favorite place of his to hold retreats.

In my roaring twenties, I was introduced to my chakras and to yoga. These were my thrilling thirties, and the expansion of love inside me was happening at a fast pace. At Rio Caliente, with the many hours of yoga practice with Charles, my heart chakra finally exploded into shimmering shards of diamond light. I was in the company of twenty-two kindred spirits committed to time spent on our lumpy Mexican yoga mats and all that could happen there. At an altitude of 6,000 feet in the magical valley of primavera (eternal spring), I knew for the first time what a chakra looked like in full bloom and I knew how it felt!

From that day on, it seemed I tasted the smell of the wild sage covering the mountainous terrain for hundreds of miles around the spa. I could feel the lithium from the mineral-rich waters of the volcanic hot river that snaked its way through the valley for several hundred miles to the Sea of Cortez; it coursed through my system once it penetrated my skin. My eyes became a brighter shade of blue from the inner light that had awakened in me and they dazzled all who came under their gaze. I was in a naturally altered state from fasting, cleansing, soaking in the steam cave or the rushing river, and experiencing massage and healing treatments from Charles and other healers like the Rolfer Owen James, polarity therapist David Fuess, and John Sanderson, who offered and taught massage. Long hikes down-river deep into shaman country fed the adventurer within me as I felt delivered into an invincible state of vitality, health, and expanded awareness.

Between the intoxicating location with its beauty and warm sunshine, the six hours a day of yoga practice, the new friends, and the guidance of Charles Muir, who was fast becoming a friend as well as a deeply inspiring yoga teacher, the experience at Rio Caliente was life-changing. I knew that feeling this much love for everyone and everything was the way I wanted to live my life. I worked to maintain this state when I returned home to Ojai and continued my yoga classes, long hikes, and bicycle rides through the orange groves in bloom. I continued seeing Rick every week as our marriage transitioned into a friendship of wishing one another the best that life could offer.

In July, on my second trip to Rio Caliente, I stayed for two weeks of both beginner and intermediate yoga classes. I assisted Charles in teaching basic Hatha yoga to two husbands whose wives were in Charles' class, and I assisted David with many of his polarity and massage sessions. Gigi came to Rio for a week and had a hot love affair with one of the massage therapists on staff, while I enjoyed flirtatious early stages of a love affair with David. This passionate affair lasted a delicious six months or so before I met another man, a chiropractor from Malibu, and canceled a vacation in Hawaii with David the day before we were to go. To say that in those days I was unconscious of how my actions impacted others would be an understatement. I'm not proud of it. I just wasn't ready to be in integrity with the heart of another.

Life as a single woman in Ojai was a balancing act between aloneness and loneliness. The Malibu chiropractor turned out also not to be "the one," and I was on my own again when the divorce with Rick was finalized. It didn't take much more than a visit to a divorce lawyer in Ventura—one hundred and fifty dollars later my marriage with Rick was over. Neither of us wanted the cost or the anguish of a contested divorce.

Arnie and Rick, these two who had been my closest companions and who sincerely cared for each other, were a foundation for me as I continued to grow, living on my own and being a long-distance mom as I drove into Los Angeles every few days to help Arnie and his new wife, Nancy, with Robin, to discuss school changes, her time with friends, to give her rides here and there, and to simply have time together. I treasured the time I spent with Robin, Arnie, and Nancy, and Rick, too, all of them offering a much needed reminder that I was loved and forgiven for my inconsistencies.

And then the pioneering spirit called to me once again.

One early autumn evening, I went to a party in Malibu hoping to run into that lovely "not the one" doctor of chiropractic at a cliff-side house overlooking the sea. Not recognizing anyone familiar, I took a seat by the fire with my drink. A tall man approached and stood beside me. I looked up into a pair of piercing blue eyes gazing invitingly into mine.

"I'm Ron," he said, offering a hand. Crow's feet crinkled the corners of his captivating eyes.

I introduced myself.

"Kern?!" The name seemed to get stuck in his mouth on its way out. "Are you sure? That doesn't sound like the name for such a beautiful woman."

I laughed. "My name is Carolyn. I've always hated it." I told him I was named for my great-grandmother, Caroline, and I had thought for some time of changing my name to hers.

He tasted the name like a connoisseur tasting fine wine. "Caroline." Spoken in his magnetic, mellifluous voice, that name suddenly sounded like the most beautiful name I had ever heard. From that night forward, I would be Caroline. Everyone who knew me as Kern or Kernie would have to adapt to my new, beautiful name. That night, too, I decided to give up Arnie's last name and Rick's last name, and claim my middle name as my surname: Graham. It was my grandfather's surname.

Ron sat down beside me, set his drink on the coffee table so he could face me with all of his attention, and we talked with ease. He was divorced, a TV actor with his own series, a river guide, and a tree surgeon. I was impressed by all the ways he made a living. I also liked the soft way he spoke of his three grown children and how much he shared with them. He was fifty-one, older than any man I'd considered being with before (to a thirty-six-year-old twice-divorced woman, fifty-one was *much* older).

I searched for something to say. I wanted to be as interesting to him as he was to me. "I live in Ojai," I told him, "And I do yoga and professional massage. I've lived in Kansas, Florida, New York, Colorado, and California. I've sailed from England to Spain, and I rode horseback for a month in the Rocky Mountains with my former cowboy husband."

His eyes twinkled as he reached for his drink. "Former cowboy?"

"Former husband. We divorced not too long ago. He's a good man, just not the *right* man."

A moment passed, and then he said the magic words: "Are you free to be courted, Caroline?"

With words like that (not to mention eyes like that!), I certainly *was* free! I gave him my phone number.

The next afternoon, Ron called. He wanted to come to Ojai—thirty miles north of his home in Woodland Hills—and take me to dinner. He *was* serious about courting! And I was curious. This would be my first real date since high school.

Giddy with anticipation, I spent hours getting ready the day of our date. I called Gigi and told her about this handsome stranger. She was distracted, caught up in her involvement with the man she would marry soon, but she was happy I'd met someone who interested me so much.

I watched from the window as Ron pulled up in his yellow vintage Porsche looking relaxed and casual. I was hardly that. I had had some life experience, but I was a novice when it came to dating. And I had never dated anyone as worldly, intelligent, and unfamiliar as Ron.

We chatted in my living room and I took in every detail of him, from the brand of his boots to the way his mouth curled and even quivered at the corners when he spoke. He spoke slowly, choosing his words with care. What a relief it was when he suggested a favorite restaurant of mine. I was aware of the sexual chemistry with this man and I wanted to get this courtship under way! I grabbed my purse and we were off.

Good food and a few martinis later, I thanked my date for dinner with a light kiss on his cheek and a heartfelt embrace. I knew we would become lovers, but not yet. I undressed and slipped into bed, glad to be alone, while he drove back to Woodland Hills. How sweet it was to be courted.

Is it still courting when you have dinner at your date's house, then let your sexual chemistry go wild? I let myself be seduced, stripped bare of more than my clothes. I was alive, though unsure of myself. I didn't know yet about the difference between sexual chemistry and sexual alchemy, but I liked how this man kissed. He was sensual in an old-fashioned kind of way…polite, gentlemanly, gentle. Nothing makes a woman like me come into bloom faster than being desired by a man she respects. Life suddenly took on the glow of romance and passion, and I was happy to have a lover who shared so many of my passions in and out of the bedroom.

That fall and winter we spent many overnights in Ron's simple home in Woodland Hills and at my place in Ojai. Ron was guarded, mistrustful, but he wanted his own free-spirited and loving nature to soar with mine. I believed I could help him release that locked-up part of himself, and I was committed to trying, sure that our differences were no problem. Ron was not the touchy-feely type, while I loved the intimacy of massage and loving touch, and I often had my hands on people I cared for, rubbing a tight shoulder, stroking a hand. Sometimes our differences showed themselves loud and clear, as happened on the night Ron introduced me to an actor friend of his, a powerhouse stunt-man actor. The evening was pleasant, but I felt no real connection with this man. When I asked if I could give his friend a neck rub, you would have thought I had suggested we all go to bed together! They were speechless. But that was what I needed to feel connected.

Ron starred in his own network television series and he liked his work, but he hated the uncertainty of the entertainment business. I knew about "the business" from living with the Levines, and I knew how unpredictable it could be. What kept him going was his thirst for adventure, and his thirst matched mine. In winter we skied in California; in summer we rafted in the Grand Canyon with his river raft company. We swam in the Pacific with Jake, backpacked in the Sierra, and hiked in the hills surrounding the Ojai Valley. Courting had quickly blossomed into relationship, and once again that familiar magnet of romantic love drew me close.

When summer was coming to an end and the days were getting shorter, I decided it was time to sell my house and rent a beach house in northern Malibu to be closer to the people essential to my life now—Ron, Rick, Arnie, and Robin. The Levines had moved to Malibu Lake and we talked often by phone; they would be nearby, too.

What joy it was to be by the ocean again! I swam off Point Dune in Malibu every day with Jake, studied acting with a well-known acting coach and American Sign Language with a nearly deaf man in Hollywood five days a week. I envisioned myself becoming a sign language expert on national television. I felt such a kinship with the deaf world. So much was opening up for me, expanding my views. I always knew my higher education was never going to happen on a college campus.

That fall, Ron would be in Miami to film a segment of his show, and he suggested we meet there and take a week's vacation at a resort he knew in the Bahamas. I was due for my annual duty visit to my dad, and the island vacation with Ron was tantalizing.

My dad picked us up at Miami International wearing a big grin. We climbed into his Cadillac convertible and headed to his elegant home on the water for an evening that I couldn't wait to end, but I could tolerate it since it would be just this one night. As we drove out of the airport, he leaned across me in the front seat to talk to Ron. "Hey, you know a lady named Marco Rita in Fort Lauderdale?"

"Should I know her, Jack?" Ron said. It seemed odd since he had never met my dad before.

"Ya never heard of her? Really? This gal gives the best blow job in South Florida!"

I froze. Great. Good start, Dad. Ron shook his head and settled back in his seat. Then I began laughing hysterically. "Dad, you are so *you!*" He grinned and lit another cigarette, driving on as the wind whipped our hair at seventy-five miles an hour.

That entire night my father didn't let on that he saw me as a loser for abandoning my daughter and taking up with a cowboy a few years earlier. He still said to everyone everywhere we went, "So, who's better looking, my sexy daughter or her even sexier father?" Why was I still trying to please this man and make him a part of my life? And what was I doing with a man who looked just like my dad had at his age—handsome, with a chiseled jaw, intense blue eyes, a ruddy complexion, and dark, wavy hair? I didn't make the connection at the time. All I knew was that I just had to get through this visit and go on vacation with my sweetheart. As I hugged my dad goodbye until next time when we left for the airport in the morning, I felt hot tears sting my eyes. One day, I hoped, I'd understand.

Within the year, Ron asked me to marry him and I accepted. My need to be loved was huge, and his desire for me was irresistible. I didn't look at the reasons this marriage might not work. I didn't think about that day early in our courtship when Ron had showed me his "little black book," a book filled with nineteen pages of women's names and phone numbers and his comments about each one. (When I accepted his proposal, he burned the book.) I didn't ask myself how I could choose a man with a little black book in the first place. I thought, "Dad, this one's for you." That's how badly I wanted his approval.

Our wedding was held at the Self-Realization Fellowship Chapel just off the Pacific Coast Highway in Santa Monica, a sacred place created for students and disciples of Paramahansa Yogananda, an Indian guru who had a big presence in the West. Yogananda's book *Autobiography of a Yogi* had made a big impact on me, and Ron was drawn, too, to the energy of this place. The chapel overlooked a small lake where mallards and white swans glided gracefully through the tall reeds and grasses. I had spent many afternoons here walking the tranquil gardens, sitting in front of the statue of Buddha, gazing into the eyes of a playful Krishna who towered over it all.

The monk who would marry us met with us separately several times in the weeks before the wedding. He was an honest, gentle man who admitted to me that, "Celibacy and my chosen life as a monk is a much easier path to God than it is for those of you who choose marriage and relationship." His words resonated in my soul for years as I tried to understand the nature of love and oneness with the divine. Wasn't there a path to the divine through love and marriage?

That day, Ron dressed in a camel-colored business suit and I wore a creamy silk dress, a gardenia tucked into my long hair. His children came to "give their dad away" and celebrate their expanded family. My teenage daughter, on the other hand, was not so happy. She felt no connection with Ron and she hung back, sulking, although I was so caught up in the celebration I didn't see how much she was suffering. I believed she would learn about life's abundant blessings and fill up on them as I was doing. I didn't understand that I used my relationships with men as a buffer between us (or anyone else). I was doing exactly what my father had done with his wives and me. Barry Levine had said once that what children truly need is the same insane attention you would give to your lover. I knew this was true, but I just didn't know how to do it.

Dad, on the other hand, couldn't have been more impressed with Ron. Imagine! A leading man and western outdoorsman would marry his daughter! For once Dad wanted to take that short walk with me—he wanted to "give me away." He proudly walked me down the chapel aisle, winking at the small gathering of guests and family, and I prayed that the huge gap between us would finally be closed.

For the next few years, Ron and I shared adventures, some exhilarating, some unfortunate. His television series was canceled. But my leading man climbed back up from the loss of this dream and returned to his tree-sculpting business. He'd come home smelling like chainsaw fuel, ready for a hot shower and a tall glass of Scotch, but happy to have work that kept him active. We rafted the Colorado River in the Grand Canyon, hiked into great amphitheaters concealed in the curves of ancient rock, and slept on sandy beaches under a blanket of stars. By the last day of our two-week trips I hated to leave my perch on the pontoon of the inflatable orange raft and return to "real" life.

Around this time, my inheritance was spilling out large sums of monthly income, and I decided to buy a house. We chose an area on the northern end of Malibu, where the real folks (not the movie stars) live, and I put a down payment on a chalet-style house with a huge stone fireplace on Via Vienta, overlooking the spectacular Southern California coastline. We bought yummy, overstuffed furniture, stained-glass lamps, and richly colored rugs, and we settled into our hilltop hideaway and the next phase of our marriage with high hopes.

Northern Malibu is a fairly untamed region of wooded canyons, sand dunes, and sprawling beaches. Houses are set back far from the road, and you can walk for miles on the beaches without seeing much more than the waves and seagulls and the big blue sky. I walked every day in the hills behind our house and on the rocky beaches north of Encinal Canyon, and Ron's work was plentiful, maintaining the majestic acreages of Malibu estates, as he got browner in the sun.

But life for Ron was not the paradise it was for me. His was a constant struggle to earn his daily bread while I collected substantial sums from my inheritance and investments. This kind of imbalance is a tightrope walk for any couple, and it was especially hard for a proud man like Ron. Our differences were beginning to outshine our compatibilities. Ron's friends were intellectual, and I didn't have much in common with them. My friends were involved with yoga and other spiritual-physical pursuits.

And my vitality was at an all-time high. I was fanatical about the purity of what I consumed, which was challenging for Ron, a steak-and-Scotch man. Sometimes, exasperated by our differences, he would say, "You're a twentieth-century woman and I am a nineteenth-century man." I used to like that about us; now I was beginning to wonder.

Charles Muir's yoga audiocassettes were my favorites, and I practiced yoga using those tapes and following his gentle instruction into poses, deepened breathing, and quiet mind. Through yoga, I connected deeply with myself and with friends who shared this passion and this practice. Ron felt left out. As time went on I soared in spiritual ecstasy while Ron could only cope with the challenges of his life. The practice of yoga gave me the feeling that I walked through life holding the hand of God.

Then one day he surprised me. "I want to try something, something you do with your friends," he said.

My mind flew to the possibilities. "Yoga?"

"No. I want you to initiate me into the world of altered states."

Ron had smoked pot with me a few times, but he had never gone beyond that. Ecstasy (MDMA) seemed a good place to start. It was legal, available, and relatively new to me, something I took now and then with my yoga-buddy girlfriends. To me, taking this substance was a sacrament, as I believe that what you call something empowers it to live up to its name.

Since the late 1960s, there was always some kind of drug wave moving culture into new dimensions. LSD, mescaline, and psilocybin mushrooms were very psychedelic; they took my brain beyond known boundaries. Ecstasy was different, easier to navigate while lifting my heart beyond preconceived and familiar limitations. With Ecstasy, my heart met expanded states of love, inviting me to surrender to its full potential. My girlfriends and I would laugh and pray and do our yoga on it, dance and cuddle and experience deep connections of intimacy together. (Eventually I wouldn't use it to enhance my experience of intimate connection, as its illegal status made it too risky, but for a while it played a key role.)

I can still see the moment in our rustic room at the Big Sur Inn when Ron looked at me, his pupils round and black, a clear window into his soul, and he whispered, "For the first time in my life, my dear Caroline, I feel no fear." What joy for us both! I had fulfilled my goal to love this dear man into the moment in which he yearned to reside—in the vastness of his loving heart, and fearlessly. But he couldn't maintain it once the sacrament wore off. After that first time, no matter how often he opened to the spaciousness of MDMA he always contracted back to the fear that was his lifetime companion. He clamped onto his old ways at the same time he wanted me to show him new ways of thinking, being, and loving. He wanted to learn about connection as I had learned it from Levine, but he didn't know how to keep it going.

When I heard that Charles was teaching a Tantra yoga workshop, I begged Ron to join me at one of them. That had to be what we needed to do, to learn about what Charles called "the art of conscious loving." I had lost interest in sex with Ron and didn't know why. I believed that Tantra practice would help us have deeper sexual intimacy and my interest in sex with Ron would come back.

But Ron didn't like Charles. "I don't need your guru to teach me how to make love to my wife," he would hiss. I insisted I didn't have, and I didn't want, a guru.

A week before Charles' first Tantra Yoga workshop in our area, Ron agreed to join me for the four-day seminar. Friends from Malibu came—Kevin and Jesse and Lucian and Margie—and Josie, an old friend of mine from yoga classes. A dentist and his wife from Laguna Beach were there that weekend, yoga students of Charles from Rio Caliente. All together there were twenty-six of us, and we would stay in a twelve-bedroom mansion known as Running Ridge Ranch, nestled in an orange grove high on a hill overlooking the Ojai Valley. Ron and I would have the library for our privacy, with a futon snuggled in the forest of tall shelves of books.

In class we sat in a large circle—all of us ready to expand our minds and hearts about the yoga of love. Charles taught for hours each day about Tantra yoga, one of his lovely lady friends by his side to help demonstrate positions for intimate tantric loving and meditating. Sumptuous meals were served three times each day, making the weekend a beautiful balance of class time, social time, and intimate practice time in the privacy of the sleeping spaces and bedrooms.

A woman named Sophia Roberts sang songs she and Charles had created for the *puja*, a ceremony of devotional prayer Charles led during which the group sang to one another face to face, blessed the chakra centers with light touch or simply from "my heart to yours," in intimate and sacred moments. Tears flowed freely as our hearts opened with the words of Sophia's songs and we gazed into the eyes of the other students, new friends we had made and old friends we grew closer with. We learned how to send our love to one another and to receive another's love with grace and integrity.

In Ojai that weekend I began to unravel the mystery of love and God and how they relate to sexual energy. There was classroom and private time focused on sacred sexual practices with our partner, making me keenly aware and grateful for the tremendous value and need to contain sexual energy in a group and class setting (no practices ever took place in the classroom that were in any way threatening to my safety and privacy).

A door had opened in my deep need to uncover what I did not understand about men and women, sex and love, and the nature of being human. My inner light shone brighter as the weekend propelled me into an orbit I would never leave. Tantra, the Art of Conscious Loving, held answers my soul longed for. I could see how this practice was healing as well as pleasurable, and it held hope for the healing and awakening I knew I wanted and needed.

Back at home, when we practiced together, I could tell Ron was uncomfortable changing anything that threatened his ego about being a good lover. Hadn't we learned these radical new ideas from my "guru," ideas like not *always* ejaculating as the finale of sex and deep eye-gazing during lovemaking? Ron would rage at me, "You should be with someone like Charles!" I would argue back, "I don't want to be with Charles. You are my husband and I want a deeper connection with *you*."

Our nights at home were becoming that familiar script of marriage: his downloading his frustrations of the day, my sharing my joys of the day. Could we go on like this? Ron was my third and final marriage. Period. I had to make this relationship work. But did I know how?

Wildfires swept through the Malibu hills the week Ron was scheduled to go into the hospital for a procedure to reduce swelling in his prostate gland. He was afraid, and I took on his fear, which left me confused. Meanwhile, Lucian and Margie were separating after twenty-five years of marriage, and Lucian called to share his woes the night Ron went into the hospital. I called Ron to tell him about it, and Ron encouraged me to go to Lucian's and be there for him. I welcomed this permission from my husband to spend the evening with our neighbor and friend.

I knew about the big fire in the area, but I had no idea just how huge it was until later that night, when news came that all the roads in the area were closed. I would have to stay overnight at Lucian's beautiful home on the cliffs high above the Pacific.

Sexual healing was a fascinating subject I had learned some about in the Tantra yoga weekend, and I wanted to offer my sexual love as a healing force to Lucian. Joined to my sexuality, I believed the healing balm of my love could move mountains. But I was inexperienced, sexual healing was still a new concept for me, and I fell prey to the bonding hormones and "fell in love," personalizing the experience with Lucian instead of staying strong and clear about my role as healer. As a new student of Tantra and not a Dakini of these healing tantric or sexual arts (Dakini has many translations but one is a tantric deity described as a female embodiment of enlightened energy), I had a lot to learn. I did not embody enlightened wisdom. With my husband recovering in the hospital, I ascended into the ethers of passion with another man.

My intention was pure, but I was unconsciously driven by unresolved needs as I surrendered to what my poetic heart would call *falling in love*. Like Alice falling into the rabbit hole, falling in love was an altered state I tumbled into without regard to its consequences. As my mother had said years earlier in a rare comment about me, "There she goes, from the frying pan into the fire." This time, was she right?

In the morning Lucian learned the fire had destroyed hundreds of homes, that roads up and down the coast were closed. The skies were black and the air was sooty. I was marooned in this heaven with no way to get to the hospital that day or even to get back home to the other side of the canyon.

When word finally came that the fire was contained and the roads were reopened, I drove to the hospital to take my husband home. It felt strange to be with him again now that I was filled with the soul of another, and worse still hearing him cry out with pain in the bathroom on his first night home from the hospital. I lay awake, enclosed within my own cocoon of spiritual/sexual fire. I knew I had done no wrong in wanting love and in my intention to use love for healing, but I was unable to comfort my mate. I feared a vengeful God would strike me down, disable me, or in some other way punish me for the evils of the flesh. *My* God would never do that, but perhaps there was a higher force who punished those who believed differently about the healing power of sexual love. Frozen and immobile, I lay semiconscious, floating just above stark reality.

When Ron was feeling better the next day, he asked to hear of my night with our friend, Lucian. I told him my story. I didn't know if I was in love with Lucian or simply felt compassion for him, but it felt divine.

Ron was calm, maybe in shock, but he didn't react too harshly about my actions with our friend in crisis. There was a part of him that also wanted to believe in this tantric thing called sexual healing. He told me he, too, had made love with someone else during that last year, a woman he had known and loved for years who reappeared, and one thing led to another. I remained calm and supportive. Arnie and I had been through something just like this.

But none of this answered the question of what to do next. I longed for my own "beloved," someone I could truly connect with in a soulful way. In Tantra class we had learned about seeing the beloved in one another—it didn't have to be a lover—but I couldn't see the beloved in Ron. Was Lucian the right person for me? I didn't know for sure. What I knew was I couldn't live any longer under the same roof with a man who was not my beloved. What I didn't know then was how the alchemy of sexual love can create the beloved from the mundane into the sacred. Our marriage had become a sacrificial offering for the next level of our spiritual growth.

If friendship had been more of a foundation during our nearly four years of marriage, I would have stayed with Ron until we could unravel the knots that kept us from becoming beloveds. But there wasn't that friendship as foundation, and within the week I moved out of our lovely home in the Malibu hills, driving away from the man, the marriage, and the house we called home with nothing but a suitcase and a few photographs. Jake would stay with Ron, as they had bonded deeply, just as Jeremiah remained the companion of Rick.

The charred remains of the Malibu hills seemed a metaphor for my power to destroy what I had created, as I moved into Lucian's family home on the invitation of Lucian and his estranged wife. Reality TV must have been inspired by the true stories lived in Malibu, California.

A few weeks later and before my mind could clear or my heart process what had happened, our affair ended as suddenly as it had started. Lucian's wife (and my friend) Margie changed her mind about leaving her husband and came home to her rightful place in her home. I packed my few belongings that day and left the master suite on the top floor to move into a chilly, dark room in the children's section of the house on the lower level. For the next three sleepless nights I prayed for a miracle while the lovers found their passion for one another again. I had done my job well, I had brought healing to a splintered family, but I was in the waves without a surfboard.

And then a life raft came. It was my friend Josie. "Come stay with me, Caroline," she said. "My room is small, but I would love to share it with you."

In less than an hour my car was packed and I was on my way to Topanga Canyon, where I would unload my things at Josie's. She lived with her lover, but she had her own room, and she suggested we spread out our yoga mats in there and pray for guidance. What a good idea! Deep breathing and gentle stretching quieted the chaos in my heart and mind. I was grateful for her reminder of what I needed.

For the next three months, this rustic house in Topanga Canyon would be my church of penance and self-absolution, and Josie's friendship would be invaluable. When we weren't on the deck upstairs practicing yoga in the sun to the sound of Charles' voice on tape, we were in our little womb room, talking, meditating, resting, or reading. Josie was there for me night and day, to talk or to be quiet, to cry or to laugh with, to know or not know what was next. But alone, on long walks each day through the Topanga hills, I battled the demons in my mind. I tried to look happy, but despair weakened me. What a mess I seemed to be making of this life of mine.

During those months with Josie, Charles and I talked occasionally by telephone from his home in Carmel Valley. He had followed the recent chaos in my life and he was concerned for me, as my friend and as my yoga teacher. He reprimanded me for thinking I could give sexual healing to a friend's husband without deeply hurting my husband and my marriage. "Sexual healing is a huge responsibility," he said. "There's no room in it for *falling* in love." He suggested I return to my husband and work on our marriage. "Only good can come from rising into more love, not falling in love, and taking your significant other with you." He also suggested I attend a Tantra support group he was holding in December in Topanga. "You can't just lick your wounds and become a recluse out there with Josie," he said, advising a student in the manner one hears from her teacher. "Come and get some healing and connection to loving friends in your community, Caroline."

Josie came with me to Charles' support group in Topanga, but it was with Charles that my breakthrough came. In one of the exercises one person was invited to lie spoon-style between another woman and a man and be nourished between the couple, breathing in the energy that flowed from their chakras and through the "guest" lying between them. I chose to be nourished by Charles and his lady friend Diana, whom I knew and liked. I let myself relax and be held by these two sweet beings, and the tears came pouring out. Their loving gaze, while they held me in the arms of unconditional love, was a healing balm. I hadn't felt such a stirring of hope in a very long time. Maybe I was right in taking these steps, how ever painful they were, to find my spiritual and emotional fulfillment. And maybe, just maybe, I'd find it.

Through the holiday season, worry, fear, guilt, shame, and desire pulled at me, but I harnessed that wild stallion of my mind through discipline and daily yoga practice—meditating, breathing, stretching, and sitting in stillness. I bought a huge oil painting of a strangely androgynous seraphim angel from a local artist and hung it on the wall behind the bed. Swirling wheels of colorful chakra energy coursed from its core. This angel, I hoped, would guide me out of my emotional turmoil.

Chapter Six

The Beloved Truth

Mira was still my soul sister long after we'd gone our separate ways after the Levines. I visited her in San Francisco and we followed the ups and downs of each other's lives, always a treasured support. One day, as I prepared to go to Charles' yoga retreat at Rio Caliente in Mexico in February, she phoned.

"Hon, I'm going with you," she said. "You've got a lot to tell me about your marital fiasco, and I've got some stories for you, too." We would room together and catch up. My spirits lifted. We met at the Los Angeles International Airport and talked nonstop until the airplane slowed on the runway in Guadalajara. A taxicab took us to Rio Caliente, where we hugged our hellos to women and men we knew from past visits there and greeted the new people. We all shared a love of yoga and our teacher, Charles, and we were excited for the journey into nourishing our bodies and spirits.

Alma, the warm-hearted spa manager who greeted us in the front office, showed us to our adobe room—two beds and our own fireplace. We unpacked and changed into leotards for the first yoga and meditation session. Every day there would be two two-and-a-half-hour sessions, one in the morning, one in the afternoon. In the evening we all would come together for one of Charles' talks. Tall and lanky and dressed in his purple poncho and rope sandals, his impossibly deep blue eyes shining with joy, Charles would inspire us to make an even stronger commitment to our yoga practice. It didn't matter that I'd heard about all of this from him before. Everything about Hatha, Bhakti, Laya (or Kundalini), and Karma yoga, everything about Hinduism, the Bhagavad Gita sacred text, and Tantra yoga filled my heart like nothing ever had before. I was fascinated with this culture so different from my own. I drank in the world of India and her spiritual practices lying cuddled on lumpy mats in the evening light, our eyelids growing heavy after the long day of travel and our first evening class. That seraphim angel hanging over my bed back at Josie's house cast its beams across me as I lay there, urging me to *listen! Feel my peace.* I *was* listening. I *did* feel its peace.

"Ancient cultures knew that sexual energy is sacred energy," Charles told us. "For thousands of years, many Hindus and others have believed this energy can be used in a healing way and as a path to enlightenment." Students needed to be prepared by a teacher or teachers, he explained, for this healing path and then be committed to a lifetime of practice.

Over the next few days, I was reminded, listening once again to Charles leading the class, of what I had learned in that Ojai workshop.

"Central to the practice of Tantra yoga and the sharing of sexual love are a meditative and focused mind, full presence behind open eyes, deep breathing in harmony with your partner, an understanding of yin and yang, giver and receiver, lover and beloved, awareness of the presence of the Divine at all times." Hatha yoga, which I had practiced for many years, was an ideal preparation for Tantra yoga. "Hatha" refers to the principal energy channels of the body, which must be fully operational to attain a state of bliss, or enlightenment. It represents opposing energies— hot/cold, male/female, positive/negative—and attempts to balance mind and body through physical exercises, or asanas, controlled breathing, and the calming of the mind through relaxation and meditation. My Hatha yoga teachers had always emphasized a focus on the chakras, or energy centers, of the body. Awareness of the chakras also plays an integral role in the practice of Tantra. I meditated on my chakra system in my yoga practice as part of the mental focus.

Night and day, steam rose from the waters, filling the valley with clouds of luminescent white vapor. Lightning and thunderstorms awed us from where we stood beneath the covered patio overlooking pine forest, river, and the valley of eternal spring. I felt more open than I remembered feeling in a long time. Every day, one by one, each student met individually with Charles for guidance in our yoga practice. He always had a supply of chocolate-covered apricots, tempting rewards after the fresh juices and platters of steamed greens, tortillas, and rice. I looked forward to these private sessions, as much for the contraband chocolate as for the precious time with our teacher.

Toward the middle of our week, Mira, who had chosen to be celibate for a year since a breakup, came back to our room one afternoon, sparkling. I was resting in the quiet on my bed when she came in.

"Amazing!" she sighed, kicking off her sandals and throwing herself face first on her bed.

"What's amazing, hon? You look different!" I exclaimed, watching her closely. "Where have you been?"

"Charles gave me a sexual healing."

I jumped on her bed and lay down next to her. "You're in love, aren't you? You can tell me."

"It's not like that," she said, rolling onto her back. "He woke up my Shakti, that's all I can say, and trust me, it's been sleeping for a long time."

I knew my Shakti energy was sleeping, too, there was no question about that. "Do you think he would give me a sexual healing?"

"Ask him."

I told her I was worried it might feel strange to be with him in that way. He was my friend, after all, not my lover. I couldn't imagine being sexual with Charles.

"It's safe and very sweet," she assured me. "I promise you. And it's not sexual as you've ever known sexual to be."

That evening, with butterflies in my tummy, I stopped Charles on the way to the dining room.

"But you're married, Caroline, and you and Ron are both my students. I can't do it without Ron's permission."

Anger swelled inside me. "You don't need Ron's permission!" I said. "We've been separated for three months. I'm sovereign over my body. And I know I need this healing."

Charles hesitated, holding my gaze. "Let me meditate on it," he said, gently. "I'll tell you in the morning."

And with that, he turned and continued along the dirt path, his brown curls waving in the soft light of dusk.

That night I soaked in the outdoor pools until past midnight, and after sweating it out in the steam chamber carved deep in the earth, I lay in bed under the rough wool blankets, too excited and nervous to sleep. I was pretty sure he would say yes, in fact, there was no other option as far as I was concerned. I was determined to have the experience that helped Mira come alive again.

In the morning, dressed in sweat suits, my sleepy-eyed yoga buddies filled the long table on the patio where fragrant piñon pine crackled in the fireplace. Bowls of hot oatmeal topped with raisins and toasted pecans were placed before us, along with plates piled high with scrambled eggs with salsa and hot tortillas dripping with butter and honey, and pitchers of fresh orange and grapefruit juices. "Buenos dias!" the women serving us sang. I took it all in, eating my meal as the warmth of the fire softened my shoulders and warmed my bones.

When Charles came in he greeted everyone with a smile, then crouched beside me at my table. "I can see you at two o'clock today," he said. "But I'm still not sure about the sexual healing session. I would prefer a blessing from your husband." I stood and hugged him.

For the rest of the morning the wildest dance of nerves took place in my belly while I attempted to appear calm. I wished there were phone service from this remote mountain spa so I could call Ron for his "blessing." Then I realized that my estranged husband had no right to make this decision for me! And estranged or not, even in marriage, my sexuality and my body could not be owned by another.

At last it was time to walk the path to Charles' adobe cottage in the woods. I knew with each step that I would never be the same after this time with him. And that was fine with me. The old me had reached the end of the line.

Charles greeted me at the door, his hands folded in prayer position. Without a word, I entered his cottage, slipped out of my sandals, and took a seat on the yoga mat spread in the center of the room. Charles closed the door behind us and took a seat across from me. We breathed together for a few moments, gazing into each other's eyes.

"How are you, Caroline?" he said, finally. "And how are you and Ron?" Butterflies chased each other inside my belly as I told Charles that Ron and I had been seeing a marriage counselor. "But I can't go back to this marriage. I'm getting the courage for it while I'm here. I'm going to file for divorce … *again*."

Sorrow choked my throat at the sound of my own words. I wanted Charles to reach out and hold me close, but he stayed in his calm pose, compassion softening his gaze. I could see he was leaving it up to me to feel my feelings and say what I needed to say. "Ron is a good man," I went on. "He has never hurt or mistreated me, he has only loved me. But I can't find a soul connection." Charles listened. I looked deeper inside. And there it was. "I don't want a life without knowing the beloved in relationship," I sobbed.

Charles reached for my hand. Quietly, he stood, and I stood with him. "Come and be held in the arms of love, sweet friend."

We walked to the bed and lay down, facing each other. "How many years have we been friends? Seven? Eight? I have always seen you as happy and carefree, in love with life. This last failed marriage has taken its toll on you, hasn't it?"

I sobbed from a deeper place than I knew was there—it seemed bottomless. Charles handed me tissues and put drops of calming Bach flower remedies on my tongue. He never asked me to calm down or to stop crying; he just offered support while emotions coursed through me.

Eventually, my tears subsided and Charles offered to give me some bodywork. We had exchanged massage many times over the years. I didn't hesitate a moment. My clothes were off and I was lying on the bed, moaning under the healing touch of his large, confident hands. He knew just where to find the blocks in my body and how to release them. He asked me to turn over so he could do some energy balancing work on my neck and sacrum. By the time he sat cross-legged at my side, one hand resting lightly on my heart and the other on my forehead, I felt steady and calm.

"Dearest friend," he said, gazing tenderly into my eyes, "I feel right in giving you a healing session. May the intention for this session bring more clarity to your life and to the decisions ahead. Trust in love and your God will show you the way. Let us share in the energies of Tantra. Just receive, and let my love in with every breath."

My heart racing again, I began deep, complete breathing, just as I had learned in yoga classes for so many years. As Charles massaged my breasts, belly, pubic mound, and thighs, I gradually relaxed more and more. It felt so good to be touched everywhere while the eyes of love never left mine. Finally, his hand cupped the opening to my vagina while his other hand rested on my heart center. Gently, he said, "May I enter and explore your sacred space, your yoni?"

I nodded.

No one had ever asked for my permission before entering my body. I felt the return of tears as he slowly lubricated my yoni with his fingers until my body opened and welcomed his fingers inside. As he did this, he described the beauty of what he was feeling. "You are soft and moist, Caroline. Your yoni is beautiful, very sexy. With your permission I will explore and massage your entire yoni."

I nodded my permission.

"Please let me know what you are feeling, not so much in words but through breath and sound."

How I felt inside my yoni? Numb. This seemed more like an examination than anything pleasurable, at least so far. Charles coached me to inhale deeply and release my breath with sound. This was hard to do! I never made sounds during sex. And I had no context for this healing other than having sex. Clearly, however, this was not sex!

To help, Charles made sounds along with me as he explored the deeper reaches of my yoni, our gaze staying connected the whole time. I squealed and squeaked and hollered, feeling mostly numb inside except for the occasional unpleasant burning sensation. This was not about arousing my clitoris, a very reliable source of pleasure. This was massage deep into the tissue of my yoni and sacred spot (G-spot) area. No one had touched me here before. At times I felt like I was on the examining table at the gynecologist's office, and I was more than ready to be done with this exam! But I endured it all—being seen, being numb, being self-conscious, being loved, feeling like a failure.

"Feel the connection between your sexuality, your yoni, and your heart, my friend," he said, guiding my breath to follow this energy conduit.

I thought of my surgeries and my hysterectomy. The scars were obviously permanent. More tears, more pain. Had I ever made this connection before? No, never.

"Now breathe all that energy up to your brain, sweet friend, and exhale with sound," Charles said, coaching me like a midwife would coach a birthing mother.

My mind ran away. Did he have an erection? Would we have sex when the healing was over? Would he go down on me? Why was he still wearing pants? The man led the way into sex, didn't he? I just had to be patient. He would want to have his way. They always did.

At last, Charles very slowly withdrew his fingers from my yoni and rested his hands on my heart and brow centers. We breathed together, gazing into each other's eyes for what seemed like hours but was probably only a few minutes.

"Thank you for allowing me to bring my healing love to your sweet yoni, dear friend. I am honored."

I had no words.

Charles then lay by my side and held me, stroking my hair from my forehead the way my mother did when I was a child. My tears flowed again, but softly this time.

"Tantra yoga will be good for you," Charles said quietly. "Sacred spot massage will arouse your sexual power and Shakti. You can claim your birthright as a multiorgasmic and powerful sexual-spiritual goddess of love."

A goddess of love? Me? With all of my female organs removed, I doubted if there was a goddess of love inside me. "We'll see," was all I could manage to whisper.

The sky was beginning to darken, and I dressed and left as Charles sat to meditate in front of his ever present pictures of Jesus and Mary. He wasn't Catholic, but he loved the sweetness these two holy beings emanate.

Later that evening, in a naturally altered state, Mira and I walked to the river hand in hand to sit under a waterfall of warm, lithium-rich water. "It was the most amazing experience of my life," I told Mira. "I felt so safe. He's not just a yoga teacher, he spreads the love of God." In some ways, I was surprised by that observation.

Mira nodded. We agreed that real love given to emotionally wounded sexual centers was something more women needed to experience. Suddenly, Mira shouted above the roar of the waterfall. "Let's live our dreams! Let's move to Maui with Charles! Let's help Charles get this work out to the world!"

Maui? I knew exactly what she meant. We had traveled to Maui together when we were with the Levines, and we had dreamed of one day living there. "Let's do it!" I shouted back.

We grabbed each other and held tight, sobbing and laughing, birthing our beloved truth into our beloved river, like indigenous women the world over have squatted on the earth to birth their babies. This was it, this was my chance to be with loved ones who understood my commitment to my healing and the healing of others. I wanted to be with my spiritual family, to be where the most love was. An awakened heart would be my path.

The next morning at breakfast, Mira and I found Charles.

"Charles," Mira said, taking him aside, "come to Maui with us. We want to help you get this Tantra work out to the world." Love sparkled in her dark, exotic eyes.

Charles was stunned. "Move to Maui?"

"We'll live in a goddess temple, all of us together," I said, following Mira's lead.

"No strings attached," Mira added. "You can be with anyone you like. Teach your workshops, heal our sisters, choose your beloved. We'll make the house happen. We'll even do your laundry." Or did I say that? God knows!

Charles' face lit up. It seemed he realized as suddenly as we had that this was exactly what needed to happen. He looked first to me and then to Mira, smiling like a happy clown. "I would *love* to," he said. "Maui is the perfect place to teach people how to love. Maui is the heart of Divine Mother."

Two days later, the yoga retreat ended and Mira and I said goodbye to our dear friends and stayed on with Charles. I had brought some MDMA (Ecstasy) with me, hoping to merge with Rio and the river before I left. I offered to share this with my companions, knowing the sacrament of ingesting this benevolent substance would further open our hearts and sexuality with expanded consciousness as we sealed our decision to live together.

Sitting on our yoga mats on the floor of Charles' room, we set our intention: "May this sacrament illuminate our hearts and minds into an offering of Tantric love. May our bodies join in the art of conscious loving as a prayer to the god and goddess of love who dwells within us. May the love and pleasure we share this night bless all who ever follow us in their path toward more love. And so it is."

We lit candles on the altar by the fireplace next to the pictures of Jesus and Mary, then stretched our bodies in Hatha yoga poses, our breath deepening as we allowed the energies to course through. Sophia's enchanting melodies played in the background, songs about loving the god and the goddess inside us. We had listened to this music in classes, songs like "I Open My Heart to You" and "Goddess You Are Filling Me Up with Your Love." Her music played the strings of my heart.

After nearly an hour, we turned off the music and sat in silence, meditating, then joined hands to meditate together, the crackling fire in the fireplace and the birds in the trees outside the only sounds. When we each felt a natural closure to our solo practice time, we opened our eyes to behold the beloveds seated before us. The sacrament illuminated the light already filling our hearts and eyes. Could anything feel this good?

We embraced and felt the spirit of love moving us toward our true home. It was time to consummate this union. Without words we began kissing, eyes, hearts, and bodies wide open now that we were in the most natural pose of all, that of giving and receiving pleasure in the union of open-hearted love. Without resistance I joined with these dear friends in a night of the most beautiful lovemaking I had ever experienced. That two close girlfriends could join in loving one close man-friend was spiritually and physically joyful every moment of the night.

And Charles, in his tantric wisdom and mastery, was in no hurry to "get off." He was interested in getting the evening "on" in ways that would thrill both Mira and me, and his orchestration was impeccable. Mira and I tasted one another's yonis, learned the term "honoring" for this, as we felt honored by the preciousness of this experience. We sipped each other's nectar. Our eyes remained open as we followed the guidance of our Tantra teacher, who reminded us to breathe, suggested words to use and positions of energy we three could create with our bodies. We took turns being the receiver, with the other two joined in love for us, testing our ability to be loved and pleasured. We took breaks from sexual loving to move into therapeutic and healing touch, massaging and pleasuring each other in these ways, too. All forms of true love were invited in as we surrendered to the joys of loving one another. We were present and grounded as we soared into pleasure and bliss.

I had strayed out of the safety of conventional sexuality before, but tonight I was clearly in a new dimension. It was the first time I had had a sexual experience on MDMA. But this night was more about heart expansion and feeling the orgasmic pleasure of love than it was about pleasure in my genitals. All of me felt alive with love for the first time ever.

Sometime after midnight, storms filled the valley with a heavenly opera of exploding light. We dressed and walked to the river, holding hands. Mira said she saw Charles and me as the divine couple who would entwine in holy relationship and teach together. She would be our consort and together we would manifest her beloved, someone she didn't know yet but was sure would come. Charles and I looked deeply into each other's eyes, acknowledging that this was the beloved truth. It seemed so easy and so right.

From that night forward I would help bring Tantra yoga to the world by living its teachings with dedication, discipline, and purpose. I would awaken the goddess in myself and in all women whose lives I touched. I would commit to practice loving and being loved on every level. Tomorrow we would part, Mira returning to San Francisco, me to Topanga, Charles staying on at Rio Caliente a few more days before joining me. My apprenticeship with him would begin in less than a week, on Valentine's Day, 1985, in San Diego. After that, I would spend six months traveling with Charles to seminars and learning everything I could about the teachings so I could co-lead the seminars, "Tantra, the Art of Conscious Loving." The answer to the question I had been asked so long ago—"Who are you?"—was getting clearer all the time.

Chapter Seven

A Queen Is Born

Josie picked me up at Los Angeles International Airport where I had departed from a lifetime and a little over a week ago. "Charles?!" she cried. She was friends with Charles and had shared tantric love with him before. I told her about Mexico and our plans for Maui as she helped me organize my stored belongings. There wouldn't be much to pack since I had left nearly everything with Ron. Our divorce would be complete before I moved to Hawaii at the end of summer.

Charles arrived a few days after me, and this time I drove the hour south to LAX to wait for the arrivals from Mexico. When I saw my long-legged yoga man loping toward me down the long corridor, my heart sang.

That night, we dined and cuddled, then climbed into bed together with Josie and made love as three. It was easy making love that night with them both. It was as if the high priestess inside my dear friend blessed my union with Charles. With her as our witness, Charles looked deeply into my eyes and said, "Will you be my beloved?" With every cell in my body flooded with love, I said, "I already *am* your beloved. I am a fool for love just like you." Charles said, "I marry thee," still gazing deep into my eyes. We sealed our tantric union with a three-way kiss.

"Hurry, beloved! We don't want to miss the plane!"

Charles and I raced through the crowded corridors of LAX the

following day, Charles tugging my hand. I was going to have to trade in
my high heels for something easier to run in if I was going to travel with
this man! We were on our way to San Diego for my first evening as ap-
prentice to Charles, and we caught that flight in the nick of time.

Charles' "Introduction to Tantra" talk was held in a Chinese restaurant downtown. At this talk Charles would describe Tantra as the yoga,
or union, of sexual love joined to spiritual union. He would explain that
Tantra yoga is a type of yoga used to awaken the Kundalini energy in the
body. Charles was the first person I knew of to suggest sexual healing
as part of Tantra yoga. If teachers of Tantra in the West before Charles
taught any of this healing work, I did not know of it. Margo Anand
wrote the early book on *The Art of Sexual Ecstasy*, based on her tantric studies in India with Osho (Bagwan Shree Rajneesh). Sexual healing
through sacred spot massage was introduced by Charles Muir and is a
trademark of his work.

I had imagined an incense-filled temple, Persian rugs circled by exotic
flowers, fine silk cushions, and statuary of Hindu gods and goddesses,
but here we were, a gathering of about twenty people seated in a circle
on cushions from the booths placed on the stained carpet, empty dinner
tables off to the side. "How do you like it so far, my beloved?" Charles
asked, a twinkle in his eye. All I could do was smile as I lowered myself to
the floor by his side, making sure my skirt didn't make contact with the
remains of yesterday's pan-fried noodles.

Just stay in your heart, my mind suggested … *don't look at what you
don't want to see.* This became a metaphor that delivered me through
many opportunities to choose separation rather than connection.

Charles knew how to set the tone, and the energy of his ideas about
loving transcended the bounds of the room. Everyone there seemed to
hunger for connection with their core and for connection with the spirit
and love of others. Charles covered many aspects of the ancient art form
of Tantra, interpreted for the contemporary Western world. The word
yoni, he explained, is Sanskrit for female sexual organs (divine passage,
sacred temple, or place of birth). He described *amrita,* the ejaculatory
fluid, or divine nectar, of the female. I didn't have experience with amrita
yet myself, but I was curious. *Female ejaculation?* The sacred spot, which

everyone knew as the "G-spot," is called *Yoni Nadi* in Sanskrit. The male sexual organ, he said, is called the *lingam,* wand of light or wand of God. He talked about *Shiva,* the masculine energies of the universe, and *Shakti,* the Hindu concept or personification of God's female aspect. Shakti is also known as Divine Mother, or the universal Divine Feminine life force. It is present in the sexual and spiritual energies of both women and men.

Tantra seemed foreign to me as Charles spoke about it, a radical way of perceiving sex and love. Tantra is not a religion. It is a body of ancient knowledge, much of it lost in translation. I wanted to be open, but my chest felt tight and I barely said a word. I struggled to find an authentic comfort zone with my sudden new life. This is understandable, since it seemed like only yesterday I was living with Josie and before that, in my home and my marriage. I could barely keep up with the changes I created in order to move toward the energy that was moving toward me.

During the last part of the evening, we were asked to stand in an inner and outer circle facing a partner. Charles then suggested we gaze into each other's eyes as we placed a hand over the partner's heart center and imagined our love entering the other's heart. We went around the circle, trading partners one after the other. This again was a *puja,* an intimate celebration of respectful reverence for everyone there. How good this felt! How natural! My comfort zone found at last. I was in the right place, no question. Tears streamed from my eyes as I moved from one person to the next, gazing into strangers' eyes like they were eyes I'd looked into all my life. On some deep level, we all knew each other. This was a pure recognition of love. I didn't have to *know* the person and they didn't have to *know* me for this love to be present, to be real. What great power there was in this, what possibility for healing there could be in this simple act of acknowledgment and respectful reverence.

That night we stayed at the home of our host, Dr. Katz, and made beautiful tantric love as we slept entwined in the arms of the beloved that began a life-long journey. In the morning we learned there were not enough sign-ups to hold a seminar that weekend, but our host assured us there was a growing interest in bringing conscious teachers into communities. It was only a matter of time before a steady stream of supporters would offer to host us. We looked at one another, love beaming from our eyes, holding the knowledge that Tantra would become a household word and, one day, a practice for all lovers.

Back in Carmel Valley a few days later, I became part of the household with Charles and his housemate, Sophia, in their simple rental house under a cluster of California oaks. We would live together there for the next six months while Charles completed his yoga series of classes and I made visits to Robin, while also arranging for my divorce from Ron. In June we joined our group of Tantra students who had signed up over the past year for the rafting trip down the Colorado River in the Grand Canyon. How much had changed in that year!

I shared with Charles the belief that we would choose one mate and one beloved for life—each other. I was eager to live a life of Tantra, forgetting that I knew so little about what that meant. We agreed to open our hearts to include others where the healing power of our love could make a difference for them. I had experienced that with Levine, Mira, Lucian, and recently with Josie—all the pages of my life have to do with how love makes a difference as well as how difficult sexual *love* can be. Surely I was cut from the same cloth as Charles. Yet how naïve I was, ready to live outside the parameters of the cultural milieu. Or was this the new paradigm, Tantra yoga? The old ways no longer seemed to work. The divorce rate was over fifty percent, largely due to people having sex with someone other than their mate.

I saw how our love was impacting Mira. She was in San Francisco finishing up her commitments before moving with us to Maui in August, and she visited us in Carmel a few times. We called her our lover, but I was and always will be Mira's *friend*. I was astounded, even frightened, by the power of her orgasmic releases when Charles did sacred spot work on her. I had never seen a woman enjoy her orgasmic energy this much, except for Gigi.

I compared myself to these women. I knew I didn't have access to myself in the same way they did. "Beloved, all women have that potential," Charles assured me. "Be patient." Eventually, I would feel that power as my own.

Yet I would only stay for a little while when Mira turned her focus toward Charles and sexual awakening. Leaving them, I would hike in the hills, choked up and wrestling with my fear of this huge power of sexuality. I didn't know how to resolve my discomfort seeing my beloved "play" with this energy in our friend. Determined, I vowed to overcome the blocks to my resistance and assume my role as his "first mate" in the awakening of female sexual power…as the queen of my beloved's work, life, and heart.

"My queen," Charles would later console me, "there is no yoni more wonderful for me than yours, no Shakti more desirable than yours. You are my beloved and no one can take your place in my heart." He knew there was always more than enough love for me, encompassing all the others who would practice with him. But did I know?

"Why do you have to involve your penis?" I would ask. "Why can't your lingam be only for me?"

"I'm a tantric yogi," he would say. "I use my lingam as a healing wand just as I use my fingers to awaken and massage her sacred spot, just as I use my eyes to love her soul and my hands to touch her body." With unmasked enthusiasm, he captured my fascination to join him in loving others. "Nothing is more powerful than lover and beloved joined together in love to awaken and bring about healing in another."

It was true: we needed to understand, to pioneer, sexual energy joined to love in order to be good teachers. Exploring sexuality in a conscious and spiritual way was the joy of his existence, and I wanted to transcend my limits about sex and love, go beyond my Midwestern conditioning. Although I wanted my beloved all for myself, I had chosen to share him. I wanted others to know and experience his gifts. After all, he was breaking the news to his lovers that he had found his beloved. The beloved truth was unfolding as I had intended it would.

Wisdom now tells me that it takes a lifetime or more to become the beloved. But a passion for pioneering into the outer limits of love and pleasure under the guidance of an ancient system of yoga lit all my fires. I was willing to risk all for the truth of these ideas … willing to scorch my edges by the fiery heat of these flames.

We both knew that one of his lovers, Emily, was pregnant. We knew she was carrying a boy. She was unclear about who the father was. Charles and I spoke at length about this situation. "But if I am the father," he confided to me, "I want to really be his dad. Even though I am clear with Emily that I will never marry her, I am willing to love this baby and assist in his care. I love kids. I'm a dad to my sister's boys, Chris and Paul. We will come to Carmel to see Mama regularly. Emily's child should have a good father."

I couldn't imagine how a baby would fit into what we planned to create in Maui. Orion was born in January in Monterey. Charles claimed paternity soon after he held that boy in his arms. Orion would visit us, and Charles would take quality time with him, but he would never be a live-in dad. I struggled with my own abandoned fertility and mothering limitations, yet I knew that if Charles wanted to be Orion's dad, I would support him. Years later, blood tests proved that Charles was Orion's biological father.

While Charles unwound his current life in Carmel, I drove to Malibu to finalize my divorce. I chose peace over divorce court, choosing to grant Ron the Malibu house and everything in it. I wanted to make an offer of healing to this good man who had trusted me to love him and be his wife. With this house he could continue to live in nature, where his spirit soared. And now my spirit would also soar, free to ascend where only the bold dare to go.

Ron met me outside the Bank of Malibu. He seemed agitated as I handed him the signed Quit Claim deed. "Thank you, Caroline," was all he said, without looking at me. Then he turned and walked to his pickup, where Jake waited impatiently. I knew this scene—the pickup, our dog, even those slumped shoulders that had once been strong and proud. It was so familiar. As he drove away, I ached for him and for everyone who gives up someone because they have to do something else with their life. I prayed that only good would come of this for us both.

Before I left Los Angeles the next morning, Arnie called. Robin had been in a serious car accident the night before and was in the hospital with a broken pelvis. "You don't need to go," he said, just before I hung up.

I raced to the hospital to find Arnie in the lobby. "It's a miracle she's alive," he said. "It was a head-on."

I was frantic. "I need to see her! What room is she in?"

He assured me there was nothing I could do. "Just go home, Kern," he said, "wherever that is for you now."

"Wherever that is?" How could Arnie make a comment like that at a time like this? I stormed out of the hospital feeling as if I was sent away. *There was nothing I could do? My daughter didn't need me?* I knew exactly where home was. I headed north on Highway 101. In the next few days I would learn that Robin would recover well, and, she assured me, she had more friends helping her than she knew what to do with.

But the surprises weren't over. On my return to our love nest in Carmel Valley I learned from Charles that he had an evening of tantric loving with Emily and with a Russian woman while I was away. I screamed a lot of "how could you's?" at him as he sat centered in his truth that this was how he had to live his life. I was doing so much to devote myself to him while he was writing a new definition of "devoted."

I closed myself in the bathroom and drew a hot bath to calm myself down. The water restored me. The only way I could go forward, I knew, was to put Emily out of my mind and continue to give myself over to getting to know Charles in the intimacy of morning, noon, and night, making love, taking walks, preparing delicious vegetarian food, practicing yoga, and helping to teach it. Long walks in the hills helped me through the shift I was making from one life into this leap into love with Charles, and lots of tears did their part, too. Sacred spot sessions with Charles moved mountains of guilt, fear, and shame I carried, and I felt new aspects of myself emerging.

Together, we began to embody lover and beloved, Shiva and Shakti, God and Goddess living Tantra in daily life. Our passion for each other and for healing, wholeness, and happiness radiated from us. The seminars began filling up once people began to understand the seminars had something to do with having better sex. Many who came practiced Hatha yoga and were already on a spiritual path. They welcomed the teachings about Tantra and conscious loving as I had, excited by the expansiveness it brought to their lives. Our dream was starting to take shape.

I had never been with a man so eager to give me pleasure, and I had never faced the blocks I had to feeling pleasure. Charles had learned from experience that emotional wounds live inside a woman's yoni and their imprints can be released as the sacred spot is gently urged into an awakened state. (In men, the anus, perineum, and the entire sexual center can be a storehouse for emotional wounding.) Charles massaged deep into the crescent moon scar that had been opened three times in my abdomen in my twenties, at the same time holding points in the scar tissue inside my yoni. I howled remembering that early trauma, his loving and tender gaze always on me. Eventually, the numbness gave way to sensitivity, and Charles and I proved wrong the doctors who said I would never have vaginal orgasms. The pleasure I felt in my clitoris filled the deepest reaches of my yoni, and I appreciated my yoni in a new way. I understood it as sacred through the loving attention, healing, pleasuring, and tender gaze of my friend, lover, and beloved. This area is an energy center, and I became more and more aware of the power it holds.

I had always had silent orgasms, eyes closed. After the few seconds of clitoral release, just as suddenly, I was "done." Now I was learning to vocalize when we made love—to use words like "Yes!" or "Thank you, God!"—whatever expressed what I was feeling.

And I was ejaculating amrita, and often. What a surprise! At first, I was baffled by it. After many experiences of doubting, by tasting, smelling, and reading about it I finally believed this was really happening. It wasn't urination, like so many people believed it was. I wanted to teach other women how to release amrita. I wanted all of my sisters to receive what I was receiving, to feel the joy of coming alive into our sexuality. We would place a pile of soft, fluffy towels under me to collect this copious, watery fluid that would gush from my urethra during lovemaking. We celebrated the ecstasy of these releases with laughter and prayers asking for my divine nectar to be a blessing for all. "Blessings, blessings, blessings," we sang together, as my amrita flowed.

"We will bring Tantra to the world," Charles would sing as we walked hand in hand along the spectacular Carmel beaches. "We will teach people how to have this kind of love and pleasure." He would drop to his knees before me, hands pressed together in prayer position, his eyes lit with radiant love. "I will live my devotion to you, my beloved Caroline."

That summer, I spoke for the first time to a group of women attending a Tantra weekend. The women's eyes were wide as I spoke, and my heart filled. I knew I was on my path. "In the past four months I have awakened more feeling than I've ever had in my yoni," I told them. Could they do this too? they wanted to know. I explained that the giver of sacred spot massage must be skilled in staying fully present for the frequent changes in response by the receiver. She may be wildly orgasmic one moment and sobbing the next, as stored negative charge and emotion are released. The women couldn't wait to practice that night with their partners.

At that weekend seminar, Mira met a man named John-ji. How I relaxed when I felt their connection and heard he would join us in Maui. John-ji would be Mira's beloved for the next twenty years. Everything was falling into place, and effortlessly.

In late June we took our river trip in the Grand Canyon with a group of Tantra students. A few days before we left for the trip, Lucian called. "I saw Ron this morning," he told me, "waiting at a stoplight." Ron had leaned out the window and asked after me. "I told him you were up north with Charles," Lucian said. "And I told him you were moving to Maui." "So she's the sex queen of the universe now, isn't she," Ron said.

Sex queen of the universe! Charles laughed out loud on hearing it, but I didn't find it so funny. I was leaving the world of sex and entering the world of sexual love and conscious loving. But it was true, if I were to be queen of anything it might as well be sex.

Charles loved it. He wrote "SQOTU" for Sex Queen of the Universe across one of my waterproof bags, and he wrote my new nickname, "Queenie," on another. The name stuck.

The raw glory of nature in the Grand Canyon filled my spirit as it had when I'd rafted this river with Ron just a few years earlier. Charles and I were like a honeymooning couple for those two weeks on the river, our friends and students cheering us on. Our tent was dubbed "the orgasma-tron." My "job," if you will, was to make enough sounds to inspire others to practice. Most of them were too tired and hungry from the day on the river. But it was easy with Charles as inspiration and guide.

After the river trip I flew to Los Angeles for Robin's graduation and to say goodbye before the move to Maui. She was receiving her master's degree in child psychology from the University of Southern California. She planned on going to school in Pasadena to earn her Ph.D. Arnie, Nancy, and Rick were there, with armfuls of roses for our girl. With me, Robin as always was guarded. I had prayed for years that our connection would deepen. Now I stood before her, seeing the bright, beautiful young woman she had become, and I wondered, would she ever understand and forgive me? I had only been trying to live true to myself. I wasn't becoming a sex teacher; I had high hopes for my healing in this new relationship. One day, I hoped, her admiration for me would be as big as mine was for her that day and always.

My next stop was Topanga, where I packed up the last of my things at Josie's house and shipped boxes to Maui. I said goodbye to friends who had been with me in Charles' first Tantra seminar in Ojai nearly two years earlier—Josie, Lucian and Margie, Jesse and Kevin.

"What are you doing, having sex on stage? Have you gone completely insane?" my dad said when I called to say goodbye. My brother Johnny didn't understand what this was all about either, but he wished me well. He understood that the winds of love had swept me into their orbit again. I was ready to step into the future. There was no looking back.

Chapter Eight

Land of Aloha

Charles was waiting at the airport to greet me when my plane touched down in Honolulu, placing gardenia leis one after another around my neck. "You're here, beloved, you're here!" He took me in his arms and kissed me passionately, holding me as if we hadn't seen each other for years, then we joined hands and he led me to the inter-island terminal for the short flight to Maui. Our great romantic adventure was beginning and my feet hardly touched the ground.

Charles had come to Maui a week earlier to see two women he was deep in sexually loving relationship with. He knew the fragile nature of attachment and he didn't want to end things abruptly; he wanted to be gentle with them as our new and skyrocketing relationship took off. He always wanted to leave people better than he found them, he liked to say.

Once the doors to this new love swung wide open, I couldn't remember a life that didn't include this. I was breathlessly in love on the beaches and in the arms of a man who enchanted me from the first light of dawn until we drifted to sleep in the balmy Hawaiian night. Our temporary home was a two-bedroom condo on the touristy side of the island, nowhere we wanted to stay but a good starting place. We couldn't wait to trade in the land of the tourists on the sunset side of the island for the "wild" side, where the jungle meets the sea and sunrise is a blaze of inspiration. We knew this was where we would find our new home. But first, Mira had to get here, and she would in just a couple of days, and John-ji would arrive two weeks later.

Mira and I couldn't have been happier. We took care of the business of settling into our new life, applying for driver's licenses, opening bank accounts, buying cars, and scouring the classifieds every morning for the perfect house to rent. Every day we kept Charles busy with sacred spot massage sessions, and afterward, he and I or he and Mira would make love. It still wasn't easy to share him this way, even now that we were in Hawaii and living our vision of the beloved truth, but Charles was committed to his vision, and I agreed it was right to keep from getting lost in my romantic ideal of "just the two of us." It couldn't be that and be what Mira and I had conceived that night in Mexico. Still, I hadn't planned on falling in love with this man who had been my friend for years already. Deep inside, I hoped I could really do this.

One Sunday, a few weeks after John-ji arrived, Charles waved the *Maui News* in our faces over breakfast at a favorite restaurant in Paia. "Look at this! There's a two-story for rent on two acres out Door of Faith Road in Huelo. I have some good friends down that way." Charles' friends on Door of Faith Road were Cos (Cosmic Galaxy), from Charles' days in Big Sur, and Cos's girlfriend, Blue Vision. They were building an octagonal cliff-side home and developing their own two acres on Door of Faith Road. They both had been Charles' lovers for some time, and he adored them. Within minutes we were racing down the Hana Highway past acres of pineapple fields and tropical jungle to the turnoff at Door of Faith Road. There, we inched along an unpaved road, laughing as we tried to avoid the deepest potholes. I noticed a hand-painted sign in front of a small church we passed advertising "Door of Faith Church," written in uneven letters. Door of Faith Church? This wasn't just a road, it was a whole community! I felt a tingle surge up my spine. This truly was a walk through the door of faith. And it was great to be here.

About a mile down the road, perched high on a cliff overlooking the rugged coastline all the way to Hana, our house waited for us. We parked in front and threw open the car doors to go explore.

I had not dreamed of a house set back from the cliff—I had imagined our home being oceanside. But as I stood on the wrap-around deck inhaling the salty trade winds fresh from their journey across the sea and saw the swaying palms around the border of the property, I knew this was where we were meant to be. That horizon line where sky met sea would be my solace many times to come, I knew. I wanted this view. I turned to Charles, who was grinning at me. "Let's do it."

Exactly one month after I arrived in Maui, we were moving into our new home, with a bedroom that shared the first floor with the yoga room and a small office and Mira and John-ji's bedroom upstairs with the kitchen and living room. And my share of the rent? Only three hundred dollars. Maui was surely receiving us with grace.

Our first night in our new home, we drifted to sleep on our new waterbed to the enchanting lull of the waves when two warm bodies slipped in beside us. I felt soft kisses placed on my cheeks before I knew what was happening.

"Cos and Blue!" Charles cried.

Charles kissed them both as they snuggled firm, tanned bodies against us. "You're here! You're our neighbor!" they giggled.

I extracted myself from the pile and leaned against the wall to try to see these visitors in the dim moonlight. *Beloved, where are you?*

Charles nodded to me, then turned to his friends. "Hey, you guys," he said, gently. "This is our first night in our new house. Another time might be better for my queen."

"We came over to celebrate with you," Blue said. "We can't wait to love her as much as we love you."

"Tomorrow is the full moon," said Cos. "We'll see you then!" He took Blue by the hand and called out "Aloha!" and they were off and disappearing through the sliding screened door as suddenly as they came. Charles reached out for me and I curled into his embrace and lay down with him again.

"I can't imagine making love with them, Charles," I whispered. "I don't even know them."

"You can love them tantrically, and let them love you. That's how you'll really get to know them."

I couldn't imagine. "It's hard for me, Charles."

"I can see that. Have you changed your mind about sharing our love with Mira and John-ji?"

"I would be forcing it," I admitted. "I never wanted to share love with John-ji. And if we were all together I know I'd be expected to."

It was hard saying this, but I had to be honest. Mira and I had talked earlier that day and she wanted things to change, too. She was sad to let go of Charles as her lover, but it was hard dividing her attention between him and John-ji. I told her I understood and that I didn't want to share sexually with her anymore, either.

Charles lay back on his pillow and was quiet for a long time. After he fell asleep, I lay awake trying to make sense of everything. Was I old-fashioned? My sexuality was so private, my gift to the one I love. But I had turned my life upside-down to live Tantra with Charles. This was part of the bargain. How familiar this felt—one foot on the accelerator, the other on the brake. It was a long night.

In the morning I was swept from my dizzying dilemma into the excitement of celebrating the full moon, a monthly ritual for my new Maui family. Many people Charles knew took the day off to revel in the beauty of the island, and we were right along with them, hiking to the jungle pools and waterfalls to make love on the warm boulders before continuing across the guava-covered palisades to Cos and Blue's property. As dusk became exquisite night, silvery moonlight gleamed through windows of our friends' half-built house overlooking the sea, and we sat naked together on Cos and Blue's bed. I reminded myself of that open door of faith. In the moonlight, Cos stroked Charles' beautiful, erect lingam and invited Blue to accept his gift of Charles. Charles held me close as Blue seductively accepted the invitation to sit astride him, and he suggested I pleasure Cos. We would all love one another. I was reeling! But I did my best to be part of it for as long as I could.

After some sweaty, sexy loving, it was time for a break and a toke. I liked the warmth between us all, but it was enough, I decided, time to go home. "Stay, Queenie!" Charles pleaded, when I told them I was leaving. They all begged me to stay. I did, for a little while longer, but finally, with my energetic and emotional wires crossing in too many directions, I just hit my endpoint, and I stopped abruptly. "I've got to go," I whispered, touching Charles' shoulder. This new girl on the block needed to be alone. I dressed quickly and walked home in the moonlight.

Alone in bed at home, my mind buzzed. Was this "the beloved truth"? Blue hardly seemed to need healing or awakening. This was just plain fun between friends who loved their sexuality together. Would I ever like this as much as Charles seemed to? Sleep finally came when he crawled into bed with me about an hour later, purring his love for his queen.

In the morning Cos and Blue stopped in for coffee just before noon. It was good to see them in the light of day, but the sexual energy between all of them unbalanced me. I was exhilarated by all of this, and overwhelmed, a strange feeling. I wanted to demystify sex as I knew it, to recreate myself as a conscious tantric lover not only with Charles but with anyone I chose. I wanted to expand beyond my limitations and beliefs, chart new territories in love and marriage, sex and sexuality, but I had to take baby steps. I had a lot to learn about my new life in mother Maui.

Over the next few months it didn't take a full moon night to bring us all together to play sexually, and I eventually began to find my way. I watched the others make love and found ways to assist and enjoy the energy. Sometimes I made love with Charles while Cos and Blue watched or touched us or made love beside us. I allowed sacred spot massage by the others (although no one did it as well as Charles), and I enjoyed their sweet and sexy kisses on my yoni, yet I rarely surrendered to their pleasuring of me. I still believed in "saving" something sacred for my beloved. Was Kansas holding me back? My interest in sexual play usually ended before it did for the others. If we were at our neighbors', I often left "early" for bed or sent Charles off with them if we had started at our house. A few hours later I would wake alone and in turmoil, conjuring up images of losing my beloved to Blue's sexual passion. Cos didn't seem worried. He had no problem sharing his beloved. He had shared his ex-wife with Charles, too. And Charles saw this as an opportunity to not only practice his art form but to teach it as well. He loved coaching his friend in ways of conscious loving: slow down, stay connected with your eyes, increase your intimacy along with your passion. By the new year, Cos and Blue had become real friends. They accepted me fully as I stayed true to my choice to contain my sexuality, only traveling to the heights of sexual ecstasy with my beloved, and they loved showing me the beauty of every season on this outrageous edge of the world.

Everything in Maui seemed new. December and January weren't the cold months they had been all my life, and it rained often no matter what time of year. Sultry tropical weather would transform into a raging storm before you could race to shut the windows against the pounding rain. Rainbows arced across the sky, often in double or triple full spectrum. We hiked to the ocean and walked its rocky shores or hiked to jungle waterfalls, lay on warm white sand beaches, and swam in Mother Earth's waters. We celebrated her new moons and her full moons, offered our love to the awakening of god and goddess in all beings. As the verdant land of Aloha merged with the splintered and healing me, we lived our lives and our work as Tantra teachers, believing nothing could harm a love so true.

What a life. I had no children at home, my job was all pleasure, and my beloved took his responsibility seriously to keep his goddess juicy and happy. Our daily morning prayer was joining in the union of our heart, body, and soul. In this devotional practice I would look into my beloved's eyes, feel his warm arms encircling me, listen to the soft beating of his heart against mine. Open eyes, quiet minds, and breathing in union sparked our bodies into remembering our oneness. He would enter me with no goal of orgasm, though deep, soulful orgasms came easier and easier to me as we joined in spiritual union, chakras joined to one another and together joined with our God and Goddess. Without a goal we could receive and give on another level, with more play, more laughter, more focus on breathing, sounding, and gazing—more *connection*. A rewiring was taking place in my sexual conduits and my consciousness soared.

I am an intimacy junkie, a flower child of the transpersonal psychology generation, and the options for connecting in Tantra thrilled me. It doesn't have to mean having sex, or even talking. Connecting simply means I connect the innermost part of me with the innermost part of another. It might be sexual and sexually pleasurable; it might be long, or brief, or playful. It could be a connection that doesn't even involve touch—it could be "fire" through the eyes without touching.

In its simplest form, a tantric connection is a joining of energies in all of the chakras with the chakras of another and with that which is divine. It could be defined as being the love you are and sharing that essence with another. Tantra is a divine triangle, a weaving of the divine within me and the divine within another with all that is sacred in the universe.

Our practice of connecting throughout a busy day ranged from three-second gazes filled with love to five-minute neck or foot rubs, and many embraces for the pleasure of feeling our closeness. At least one connection each day included inserting my beloved's lingam into my yoni, either leading into the dance of love or into insertion and stillness, breathing our love and energy into one another without thrusting. This alone changed sex for me into something I could always be open to. The mere act of receiving my beloved into my body was all he really needed, and that was something I could always do, and particularly because the purpose was to enhance the connection of our love. From that point on, I determined what I wanted in the lovemaking. Now *that* was empowering.

Students would ask, "How do you have time for these practices?" And our answer was always, "What could be more important than practicing your love?" You have to find the time for practice; it seldom finds you. Charles might say, "It's five o'clock, my queen, time to connect!" and I'd wrap up whatever I was doing and meet him in our bedroom, our sanctuary for loving. The chakras build a charge from running this kind of energy through them, and we wanted highly charged energy centers. Just as a musician has to practice, our bodies are instruments for loving and they need practice, too.

Before arriving at the bed to prepare for daily Tantra practice we usually dropped to the carpet for a Hatha yoga stretching tune-up followed by even a few minutes of massage. When we felt more connected to ourselves, we could more fully connect to one another. I would often sit astride Charles, my legs wrapped around his hips, and I would gaze in his eyes, breathing from the base of my spine, filling my brain with light and energy. If we were more comfortable standing or lying face to face, we would use that position. (There are "conscious cuddle" techniques where partners lie back to front, using inner imagery, instead of lying face to face.) We often said softly, "I am loving you," with the other responding, "I am loved by you" or "you are my dear beloved friend (lover, husband, etc.").

"I so appreciate you...you are beautiful to me in every way," would be combined with caressing, rocking, kissing, pressing foreheads together ("the kiss of the third eye"), or simply being still, breathing in and out consciously, in unison or alternately. Our chakras aligned, he would then lay me back on the bed, inviting me to join him gazing out to sea before gazing into one another's eyes again. Our eyes could make love for hours. On and on the poetry of love would flow from our lips when we weren't using them for kissing. "Yes to our love, yes to this pleasure. I love you more than there are stars in the sky. I receive your love in every cell of my being. I return my love to every cell in yours."

The sacred and sensual daily massage of my sacred spot—which usually resulted in a series of powerful orgasmic contractions and the warm release of amrita—became effortless. It was often preceded by arousal of my clitoris (my pearl) with his mouth or fingers, or hand-assisted—unique techniques taught in our seminars, which include "painting," rubbing, or tapping his lingam gently around my yoni, belly, and inner thighs. It was an experience of bliss and ecstasy as I sang with pleasure, releasing my nectar upon our selves, our lives, our families, our work, and the Earth Mother herself. Although lovers always seem to enjoy the taste of one another, I loved the suggestion from my beloved, "Rest, just breathe me in, while I pleasure you," and then we often alternated, giving pause to both partners being active at the same time, exciting sometimes, but not always.

On weekends, our ritual of love lasted much longer, giving ourselves the gift of leisure from the work-week. We would start by beautifying our bedroom with flowers from our gardens. Gardenia-scented baths readied us for the feast of loving. Sometimes we fasted and we prayed, playing with our bodies in stretch through Hatha yoga (White Tantra) as foreplay to our lovemaking (Red Tantra). We massaged each other, laughed, talked, and touched, all the while our eyes never leaving the light dancing in the other's eyes. I learned the value of taking in a deep breath of his love, looking into his eyes, and replying to his passionately spoken words, "I love you," with connection to the feeling inside of me, "I am loved by you." This was one way I was learning to feel my own lovableness

Charles loved giving and I loved receiving, and the more loving touch I received, the more I wanted to give back. But it was a different kind of giving than I had been used to with other men. Charles prided himself on his increasing skill to have ejaculatory choice, for internalizing his orgasms, and I delighted in assisting his journey toward mastery of this life-enhancing skill. Until Tantra I never knew there was another way. All of my male lovers had ended our lovemaking with their ejaculatory orgasm.

It was important to both of us to be in good physical condition, and we had an abundance of healers eager to trade with us. Charles traded seminars for bodywork, Rolfing, and acupuncture sessions, and we each received two-hour massages every week from massage therapists, often on a massage table outdoors in the shade of our coconut palms. The tropical heat and humidity kept our eating light, and Hatha yoga kept us in good shape. My soul and spirit had found home.

As idyllic as so much of my life was now, in the bedroom some of the tantric principles, such as quieting my mind and staying present, were still a struggle. Mental wandering seemed a natural state, and bringing my mind into steady focus was like trying to swim upstream. The discipline is to bring the mind back from its wandering and focus on the connection with self and beloved. Breathing deeply and consciously was hard sometimes, too, for this former cigarette smoker. I would breathe in harmony with Charles and as soon as I moved into action, my breath would quicken and we would fall out of sync. Would I ever get good at this? I believed that healing is ready to happen and that love and pleasure are our birthright. I had to be patient and keep trying to open my heart so my Shakti and the magic of increased aliveness would continue to unfold. Charles would remind me sometimes, with "Slow down, beloved queen. Enjoy your breath and take in my love. There is nowhere to go. We are already there."

I was learning.

At the Tantra seminars, I sat by Charles' side, my self-confidence growing every time we held a session, each time addressing a larger group: eighteen became twenty-four, then thirty-six, and eventually we taught to groups numbering over a hundred men and women. As time went on, we continued to create safe environments for Tantra to be taught to larger and larger groups. Students would come back over and over to re-take the course and "just be in the energy," since there was never explicit sexual practice or nudity at our seminars. "Homework" assignments were given, and people did their healing practices in the privacy of their rooms or homes.

I learn best by experience, so teaching from experience made the most sense to me. At the seminars I prepared the women by sharing with them what I experienced in my tantric practice with Charles. I told them to expect to begin their sexual awakening by inviting God into the bedroom, however they experienced God. I described vaginal orgasm through massage of the sacred spot and told them about my experience releasing amrita, the female ejaculate.

"Take time with your partner to state your intentions for your healing and awakening," I told the women, pausing to give them time to digest this radical concept. "Give words to your fears, your hopes and expectations, and then surrender to become all you are as a fully enlivened and radiant goddess."

While I met with the women, Charles prepared the men. In that setting the men could express their fears and learn from "a guy" about things they may not have known about the anatomy or the emotional needs of women. They learned about ejaculation choice, and how to control their own so they and their partners could enhance the longevity of their pleasure together. Tantric lovemaking could go on for hours if that was desired, with both lovers rising in orgasmic and nonorgasmic bliss. These energies of love, passion, and pleasure escalate with each breath, each kiss, as the men grew more and more enthused to practice what they were learning in class. The women had their coaching and now the lovers were sent home to practice.

Wherever we taught, I noticed common themes: People are hungry to love and be loved. People are starved for the truth about joining spirit with sexual energy. People want to know how to give and receive pleasure that results in more passion, more love, more of a feeling of oneness. Everyone has ego issues about being a good or successful lover. Orgasms, other than clitoral (for women) or ejaculatory (for men), are a mystery to many. Generally, men want more sex—and more stimulating sex—and women want deeper intimacy during sex. For some, those desires are reversed, especially as more and more men claim their sensitivity as strength.

In the early days of teaching together, Charles and I focused primarily on women's healing and the awakening of her Shakti. Eventually we would devote ourselves equally to the healing and awakening of consciousness for the men, as they, too, have a desire to be passionately loved and to experience themselves as sexual-spiritual beings.

My understanding of healing was growing with every experience of it. I was learning that healing doesn't have to be painful—it can happen through pleasure of any kind, through laughter, pleasure, and orgasm, or simply loving touch. Sadness, loneliness, disappointment, frustration, emotional wounding from the past—any of it can be healed, or eased, through loving pleasure fit into any busy day. This was the power of love in action.

Daily, I learned from Charles about how love and kindness make up holy relationship. "Lie down, my queen, and let me rub your back. Turn over, my queen, I'll release any tension in your neck. Taste this, my darling, I've made a cream of cauliflower soup. Have the first sip, my beloved, this cappuccino has your name on it. " I squealed with delight at the very sight of my beloved returning home from town. The first touch of embrace, the rush of his natural scent mixed with the sandalwood oil he always wore, the sound of his voice quickened the Shakti awakening in me. We cooked for each other, feeding one another the deliciousness that came from our efforts. At the sound of tires crunching the gravel in our driveway, we hopped, skipped, and jumped out to the car to greet the other. We often headed straight for our waterbed to lie together, embracing as if we had been apart for years. Laughter shook our bodies as joy overflowed from our hearts.

And Charles always had a creative way to make life just a little more fun. "Put on your sexy new sundress, beloved, and I'll drive you to our favorite spot for a Thai feast." Or, "Let's pick up a movie on our way home, my queen. What kind of love story are you in the mood to see?" Halfway through the movie we put the film on pause, knowing that lovemaking would keep us smiling until we fell into bed for a night of sleep wrapped in each other's arms. In the supermarket we danced in the aisles to songs over the sound system—"A kiss is just a kiss / a sigh is just a sigh / the fundamental things apply / as time goes by…" Traffic lights were always an opportunity to spin around in my seat and press my heart to his chest or plant a kiss on his lips. Sexual play while driving was easier on Maui than in most places, and pulling off into the sugar cane fields in the moonlight was an event not to be missed.

With Charles, in addition to all I was learning about love and healing, I was learning, too, to be more centered in my power, to be more thoughtful and less reactive. If I said something negative, Charles might respond, "Beloved queen, is that how you want to use the power of your spoken word?" The *power* of my spoken word? If I had a worried look on my face, he might say, "Queenest of my heart, is that how you want your mind to serve you?" This was beloved wisdom.

As we lay in bed together one afternoon, Charles told me the story of his beginnings with Tantra yoga. He had started on this path more than fifteen years earlier, after discovering Hinduism while at City College in New York City in the early 1960s. He went on to study yoga with Richard Hittleman and, in 1968, followed one of Hittleman's teachers to Rio Caliente, where he discovered the mineral waters of Rio Caliente Spa. Yoga led him to ashrams in upstate New York and to gurus who came from India to teach yoga to the West. His passion was teaching yoga and in no time, he told me whenever I asked for the story again, he went from a stiff, overweight teenager to a healthy vegetarian man. On many afternoons lying together like this he told me stories from the Bhagavad Gita, love stories of Hindu gods and goddesses—Krishna and Radha, Rama and Sita, Shiva and Shakti. And he listened to stories of my life—my affair with my first husband's teenage nephew and other details of my love life. Now and then he asked about my father and grandfather, wondering if either had been sexually inappropriate with me, since he believed I had wounding trapped in my sexual center. "Absolutely not!" I always assured him. "I had a completely normal childhood."

With enough practice, anyone can awaken the sensitivity to read energy. From years of practicing yoga and massaging the sacred spots of so many women, Charles' intuition had become acute. He knew that when he touched a certain place inside me, I wouldn't be able to breathe. I felt like I was suffocating. I needed to pee. We both knew he wasn't hurting me. He was contacting hurt already there, the *memory* of hurt, which can be as or more painful than physical hurt. The area inside my yoni somewhere in my urethral sponge could feel like broken glass was embedded there when it was even gently touched. When it happened, I would rage at Charles for hurting me and suddenly lose trust in him, rushing from the bed for the open window for air. Neither of us knew what the source of this emotional hurt was, but the effect of pain was there and Charles was determined to revive the memory of the hurt inside my body in an attempt to release it and see me move on.

More often, though, my intimate life with Charles was about pleasure. I received so much pleasure I had to breathe deeply sometimes to stay calm. Charles would show up wearing a funny hat, a Groucho Marx mustache and bushy eyebrow–topped dark-rimmed eyeglasses, or act out a Broadway song-and-dance on the spur of the moment. Hot soups would appear from the kitchen, and steaming bowls of ravioli or frothy cappuccinos "for my beloved." And always, there was his shoulder bag of goodies. If Charles was there, you always had whatever you needed.

Besides his height (six-foot-four), his dazzling blue eyes, and his magnificent smile, one of Charles' identifying features was his big shoulder bag. Charles loved having exactly what anyone wanted. "Stuffy nose?" and the item was instantly in their hands. "Feeling a little off, my darling? This Bach Flower Remedy is for you." He was constantly unzipping compartments of his bag to provide aid and assistance. Once we weighed the bag: a staggering thirty-four pounds. (After that weigh-in, it dropped ten pounds!) In that bag inside small embroidered pouches were Charles' Indian brocade wallet and worn address book, cassis chews, peppermints, and licorice pastilles, pens, a hair brush, rose and aloe facial mists, sandalwood resin for his underarms, amber essential oil for third-eye and chakra blessings. I would always find some treat wrapped in its original paper, usually a yummy fudgy thing from the checkout counter of a health food store. There were demo tapes from musician friends like Steven Halpern or Stevie Bergman (Charles had the first New Age music business and was always helping his artist friends produce or distribute their music). A first aid kit complete with glow-in-the-dark Band-Aids, antibiotic salve, cortisone cream, a variety of pain meds from leftover prescriptions. Dental picks, floss, a toothbrush and toothpaste, hand cream, moisturizer, sexual lubricants, massage oil, and a variety of lip balms, from raspberry-cherry to vanilla-almond espresso, all of which felt good inside of nostrils, too. He liked large white handkerchiefs, too, with his initial "C" or "M" on them. Traveling with Charles was easy; if I forgot something, he usually had it.

And travel, we did. Every few weeks we taught Tantra in different locations—in Honolulu, on the Big Island, on Kauai, living out of a suitcase and sleeping on a friend's futon. We flew to the mainland every month, holding seminars in Santa Cruz, Carmel, Marin County, Los Angeles, and San Diego, and in Colorado Springs and Boulder. Eventually, we would hold annual seminars in Houston for the PAIRS (Practical Application of Intimate Relationship Skills) couples, and in Atlanta, Georgia, and New Hope, Pennsylvania. We would schedule weeklong vacation seminars at Rio Caliente as well as on Maui. I wanted to teach at Esalen Institute in Big Sur, and Charles booked us at that great landmark of personal growth, and we gave our first popular workshop there in the early '90s.

At last I had a big enough love to satisfy the great longing in my heart. Our island life had its demands, to be sure. It takes much longer to get anything done in the land of aloha, tourists, and hot tropical weather. Business moves slower, rental cars drive at a slow enough pace for the tourists to see the view, but being young and in love in the land of honeymoons kept us remembering to relax and live in gratitude for the choice we had made to live our love on Maui. Mira and John-ji were in their own bliss, often swimming in the ocean, walking on the beach, making love in the cool of the day, keeping house, and living their island lives while Charles and I taught our seminars and practiced conscious loving at home every day, enjoying the deliciousness of each other's company every moment we could. Students expressed their gratitude to us at seminar after seminar in city after city. Even Charles was amazed at what was happening. "What better job could we have than teaching people how to love better?" I had to agree. What a gift to have the opportunity to awaken people to more love and pleasure than they might ever have imagined! I had wanted to live differently and to make a difference in the world. I couldn't think of a better way.

Chapter Nine

The Island of Our Love

Two important women showed up on our doorstep that first year on Door of Faith Road—Jahlia and Singie. Jahlia was a refined wild woman. She was from England originally and had the manners and accent of a fine English lady, but Jahlia had lived for the past two years on the slopes of the Haleakala Crater planting sandalwood trees and writing songs. When the cold became unforgiving at 5,000 feet, she moved to Makena Beach, one of the great beaches of the world, where she had slept outdoors for a year. She had heard about us and she wanted to meet us and be part of our lives. We invited her in right away.

"I would like to give you a song," she said, "but you'll have to forgive me. My lyre was stolen from my car last night at Makena."

We assured her we were grateful for anything she offered, and so, with her voice her only instrument, Jahlia kneeled before us, her long, sun-bleached hair cradling her heart-shaped face, and with the sweetness of a songbird she sang us "Lady Eagle" as she gazed into my wonder-filled eyes. When she finished, I took her hands in mine. "Please sing for us as often as you like!" "Please sing at our next seminar," Charles said, bowing to her with respect and thanks. She heartily accepted.

Singie was also a musician and a dear friend of Jahlia. I had taken the celestial journey of her songs and chants many times over the years while practicing yoga on my own or making love with Charles, and I asked Jahlia to introduce us. Without a doubt, she was a connection to the divine.

What an impact Singie had on me! When I opened the door to greet this dynamic woman with the blue eyes and wild red hair, I knew instantly I could get lost in her passion. I hoped I would.

"I'm *so* happy you're here!" I said, throwing my arms around her. "Please come in."

Singie followed me inside, looking around as though she was checking for the emergency exit in case she needed it. Singie seemed feline, timid yet ready to pounce—or fly from the room—at any moment. I took her hand and guided her into the yoga room. "Beloved? The Songs of the Lord's Love lady is here!"

Charles came in barefooted and all smiles, and he knelt before her, pressing his hands together in prayer position. "Namaste," he said reverently, gazing up at Singie.

She smiled. "Nice welcome, guys," she said.

I suggested tea to loosen things up.

Throughout that balmy afternoon, we sipped tea as Singie enchanted us with her stories. She told us about living in a spiritual community as a teenager after running away from her broken home, about the arranged marriage her guru had directed her into when she was eighteen, to a man she didn't love. With horror, I listened to her accounts of their intimacies, which bore them two children. At last she had chosen freedom, even though the price she paid for it was high: her husband had refused to let her take the children with her. To save her soul, she'd left anyway.

Singie and Jahlia quickly became a regular part of our lives. Jahlia was easy, grounded and honest, always ready to make a fresh pot of tea or write a new song. We inched closer over cups of English Breakfast tea and her vast repertoire of songs, with lyrics that pulsated with soul. We would take a journey of healing and awakening together over the next twelve years, as she became a part of our intimate home life. Sometimes she would strum her new lyre at the foot of our bed while Charles and I made tantric love. Now and then, she would allow us to stroke her lovely lean body, massage her, or even arouse her in subtle, sensual, teasing ways, as she shared stories of her heartbreak and disappointment in love and sex. In Jahlia I saw many of the same fears and truths I recognized in myself.

My friendship with Singie was very different. Singie was fiery and animated, and our friendship grew fast and hot. We were entranced with each other. She joined me often in the mornings for yoga and breakfast with Charles. Sometimes Mira and John-ji would join us, too, or come along with us on a long hike to a jungle waterfall or to a favorite beach, but Singie never bonded with them as she did with us, and particularly with me. Her sexual Shakti was palpable, and I was magnetically attracted.

Our Maui family was expanding in many unexpected ways. Next on the scene were Michael and Marbie, two former students of ours from Honolulu, offering their services—anything to help the expansion of Tantra. Michael ran errands for the business, his long legs appearing to race ahead of a mind filled with so many things to do, a smile that never left his face. He loved us, loved Maui, loved being Charles' right-hand man and business assistant. Before long, with his dedication and Charles' vision, the business was paying real salaries. Marbie, Michael's sweetheart, became our first *dakini,* magnificently serving our students with her massage skills when they attended seminars in Maui. A dakini is a teacher of love, poetically described as a "celestial messenger," someone who could teach the techniques of Tantra to couples in the privacy of their bedroom. Marbie became a dear friend and confidante, available to help and assist in every way.

Other new additions to the family were two kittens, Tai and Chi. They showed up one day at the beach, jumping at our sandy ankles and feet, their eyes still closed as they meowed their way into our hearts. We took them home, where Marbie showed me how to feed them milk from a baby's bottle while cradling them in the crook of my arm. We nursed and cuddled them into spry young adults. Tai and Chi always remembered Marbie, purring even louder when she visited and jumping up to cuddle in her lap. And it was a love fest with us, too. Sometimes it was hard to know who was purring louder when Charles and I lay snuggled with the kitties in bed at night .

Huelo is a series of valleys along a tail of land on the north shore, an untamed area between Kahului and the one-lane road to Hana. Jungle meets the sea in Huelo, and the rain comes often and furiously in sheets so dense you can't see the highway in front of you day or night. These intense tropical storms keep tourists away, and only the locals are around to witness the spectacular sunbeams and moonbeams that grace heaven and earth after these storms. Giant mango trees offer shade on hot summer days, and waterfall pools deep in the jungle beckon. Many of the Hawaiians in this area live in makeshift screen and plywood houses; they've been here for generations. Fire trucks and ambulances need at least thirty minutes to reach homes on Door of Faith Road.

Two churches dot the landscape in Huelo, one Baptist, the other Pentecostal. I became a regular at the Pentecostal Door of Faith Church. It wasn't for the sermons on Sunday mornings—it was for the connection with the locals. After all, I was a resident of the "hood"!

Jahlia or Singie often joined me for the music, or I would go alone. The minister, Dolly Kahiamoe, a grandmother in her sixties, delivered Sunday sermons with frenzied emotion, waving her arms and speaking in tongues. Amidst this, the men nodded off in their seats while the ladies, decked out in pastel church hats and flowered muumuus, swooned in the pews in altered states, intoxicated by the love of Jesus. Children sang sweet love songs to Jesus, accompanied by the strangely lyrical ukulele, and if Jahlia or Singie were there, they offered a rousing solo or added their voices to the chorus.

After the service, Sunday dinner was served in the church lanai—plates of steaming shredded pork *(lau lau)*, bowls of *poi,* mounds of steamed greens, roasted white, orange, and purple potatoes, and creamy tapioca pudding. I loved the mix of locals and "haoles" (mainland whites). This was community, and I craved community. On the outside we were so different, but in a deep heart space we were one.

Walking home after church dressed in our Sunday best, we felt as if the air pulsed with magic. Parrots screeched in the banyan trees as we stopped by the house to collect Charles and head to the Bamboo Pools or the Emerald Pool through a forest of bamboo so dense only shards of sunlight could get through. At the pools we would strip off our clothes and jump into the cool rainwater that collected in those ancient lava formations nearly buried in the jungle. Lying naked in the Hawaiian sun on baked lava that had once boiled inside the earth seemed far more spiritual than being in church. This was where we truly worshipped.

It was after church on one such Sunday that I received the fateful phone call from my neighbor, Joe Stephano. Joe owned the three acres in view from my kitchen window. "Caroline," he said, "I'm putting the land on the market for $99,000. I thought you might be interested."

Interested? Sure, I was interested, but I didn't have that kind of money! I thanked him and said I'd call if anything changed.

That evening Charles and I joined Cos and Blue for dinner at a Thai restaurant in Wailuku-town. "Joe Stephano called this morning inviting us to buy his land for just under a hundred grand," I told the table of hungry playmates.

Cos nearly dumped his plate, he jumped up so fast. "You're kidding!" he cried. "Buy it!"

I motioned for him to sit back down. "But it's covered in scrub brush and has a falling-down old shed in the middle," I protested. "Besides, I like my view out the kitchen window. And who has $99,000?"

Cos wouldn't hear it. "There won't be land left in Huelo to buy soon." He sat back down. As an architect and developer, he knew the potential of real estate on the ocean. "There's only so much oceanfront and ocean view land in the world, Queenie. I'm coming over in the morning and we'll walk that land. I'll show you the house I see for you up there."

Owning land had been my lifelong dream. Nank had grown up on acres of farmland, and he had told me many times over the years that he hoped I would one day have the same pleasures. When Rick and I lived in Colorado I had dreamed of owning land, but now? In Hawaii? I loved my freedom to play as much as I worked. Owning land and building a house would be like having a jealous lover.

Charles had a different idea. He was a visionary. He had seen what Cos had built in Big Sur and was building now on Maui. He believed we should have our own home, and he thought this could be the perfect place.

The next morning at eight a.m., Cos was at the door. "Ready?" He grabbed my hand, I grabbed Charles' hand, and we were off.

Cos walked us around the acreage, scanning the elevations with his passion to get things done. "I promise you," he said. "I'll draw up plans for a home fit for Charles and his queen."

I could see the property was set back about 600 yards from the cliff edge. "I want a house right at the edge of the cliff," I told him. "Oceanside. Like yours. There's a place down the road that's right on the edge of the cliff looking into Waipio Bay. Why don't we try to buy that?"

"It'll cost a lot more, Queenie. I can make you a cliff edge of your very own right here. Trust me. This is the property to buy."

I left the men to walk together and climbed alone to the crest of the hill to think this out. There *was* that view of "forever" I loved so much. Puffy white clouds rested on a horizon line that I knew so well by now. That line that was steady and reassuring. I imagined watching the whales pass by on their annual migration south from Alaska from a seat in my new yard. But I didn't have that kind of money! I had given my last house to Ron to buy my freedom.

Two weeks passed, and I got another phone call. It was my grandfather Nank's bank calling, from Kansas. A small trust he had set up when I was a child was due for disbursement. "Where would you like the $150,000 sent?" they wanted to know.

Some things are simply meant to happen.

For a few weeks, we looked at other parcels in the area, and then we turned again to the land in view outside my kitchen window and made an offer. Joe accepted it. We "settled" for 180 degrees of ocean views set back a few hundred yards from the cliff and an architect eager to design our home for a very small fee. Blue assured me we could get the landscaping done before the house went up, using cuttings from her property and hiring local workers to help us plant. With her guidance and star power, I knew it could be done.

Right away, Cos drew up plans for the estate—twenty-three pages of them. I pored over big sheets of heavy tracing paper, looking at outlines of elevations, berms, driveways, ponds, and garage pad, even hand-drawn trees, shrubs, groundcover, and fruit trees that would do well on our little piece of paradise—starfruit, lychee, papaya, banana, passion fruit, avocado, mango. Cos's signature style was grand entrances, lily/lotus ponds, tropical foliage for privacy from the outside world, and regal columns in the style of Grecian temples. The bed in the master bedroom would be in the center of the room under a Polarized skylight for viewing the night sky and for bringing in the radiance of the sun by day.

"Queen," Cos announced one day, his silky hair falling over his eyes as we hovered over the blueprints, "you and Charles have to sleep under the skylight. When you and Charles dream together your spirits need gateways to keep celestial contact. And the skylight can't be domed. It has to soar upward at forty-five degrees."

I didn't doubt that constellations from the stellar landscape would want to use our home as a contact for Earth. Sure, it was "out there," but weren't we members of a cosmic tribe who liked to live outside the box? "Let's do it, Cos," I said. The fact that we nibbled on some fine-quality blotter acid one evening as we proceeded to draw the kitchen only made the outcome more perfect.

While we waited for the stamp of approval from the county, Cos gave me a list of what seemed like a million things to do—phone calls to make, bids to get, tools to buy. At first the tasks seemed daunting, but I rose to the occasion, focusing on the opportunity and the goal. Blue and I began clearing brush and readying the land.

Blue was half my age, petite and muscular, with a mane of curly blonde hair and creamy mocha skin. Her favorite outfit was a G-string, work boots, and a shimmering scarf draped around her neck, artfully covering her small breasts. I was proud she was "our" lover. Days were filled with sunshine and shovels, more plans, and dreams come true as we worked topless and clad in G-strings, the trade winds cooling us. Local women helped us plant eucalyptus, paperbark, and ironwood seedlings, baby palms, and ground covers. Surfers helped haul and dig.

At day's end, Blue and I showered with coconut soap, scrubbed ourselves clean, and emerged for the evening in silky sarongs and beaded necklaces and bracelets handcrafted by Blue. We'd meet at our place or theirs for a smoke of fine local hemp and line up the next day's work plans while recapping what we'd accomplished from sunrise to sundown. Later, Cos and Blue were often open to lovemaking with us if I wished, but I usually preferred to call it a day and go to bed alone.

One day, Mira surprised me with some news. She and John-ji would be moving out. Mira hadn't been involved in all that my life had become, and she was entirely devoted to John-ji. We were far from the vision of the beloved truth we had shared that night in Mexico. "We have been thinking long and deeply about this, Queenie," Mira explained. "You and Charles have your land, your work is flourishing. We're not part of your business. It's time for us to go and create our own life."

It was true. Charles wasn't interested in owning the business with anyone else. In our arrangement we each served a clear purpose, and our combined efforts were integral to all that "conscious loving" had become. And we hadn't been able to connect as deeply with Mira because of her involvement with John-ji. I didn't want to be involved tantrically with him. By avoiding them at that level, I had avoided getting closer to them both. I wasn't proud of maneuvering around discomfort, but I wasn't willing to do it any other way.

Now that Mira was leaving, I realized I had taken her presence for granted. "Things haven't unfolded like we planned, have they?" I said. We embraced tearfully.

Two weeks later, when Charles and I returned from a seminar, we found the upstairs room empty. Mira and John-ji were gone. My friendship with Mira would continue, but a new chapter of our lives had begun. Jahlia and Singie kept my spirits up, visiting often and regaling us with new music they had written, brightening our days with more love and laughter, or luring us away from our day's duties for a hike. One of our favorite adventures was a walk twenty minutes down the cow trail to the north shore and its rocky beaches. We would soak in warm natural pools or jump into a channel of the Pacific where it looked safe to swim. Humpback whales, dolphins, and sea turtles were our companions, although sharks lived in there as well. Would the predators come around? We were willing to take the chance.

Everything seemed perfect, and my confidence in its continuing that way strengthened every time Charles came home with news as surprising as he did one day after a trip into town for more building supplies.

Charles had an uncanny ability to manifest whatever and whoever was needed to make our life work. In a Sears parking lot one day, he met a man he knew from the island who could "do just about anything."

Larry was a builder without a license or a home, having left the mainland several years earlier, and some debt he decided not to be accountable for. He thrived on living off the grid, like so many of Maui's star children. Attractive, intelligent, and thrilled with the invitation, Larry moved onto the property with his van, his collection of crystals, blue jeans, western boots, and tank tops. We offered him the empty bedroom upstairs in trade for first-assistant-to-owner-builder status. I would need his help night and day—eventually he put up a dome tent on the acre below and out of view from our home. He lived simply, kept to himself, loved Tantra, and knew how to get a house built.

In July the cement pad for our house was poured and construction began. There were trenches to be dug for water, electrical, and telephone lines, questions about what size PVC pipes were needed, finishings that would promise years of service, water tanks to install, and a lot of dirt to move around so we could sculpt our three acres into a tropical paradise. Larry was my right-hand man, always ready for his next assignment, confident that either he or Cos or Jack the builder would find the solution to any construction problem. And when we were away teaching, he could be counted on to give me an accurate accounting of where the money was spent from the signed checks I left in his care to keep the project moving forward.

At times, though, I was stretched to the limits of what it seemed I could endure emotionally, financially, and physically. Charles was under pressure, too, to finish the final polishing of the Tantra book we were writing, keep the business running, and support me in moving the house project along. When I saw our money dwindling and learned that banks don't lend money for unfinished houses, I hit a wall for the first time. "We're doomed!" I cried. "We can't borrow money until we have our final inspection but we can't get the house finished for the final inspection without at least another $150,000." I was tense from juggling the budget to try to make it all work.

"Don't worry," said Charles, optimistic as always. "Sex magic will help us manifest whatever we need."

I glared at him. "You think love can accomplish anything! Don't you understand? This is a genuine crisis!"

"My queen," he said, "our vision for the house holds the energy to complete this."

Sex magic is when two people hold an emotional and a visionary picture of a result they want and they bathe their vision in their love as they make love in a connected, tantric way. I thought about it for a moment. Maybe he was right. What good would it do to surrender to a feeling of doom? We needed money and we needed help. We needed good carpet layers, talented finish carpenters, a bank that would lend a mortgage in the boonies of Maui, the commitment not to stray from our vision and go for anything less than blue Japanese roof tiles if that was what we wanted. I agreed to join him in shifting the energy.

After a shower, we went into our bedroom, which was mostly taken up by the waterbed, side tables, and a koa wood desk Charles had a friend build for me so I wouldn't have to manage the house project spread out all over the floor. The desk was piled high with notebooks, construction material samples, roof tile samples, a calculator, my "to do" lists on yellow legal pads, rulers, pens, and pencils. We camouflaged the chaos with a colorful Balinese sarong and began our practices of love.

Meeting in our adjoining yoga room, we began with some gentle Hatha yoga poses joined to deep breathing. This opened and stretched our bodies and assisted us out of our busy minds and into the moment. Once we felt connected to self we moved toward one another before our altar, an eclectic collection of his and my spiritual artifacts, photos of Jesus and Mary, our kids, our Mama, and tall, carved candlesticks we found in a thrift shop. I sat astride my beloved for more breathing and meditation, and then we opened our eyes and gazed into the love waiting there. With our hands in prayer position, we spoke of our gratitude for all we had been given, thanking our God/Goddess for the love we shared and for this good life and good work we had come together to live. We stated our intentions for the manifesting of the funds to finish the house and wrote them down on one of those yellow legal pads.

At the top of his page, Charles wrote the word "FUNds." "First, beloved, we must always have fun," he reminded me, winking and smiling. We estimated what we needed for the dry wall with rounded corner bead, glazed Japanese blue tile roof, koa wood kitchen cabinets, appliances, flooring, carpeting, and on and on. Next was directing the flow of our creative life force in transformative lovemaking.

Returning to the comfort of our bed, our eyes were wide open as we entered into the infinite grace of sexual pleasure to pray and manifest. As we made love, I sent my orgasms into mental pictures of all we needed to manifest. "Thank you, God, for delivering the blue tile we need to finish the roof as we have envisioned it. Thank you, Goddess, for the rich koa kitchen cabinets that will give our temple the richness and luster of this local wood. Thank you, Goddess and God of love, for the best appliances our money can buy. Thank you, God and Goddess, with all my heart for finding us the perfect dry wall finisher and for more than enough money to have rounded corners instead of square ones, cedar ceilings rather than dry wall, and handmade bronze pyramid skylights. Most of all, thank you, God and Goddess, for everything, especially for my beloved with whom all of this is possible!" The power of prayer along with the presence of the divine made our lovemaking both spiritual *and* sexy.

In the time we had been together, my orgasms were too numerous to fathom. I would simply say thousands and thousands and thousands. Charles' mastery of ejaculatory choice also gave him many thousands of orgasmic experiences, but he released his seed only once or twice a month. That day, he imprinted the release of his life force along with many of those same prayers and affirmations. Many orgasms and much laughter later we had thanked God countless times with a clear goal of $150,000. That amount would take us into final inspection day, at which time the bank would give us a mortgage for this house built on love, faith, vision, Tantra, friendships, and multicolored orgasms.

About a week later, a dear friend of Charles' called from San Diego. "Hi, brother Glennie," I heard Charles say, as I stood in front of my vanity brushing my hair. "Queen and I are wonderful, though the building is at an impasse until we raise a bunch of money to finish it." Suddenly, Charles cried out, "What? Are you serious? Glennie! That would be so wonderful. Yes, of course, draw up a loan agreement and we'll sign it. I love you, too, brother. I need to tell the queen." With that, Charles hung up the phone, sprang from bed, scooped me up, spun me around, and laid me softly down on the bed. "I told you so," he purred, grinning. "Glennie has seventy-five thousand sitting in a money market account and he would love to loan it to us until we get our final funding."

"My God!" I howled. "I believe in love, I believe in love, I believe in love!"

There was more to do than ever, and just as the need came, it was fulfilled. The business was expanding, and Charles and I decided to put everything under one entity, shared equally by Charles and me, and incorporate our Tantra school, giving it the name Hawaiian Goddess, LLC. It was time for a bigger office space, and we rented a funky three-bedroom beach house on the north shore, in Kuau, minutes from the plantation town of Paia. I could swim in the ocean right from the backyard of this house/office, and I did. A roomy hammock hung between the coco palms out by the lava wall that kept the sea from drowning the backyard, and a funky lanai faced the ocean. Visiting my beloved "at the office" was a visit to our second home, as almost daily I had errands to run in town, never wanting to miss a hug and a swim on my way home. One of my greatest joys was swimming in the waters off Maui. At our beach house/office, it was no exception. Stretching my body in a swimmer's crawl in water temperature always perfect for comfort continued to be an experience of dreaming the dream. I often swam alone, far from shore, fighting with my mind and its ability to feel *fear* when there was none. Oh, the stories of sharks and scary shark movies are a never-ending reminder to control imagined fears. Every day that I swam in these heavenly waters, I became less afraid and more at home in what always felt like moving through embryonic fluid inside of Divine Mother. I would sing to the mother-ocean while I swam, a type of prayer that nurtured my very soul. I was never threatened and I always paid my respects to the sea before I entered her.

When Mira and I first conceived of life on Maui not so long ago, we had said there were no strings attached—for Charles or any of us. I could laugh at that now. How innocent! "More love" was everywhere in sight for us both. Wherever we taught, Charles and I were first choice for at least one of the female students, women who asked to be invited to our room for sexual healing and tantric practice at the end of the day. (Men were learning this art form, too, but I was not comfortable teaching them how to love and be loved in private session "after hours," so I didn't.) I had to learn how to navigate this kind of popularity with the women. I wanted women to receive sexual awakening and healing, but not always on my alone time with Charles. Then when? On Sunday nights I was more interested in resting or connecting with Charles than in doing sessions with others. But nighttime was the only time we could work with someone after a day or long weekend of teaching. So I pushed myself by creating time limitations. This worked as I enjoyed tantric connection, which was rewarding, healing, and pleasurable for me as well. I noticed, however, that I kept a close eye on the clock. Protecting the limits of my energy output was the only way I could keep from burning out as love, sexuality, and intimacy are like life on top of the mountain. The air is intoxicating, the passion enticing.

In these nighttime sessions we often practiced our own Tantra (mostly sacred spot massage) for the woman to watch and learn from, and then she would be invited to receive from Charles or from me while he or I assisted. I often initiated her into sacred spot massage while we held her, spoke lovingly to her, and breathed our way into more intimacy together. I was always ready for the evening to end sooner than the other players were, and there was often tension between my beloved and me over this. But life was moving at such a pace we barely had time to process it. On top of everything else we were doing, there were two weddings to plan: we would marry, first, in a church wedding in Central California, with family and friends, and next, in an outdoor wedding on Maui, island-style. When love is your priority, everything else pales.

Chapter Ten

Over the Rainbow

Charles and I were not formal churchgoers by any means, but we had grown up as members of the Episcopal Church and we wanted our married life sanctioned by the church and blessed by our community in Hawaii as well. St. Mary's-by-the-Sea in Pacific Grove was a church we knew well. We sang there on Sundays when we took Charles' Mama to worship before we moved to the island and when we stayed with her on the mainland. Our Maui wedding would come at the end of our annual February Intermediate/Advanced seminar so that each year we would be able to re-take our vows along with our students in the final puja ceremonies.

Based in Hindu worship, our form of puja is a celebration of the interplay between divine male and divine female energy. In our ceremonies, we worship one another in circle, through eye contact, words, song, or light touch and embrace. The purpose is to see and feel the divine in one another, as well as in one's self. In this simplified, Western form, the puja is the heart of our closing ceremony in all of our seminars and workshops. The puja at the end of our Intermediate/Advanced seminar added an element of ritual to those weeks of study and practice and would become a yearly tradition, with couples "re-marrying" every February along with us.

I loved weddings and I loved marriage, so planning my nuptials with my beloved was nothing short of ecstasy. The wedding in California would be small and was easy to plan, with support from my sweetheart when I needed his help. In the fall, I flew to San Francisco to buy a wedding dress—a pale peach silk and lace dress that fit me like a glove. I chose the florist, made reservations at Pasta Mia in Monterey for the reception, and chose several sweet Monterey B&Bs to house our honored guests.

Robin would be my only family member at the California wedding, and she and Mira my only bridesmaids. Johnny would wait for the Maui wedding. I didn't invite my mother or father to either wedding because they didn't support me or my choices and I didn't want that energy present at my sacred marriage. When I had told my mother (whom I talked with by phone whenever she would answer and speak to me, about once or twice a month) of my plans to marry Charles, she said, "Here you go again, out of the frying pan and into the fire." Whatever that meant. My father wasn't even going to get the news of the wedding. When I had told him a year earlier about teaching sacred sexuality with Charles, he had said, "What do you do, get out on a stage and have sex? Don't people know how to do that?" I myself could barely keep up with understanding my sudden new life, but I didn't want anyone's misunderstandings or judgments to mar my special day.

On December 27 Charles and I arrived at St. Mary's early and went our separate ways to prepare for the ceremony. I wanted time alone before my bridesmaids arrived. I went into the "bride's room" and closed the door behind me.

Here I was, forty-four years old. Every action and decision I had taken thus far had led to this perfect moment. Three ended marriages didn't mean they were failures or mistakes. I knew I was in integrity to have left New York and to have left my marriage with Arnie. I was at peace with myself and my choices. Now I was making a commitment to so much more than a beloved mate: I was committing to climb the steep slopes of higher consciousness through love in action. My years of yoga and my spiritual path were completing a cycle. I was at home in myself as never before. A river of energy flowed from my center into all of the tributaries that make up my nervous system. Shakti, the sexual/spiritual life-force energy of the universe, coursed through me. Like never before, I felt fully alive.

I thought of my love for so many people who were not present—for Ron, who had weathered the storm of my departure two years earlier; for Nank, who would never see me this happy; for dear Johnny; for my first love, Arnie; for the beauty and adventure in life that I had shared with Rick; for the teachings of the Levines; for the friendship of Mira—and so many more. Gigi was uncomfortable with the way I had left Ron and she thought Charles was beneath me. I wished she could be here and be happy for me, but she'd left Carmel when she'd remarried and said she couldn't make the trip. Friendships change, love lives on forever.

Through the walls of the old church, I could hear our friend Sophia singing "God of Love Is Reigning in the Temple of My Heart," accompanying herself on guitar, as guests took their seats. The door opened and Mira peeked in. "It's time to start, hon."

Charles' best man, Glennie, walked me to the main altar. As Sophia sang "O God, Beautiful," Glennie squeezed my hand and, with tears in his eyes, wished us a lifetime of love. Charles stood there, so handsome in his Italian white linen suit, beside nephews Chris and Paul, smiling with all the beauty in his heart. I overflowed with joy.

Several months earlier, after making love on one of Maui's perfect, lazy afternoons, Charles and I had written our wedding vows. Father Edwards read these sacred vows to us now, and we repeated them, feeling the embrace of spirit around this union witnessed by family and friends.

Before Christ, our God, our families, and our friends we do make these our Sacred Vows: We vow to love one another fully and without conditions, and allow the flower of our love to open in its own way, in its own time. We vow to express our love fully as an adult, with the openness and freedom of a child. We vow to bring each other up and never put each other down. We vow to function as a team in the service of God. We vow to always journey deeper into the energetic, physical, and spiritual bond between us. We vow to consciously and creatively care for each other, and always to help each other care for ourselves. We vow to never possess one another. We vow to honor one another's path toward oneness with God and the fulfillment of our beingness on the earth. We vow to uphold our togetherness, walking hand and hand through life, committed to working through our challenges and toward our dreams. We vow to cultivate harmony in our relationship, realizing that nothing is more important than this, not even being right. We vow to honor one another, serve one another, and assist one another in bringing that which dwells in the kingdom of our heart, outward to the earth.

After the ceremony we left the church arm in arm to share in the merriment with loved ones in the garden as a chorus of seagulls hovered overhead. A reception followed at Pasta Mia, where we filled long tables with guests and many Champagne toasts. In our toast Charles and I vowed to live our lives as one long honeymoon. Love is something that can be generated at will, and we had within us a bubbling source of passion to love.

The year 1988 was off to a running start. With Michael's invaluable help, *Tantra: The Art of Conscious Loving* had found a publisher. It would be in print the next year. Meanwhile, in February, this time under a cathedral of swaying palms and draped in tropical leis, we gathered for our Maui wedding on Cos and Blue's private estate on Door of Faith Road. Our beloved friend Susea made hand-painted sensual silk clothing for us to wear, and in this ceremonial cloth we walked barefoot across the lawn to the cliff edge, where the devotional musicians Michael and Maloah Stillwater officiated at our nuptials. We read our vows again after Cos and Blue "gave us away."

It was a colorful celebration of love island-style. Johnny was there, and Mira and John-ji. Two women whom Charles had considered for his beloveds before me were there, and they both gave their heartfelt blessings. Besides these special people, many other dear friends and tantric lovers and thirty or so intermediate Tantra students attended. Fantuzzi and Friends, Sophia, and others made music throughout the afternoon and evening, and Yaz, a lover and friend of ours from the Big Island, performed for the wedding party later in the evening.

Yaz was an eyeful—and a handful—a beautiful, sensual woman I met and was taken with during a Tantra seminar on the Big Island. I could tell she had never met a conscious lover and knew she deserved one, so I offered Charles to her. But sharing him with her had been hard for me, as I tried to ride the rollercoaster of fulfillment of the beloved truth. Yaz was in every way my friend and sister, and she was so honored to be our lover. But once I witnessed how big her Shakti was (and how enthusiastic my beloved was to play with her), I wanted to slow the speed of our connection and friendship. At the wedding, at least, I knew I was the only woman going home with Charles afterward. (Although in his Tantric soul, Charles would have loved sharing our wedding nights with women we loved and who loved us. Even a Tantric Queen has her limits!)

I had asked many questions of myself before entering into our co-creation of sacred marriage. I had questioned who determines how love is expressed during a lifetime. All I knew for certain was that love is a quality of the heart that surpasses all understanding. I was claiming the freedom to enter into its mystery and in that passage I would gain more experience and greater knowledge of the mystery itself.

Still, after our weddings, the issues of expanded Tantric loving still spun me in circles. I had prayed—even believed—that over time our marriage would end Charles' desire to practice Tantra with other women. How could a beloved want to make love with anyone other than his beloved? How could a beloved want me to teach and practice with other men as well? It was a strange sensation to know the answers in my mind and not always understand them in my heart.

I wanted so much to please my beloved. As hard as it was sometimes, I understood and agreed with the logic of having tantric lovers, and I shared the excitement and fulfillment of teaching others in intimate communion. I knew there was no better way to teach tantric love than to share love with others, to include others in the energy and passion of our love. Besides, as Charles often reminded me, it was that split between love and sex we were here to heal. Eventually I would become wiser in my choices for lovers, realizing that deep and abiding friendships would form and require time and energy. I would choose women I felt I could learn from and trust. I would step harder on the gas and lighten up pressure on the brakes as love and passion swept me into the great and fascinating mystery of this most exciting time in my life.

The year we married in Hawaii, there would be twenty-two seminars, eighteen flights to and from Maui, hundreds of adventures into the jungles and to the waterfalls, weekly visits and connects with Cos and Blue, regular visits from Singie and Jahlia, and a few important lovers who happily helped us learn how to navigate all this love and Shakti. My life was a whirrrrrrl of loved ones coming and going. Charles and I could often be found naked in our bed, wrapped in loving embrace and answering questions for Michael about tasks for the day or assuring our friends they could come in for a hug. We would howl at the top of our lungs when others appeared at the open bedroom door in a greeting of aloha that inspired hysterical laughter and a cuddle puddle. Somehow, we managed to do it all. And Cos and Blue were an integral part of every day.

From the wet winter day Cos began bulldozing the property to the day we would move into our home eighteen months later, the quality of love and respect among us four fed my soul. Cos and Blue and Charles and I walked the land in moonlight and made love day and night on the soft new grass. Blue and I practiced sex magic together, squatting under the full moon, reciting our prayers and stating our intentions for completing the planting and building and then asking permission to enter one another's yonis. When permission was granted, Blue would enter my yoni with her fingers and press tenderly on my sacred spot. I would enter her yoni and press lovingly on her sacred power spot, as together we breathed in, our eyes never leaving one another. We'd exhale with a tone or release a sound something like the birthing howl a wild animal might make. This raised so much energy we were soon releasing our amrita on the land, watering our territory and turning seedlings into trees, panax cuttings into full-grown shrubs, and helping the home where love would grow emerge from its wooden skeleton. We felt like two goddesses in an ancient ritual, falling finally into embrace and laughter. As we did this, Charles and Cos cheered us on, filled with love and fascination for the beauty of our Shakti. The night often ended with the two men making love to Blue, who could so beautifully open up to them and enjoy her sexuality. I would join as assistant, bringing glasses of water or kissing Blue and offering her encouragement and waiting patiently for Charles to be ready to spend time alone with me before our need for sleep called us to bed.

For months, Blue and I worked with local young women we hired to plant lawns, shrubs, and trees. In the hot afternoons we often took a break to cool off in the jungle pools a short walk through Cos's property. His half-built octagonal home was perched on the edge of cliffs overlooking twenty-five acres of a jungle gorge where it meets the north shore a few hundred feet below. Native Hawaiians called this magnificent gorge "home of the divine."

When it wasn't raining, raining, and raining some more, the Pacific Ocean glittered as far as our eyes could see. That is the nature of this wild, tropical tail of land. The sound of Singie's and Jahlia's voices chorusing together filtered through the trees, competing only with the screech of parrots nesting there. From a distance Cos could be heard hammering or sawing away on his own home six driveways from mine. Blue sometimes left to help out, hauling two by fours or making runs into town for supplies.

Doug and Guy, a gay couple who had left Laguna Beach to live in the apartment-like barn next door while they developed their two acres on the cliff side, became invaluable friends. They were eight months ahead of me in developing their land and they usually had an answer to any of my questions about building. They also made one of my favorite comments when they first moved into the neighborhood and rang the bell at Cos's house one full moon night to pay a friendly visit. When Cos opened the door wearing only a sarong, with all of us (Charles, me, Blue, and several friends) also barely draped in sarongs and piled together in ecstatic play, Doug smiled a handsome display of teeth and said, "I feel like we're the straightest folks in the neighborhood." At that, we squealed and invited them to join the cuddle puddle of open, loving friends high on life and high on the freedom to love and play in the tropical gardens of paradise.

Aloha is an infectious wind that permeates the very core of your being in the islands if you let it in. The original Hawaiians lived in sensual aloha. Living aloha was still a way of life for the locals on the islands in those days. Johnny Kahiamoe, the husband of our minister at Door of Faith Church, was one of these locals. Johnny mowed our big lawns as soon as they went in. He was the original owner of the pineapple fields in the area where we now lived, and the granddaddy of Huelo. Johnny never left my property without sauntering up the walkway to find me and stand with me, joking and "talking story" for twenty minutes or so before he was paid.

"Wanna sell any of dose goldfish you got in dis hea pond, Caroline?" he would say, his dark eyes squinting with laughter. "I tink you otta raise trout in dis pond!" Or "How much you charge me fo' yo' fish? Ha, ha, ha!" On and on he would go, entertaining me. More important to him than getting his check right away was this aloha-time, "talking story."

When I first got to the island I thought the locals liked "talking starry." "Let's talk starry," I'd coo, gazing into Charles' blue eyes. How he'd laugh, and "starry" we would talk. "I adore the silkiness of your skin, my beloved." "The taste of your yoni is as sweet as the mangos in May." He would lay me back on soft pillows in the late afternoon and kiss me into ecstasy as I offered my power and passion up to the gods and goddesses who created this perfect afternoon for lovers to engage in life-giving union. Amrita splashed us with cooling drops before we fell into deep slumber, wakened by the screech of the parrots in time for dinner. We made love daily, practiced sex magic often for manifesting our dreams, and meditated and prayed to Divine Spirit to show us the way to accomplish our goals. Our motto: Love first, work later!

As my Shakti awakened more and more, so did my awareness of my beautiful life in Maui. It's a short drive up the Hana Highway to Baldwin Beach, a crescent-shaped mile of creamy white sand dotted with plentiful chunks of white coral. I walked or swam at Baldwin every day. The Pacific on the north shore is slightly cooler and wilder than on the south side, where the tourists stay, and that cool, milky aqua water nourished me more than anything in the world except for the love I felt with Charles. I surrendered my skin to the intense equatorial sun and treasured every minute baking in its golden heat. In September the seaweed was an added jewel, a bountiful feast I would gather and take home for a salad or steamed greens. Rarely did a day pass that I didn't stop at the beach on my way home from an errand in town, swim awhile, and shower outdoors. In the car, I'd strip off my bikini, tie a Balinese sarong around my cool body, scrunch my curls, and drive home with sandy bare feet, barely covered and singing my joy to the afternoon breeze.

Chapter Eleven

The Ecstasy of the Singing Angels

As the months passed, the skeleton of our new home transformed into a three-dimensional version of that big set of plans. "My God!" I would exclaim sometimes at the sight of it from our kitchen window. "Would you look at our house!"

I was more than ready to be done with keeping track of the generous loans from good friends that we had manifested through sex magic. I was ready for the final inspection so we could receive the bank loan and pay people back. And the delays! Everything takes longer on an island, especially when workers have to depend on the weather or on having the needed supplies.

Fortunately, hard work and heaven go hand in hand in our corner of the world, where the sounds of pleasure rival the roar of wind and rain pounding against windows and doors. Every month gave us another reason to celebrate. The moon was full! The pagan in us wanted to play. The harmonic convergence was on the calendar, or the Wesak birthday of Buddha called to us to expand tantrically in mind, body, and spirit. Beltane, a pagan fertility festival celebrating the Earth's fecundity and anticipating the summer's powerful sun, was another good excuse on May 1st. "Our house or yours?" we would ask Blue and Cos, eyes twinkling with excitement of what was to come.

Charles would ask me, "What will you wear to walk the block in the moonlight and arrive looking gorgeously outrageous for our friends before everything comes off, my queen?" In the earlier hours of journeying with the moon, Charles and I would make love for hours on our own and so would they, and then we four would spend much of the rest of the night together, sometimes accompanied by current girlfriends, an occasional male lover of Blue's, or my favorite, Singie or Jahlia, playing music for us, wandering like troubadours with their instruments, blowing in and out with the trade winds that were a constant messenger of pleasure to my skin.

The sensuality of those nights for me was rivaled only by the promise of even more hours of loving when my beloved and I were alone again. We always had one last connect, a "best ever" series of orgasms for the tropical night of lovemaking in union with the divine, our highly charged bodies and wide-open hearts cleansed by twelve hours dedicated to Tantra practice. We often saw dawn peek over the horizon as we put on our sleep shades and curled up for a morning of much needed sleep, our faces buried in each other's curves, breathing in the scent of the beloved as we fell into deep sleep. Once rested and assisted by cappuccinos, we phoned our friends to re-cap the night. Never had I known so much awe-inspiring majesty as those moonlit nights in Huelo that were often followed by hot sunny days at the jungle waterfalls or the pristine beaches. It was always an adventure of deeper intimacy, bigger passion, and stretching the limits of our love.

In spite of all this, Charles' sexual connection with Cos and Blue was hard for me sometimes, and I was thankful they were as busy as we were. Each couple had a current girlfriend of the month, and we bragged about who we were involved with and weren't they *fantastic?* Still, I never felt the same *desire* for our lovers as my beloved did. No doubt hormonal levels were also at play here. In all fairness to Charles, he always wanted as much pleasure and love coming my way as he desired for himself or another.

I admired Cos and Blue for the creative and hard-working people they were, but my life was so full already, and my energy was focused on accomplishing my tasks, showing up fully in my marriage, and enjoying my life. For me, most friendships did not require the all-chakra joining (Tantra) that Charles held sacred.

And then my attention was deliciously diverted by Singie.

Singie was dazzling. She could pound a nail, weld steel, ride a motorcycle, scrub floors, play a twelve-string guitar like a rock and roll queen, open her throat to the heavens and release the ecstasy of angels. One day, as we lay on the warm rocks by a waterfall, Singie told me she was ready to do something to heal her heart and open her life and her Shakti as I'd opened mine. "I don't know what that sexual healing stuff is all about," she said. "I just know I need some."

I rolled onto my belly and took her sweet face in my hands. "Girl, you have come to the right place."

She grinned.

Singie showed up at our house at the appointed hour for our healing session, nervous, courageous, and ready. She knew we had no agenda other than to offer her this opportunity, which would let her open deeply to her own healing. And seeing Charles' powerful male presence in union with the beloved in me was always helpful in imprinting positive lover/beloved images in people who had never experienced such a positive experience of sexual loving before. We would navigate as we always did through instinct and love, skill, integrity, intention, unity of purpose, and a shared willingness to enter new territory.

I followed Charles' lead and did what he suggested in loving a woman in a tantric healing way. I gazed into Singie's bright eyes, spoke blessings to her beautiful yoni, and consecrated her sexual energy as a gift from Divine Mother. Charles and I gave sacred spot massage to her together, representing mother/father, God/Goddess. With words of empowerment, we encouraged her to forgive those who had violated her and invited her to take our love into those places in her psyche and body. I had great empathy for her and knew how much trust it took for her to open to us.

For most women it is healing to receive loving and therapeutic massage to her entire body, including to her pelvic region, and especially inside her yoni, in her sacred spot. In this sacred ritual a woman can learn to let go to the vulnerability of truly feeling loved, honored, and respected. This can create a deep healing of her self-esteem. Sacred spot massage can also help a woman access memory of unpleasant or painful sexual experience and bring healing through love into that memory.

She can awaken to the power of her Shakti, her life force, feeling it in multiorgasmic pleasure throughout her body. This power can give access to the Tantric Wave of Bliss, a seemingly never-ending wave of orgasmic pleasure. Eventually, I would understand the Tantric Wave of Bliss as the source of my existence.

In that first session of sacred spot work, deep rage at the father of her children came up for Singie. Her grief over his keeping them from her was huge. She also revealed grief over a recent PAP test done during a routine exam. There had been signs of ovarian cancer and a recheck was required. If she was sick, she wanted to know, would we still work with her? We assured her we would always love her and would work with her for as long she wanted. That was never in question.

Singie came back again and again, each time bringing more playfulness to the healing work as her trust in us grew. She would have her way with us, rising into her full Shakti power and switching from receiver to giver on the spur of the moment. She would push us down on the bed and dance around us, laughing as she tantalized and teased us into surrendering to *her* healing touch. I had never witnessed this quality of Shakti before, and it was new for Singie, too, to feel it. She was discovering herself as we discovered her.

With Singie I saw how boundless spiritual-sexual energy could be. She burst with life force as she claimed her goddess power. She could squat over us and release her amrita, singing prayers all the while. She could be off to the kitchen for slices of ripe mango, then come back to slather the sweet pulp all over our skin and lick the juice and kiss morsels of the fruit into our mouths. Other times, she might wet her long hair and caress our skin with her locks, so wonderfully refreshing on a hot day. And just as suddenly, she could jump up, grab her sarong and fly out the door, shouting, "See you later!" We might not see her for a week.

I knew Singie struggled. I was afraid sometimes that she would abandon our friendship, but without fail she returned, ready to admit embarrassment at having flown like she had. "I know you're trying to heal me," she'd tell us as her intense blue eyes darted from one to the other, "but I don't trust anyone, not even you guys." Charles explained that she could start to trust when she gave up control, "or at least begin to heal your fear of trusting." She'd look at us then with that expression I must have seen a thousand times—the cat about to pounce or flee. "We'll see."

My passion for Singie was huge. At the time I was still prudish enough to be uncomfortable with this part of myself. I have since awakened to the truth that love is love and sex is love and it doesn't matter which gender I am loving and being loved by. When I realized I was "universexual," a world filled with more love than I ever imagined could be possible opened up for me. But in those days I only had a little experience with it. Gigi and I had loved each other this much but we'd never explored it soulfully. We didn't know of the wonders of Tantra. Singie wanted that tantric love connection, but it was new for her to feel such tremendous love and desire for another woman.

Singie gave me huge insight into the torrential power of female sexual energy. It is indeed the creative maternal energy of the universe. When Singie held me to her heart to be surrounded by her lovely breasts and stroked my hair, I felt I'd crawled into the heart of the Divine Mother. Charles knew how much I longed for this mother connection, estranged as I was from my own mother. I also learned how confusing, elusive, frustrating, seductive, intriguing, absorbing, unpredictable, adorable, and fun a woman can be. I discovered the tantalizing, sensual, earthy magnetism of the Feminine. And Singie mirrored all that in me, which frightened us both a little. "You're married to Charles," she would say. "I can't love you this much, but I do."

It was true. I had Charles, and Singie was grieving the loss of her children and trying to make her way alone. Her cancer recheck had come back negative, but she would need to be tested every six months. Her music was the focus of her life, and we were grateful it was more of ours. She kept her electric piano at our house and the music of the spheres sailed through our days.

When Charles and I invited a friend into our loving, I was always the first focus of attention. I was honored as beloved and wife, pleasured and fulfilled for my own enjoyment and to introduce our invited guest into our sexual energy. From the strength of our love we then turned our focus on our friend as Charles skillfully led me into ways of connecting, delighting, and arousing her. I was still tentative and met with resistance within myself in lovemaking with another woman. With everyone, that is, before Singie.

It was different with Singie. Easy. Wildly sexy. I was unsure at first if there was room for my personal desire, but I resolved to open to whatever I learned. Charles watched me wake to the joy of loving and being loved by another woman. We shared with him what we wanted to try and what we weren't ready for and we welcomed his ideas about how we three could join in tantric union. Charles kept us laughing, fed us abundant bowls of pasta and the best homemade pizza around, and suggested all kinds of fun and sexy things to do together.

As the months went on, Singie more and more openly invited me into her heart, her yoni, and her soul. We were both somewhat intimidated by our passionate sexual exchanges, our eyes penetrating where no one had ever gone, yet we found ourselves creating more and more of them. We felt as if we were praying at the temple of each other's life-giving center. Sometimes Charles seemed in the way, and we preferred being alone together. When we did that we surprised ourselves by how timid we could be. His presence was the permission we needed; he sparked the tantric fire. Other times, together the two of us touched into incredible power. Our eyes widened with wonder as we felt our energy pour into each other. Our yonis merged, we pressed our breasts together and "entered" each other at the heart center, ejaculated buckets of divine amrita, howled in ecstatic glee. With Singie, amrita could come from direct touch and/or simply from the magnetism of our Shakti.

Jahlia seldom joined us in overt sexual loving, choosing instead to dance around the periphery of our unions, sometimes offering kisses of mango or passion fruit to enhance the dance of love. The sexual energy of our friendship sometimes found spontaneous expression in a deeply passionate kiss or a sacred spot session, most often outdoors under the night sky. And now and then Jahlia would join me and Singie in rituals of tantric healing practice with Charles, where we three women would shed some of the burden we carried from boundaries trespassed by fathers and stepfathers, uncles and brothers, neighbor boys, and fathers of childhood friends. In this safe and loving place Charles represented all men as he helped us replace our offending memories with laughter, love, and supreme friendship.

Jahlia or Singie often went with me on Sundays to church, and enjoying sacred spot massage naked in the sun by the jungle stream on the way home was always a highlight of the day. It was a joyful experience, as nectar-met-nectar to join with the rainwater pool. Back at home afterward, Charles would whip up one of his pizzas while we showered outdoors and met in the kitchen, hungry and happy.

Singie and Jahlia performed concerts around the island, and at our home they often serenaded Charles and me with our favorites, such as Paramahansa Yogananda's prayer, "O God Beautiful." Here was Jahlia, sitting at the edge of my bed with her lute singing this prayer to our love, the ultimate touch of grace. Could "more love" even be possible?

> *O God Beautiful; O God Beautiful;*
> *At Thy feet, O I do bow.*
> *In the forest Thou art green;*
> *In the mountain Thou art high;*
> *In the river Thou art restless;*
> *In the ocean Thou art grave.*
> *O God Beautiful; O God Beautiful!*
> *At Thy feet, I do bow!*
> *To the serviceful Thou art service;*
> *To the lover Thou art love;*
> *To the sorrowful Thou art sympathy;*
> *To the yogi Thou art bliss.*

Naked in the kitchen except for his Superman apron, many evenings at home Charles prepared temptations for any of us who might be there. It could be one of his "nuclear" cheese meltdowns (a combination of cheeses grated onto a plate, flavored with spices and herbs and heated in the microwave) served with tortilla chips or pita crisps or an organic salad topped with savory tofu strips or mini-pizzas topped with the chef's choices of the day. Sometimes we'd head into town for a Thai feast followed by coconut ice cream, hot fudge, and a good movie. Alone together in bed at night, his big hands and long fingers nourished my body, healed any aches, moisturized my breasts, gave me pleasure, and I would massage his tired or aching muscles or trade foot rubs. All of our touch was devotional practice for the beloved.

In spring 1989, the long-awaited day finally arrived. Charles and I left the lender triumphant, check in hand. At last we could repay loans and our packing could begin. In two weeks we would move into our realized dream up the hill from the first house, our temple by the sea.

Singie was by my side to help with packing up and getting ready for this new chapter in our lives. We teased and flirted, laughed and worked, while Charles carried on business as usual or made us a pizza that knocked our sarongs off. "Hey, you sure you want all these shells going over there?" Singie would toss a shell in the air and catch it. The next thing I knew her hand was reaching inside my halter to gently caress my breast. "Working and sorting … a woman's work is never done!" she'd say, offering me a quick lick of her tongue. Women are so damn distracting!

Our only furniture was my heavy koa wood desk, wicker bedside tables, stained-glass lamp, royal blue Persian rug for our yoga, and that huge painting of my seraphim angel. Charles had a few filing cabinets and a desk, and besides some clothes and his big shoulder bag that went everywhere, that was about it. In the new house our waterbed would fit inside a throne-like koa frame Cos had designed. The sleeping platform would be bordered by four ceiling-high columns and positioned eighteen feet below the bronze pyramid skylight. In time, items we used in daily life would fill the bed frame drawers—stacks of plush amrita towels, eye pillows for keeping out all that beautiful light from above, and other assorted paraphernalia. On Charles' side of the bed there was always his shoulder bag with anything I might need—eye drops, lip gloss, an endless collection of sucky, chewy candies. The top of the headboard collected an array of water bottles, sexual lubricants, hair clips, gumbos (cans of mouth-watering glycerin chews for scented breath), massage lotions, candles, flowers, and lighters. There were mirrored sliding-door closets filled with built-in shelves so we didn't need drawers. I put clothing hooks all around since we mainly hung our sarongs on the nearest one.

At this point, a decorator would have had a ball. But without the time or money to fill our home with furniture, we chose to live in infinite space. Our new home felt more like a cathedral than a house, thus earning its name "temple." Our personal stuff was there, but the yards and yards of glass sliding doors were bare, and the carpeting went uninterrupted from one end of the house to the other. This was great for dropping to the floor and doing yoga anywhere. Life at home was lived mostly in bed, on the floor, or around the kitchen island on high bamboo stools that twirled and squeaked. I picked up some floor pillows in town and we moved our majestic arc of a hammock indoors. Outside in the yard we tied a colorful island hammock to the full-grown palms we planted. Pleasure was ready to be had everywhere, especially in the bubbling hot tub that was to become a great center of outdoor camaraderie.

Goethe has described architecture as "frozen music," and here, it truly was. I had built a symphony of lyrical grandeur in the wilds of a tropical island. After hauling truckloads of boxes to the new home, we unpacked our belongings, promised ourselves the house would feel like home in no time, and, excited and exhausted from it all, decided that before we did anything more we needed a vacation, our honeymoon at last. And where better for a honeymoon when you're already living in paradise than the jewel of the South Seas—Bali.

Chapter Twelve

Polishing the Pearl

"Don't buy anything your first week here," our Big Island friend Jimmy Bolman advised us over coconut-lime spritzers as we sat on the terrace of our beachfront inn our first balmy evening in Bali. "Just look around. Make a list of what you want to buy. I'll send whatever you want over in my container." Jimmy owned an art gallery in Waimea, an upcountry town that borders the great Parker Ranch on the Big Island of Hawaii, and he used a container ship to transport art across the oceans to his gallery.

Go shopping on our honeymoon? Jimmy had to be kidding. All we wanted to do for the whole month was sleep, make love, and enjoy our lovely room at the beach. Days passed like this, with forays no farther than the beachside café to sip rich Balinese coffee and eat a light breakfast while feasting our eyes on the culture all around. Long, colorful flags waved enchantingly over the sand, and smiling men and women stopped by to offer sarongs for sale. We shook our heads, happy to return to our darkened room empty-handed for more rest and recovery, lovemaking, bathing in the double-sized huge round tub, reading a few lines from a travel book, and wondering when jet-lag would ever end.

Four days in, we felt more restored and ready to visit a nearby village. We lounged in a restaurant with huge bamboo couches and ceiling fans, enjoying spicy curries and feeling terribly obvious dressed in mainland clothes amidst sarongs and the barest of tops. We vowed to change our style right away and dress like the locals.

It was hotter in Bali than in Hawaii, and the air was heavy with the musky aroma of cloves and burning firewood. Kretek cigarettes—tobacco scented with clove—made luscious, curling waves of smoke that added to the exotic, erotic quality of life. I was fully awake to the life on Bali, and Jimmy's words of warning made sense all of a sudden. The shopping was fabulous! It had never interested me more. Everything was so inexpensive, unusual, and beautiful, and it seemed I could afford everything.

Jimmy and our driver, Arka, were our tour guides, keeping us entertained as we traveled from one distinct village to another, staying in new locations sometimes for a few days or a week at a time. Arka took us to the homes of artists he knew who made furniture, fabrics, and statues, and I bought some of their work. Arka was an artist himself, and one night he invited us to his compound in Ubud for dinner. Being a guest in a Balinese home was like being invited home by Santa Claus for Christmas dinner.

Arka was patriarch of the family compound. He showed us his oil paintings—pictures of a life that revolved around family, dogs, cats, and roosters, holidays, and infinite Gods and Goddesses, demons and deities. The women of the compound (wife, grandmothers, aunties, and daughters) worked in the hot little kitchen preparing flavorful savories they would set before us to delight in.

In Ubud, where we felt we could have stayed forever, our room cost $27 a night—a high price because of the swimming pool and because we stayed on the upper floor, overlooking the rice paddies.

That price included a delicious breakfast and steaming pot of fresh local coffee. By day we toured the area, went to Balinese dances, and shopped, and at night we immersed ourselves in secondhand novels and I pored over my purchases—gifts for friends, family, and myself. There were sarongs, beaded bags, skimpy tops, wood carvings, masks, Buddhas and Quan Yins, and all sorts of other deities in prayer or dance poses or simply posing serenely. I modeled outfits for my beloved, who "oooohed" and "aaaahed" as I twirled before him and then returned to his novel with an invitation to "come cuddle" in the dim light of the bedside lamp. Other regular distractions were for our daily Tantra practice and yoga, which we did on the bamboo floors on mats covered in one of our new sarongs amidst the soft scent of mosquito coils that circled lazily through the large room.

"Good morning, Arka," said Charles one morning, greeting our lovely friend before a day's tour. "You sure look happy."

"Why not?" said Arka.

That was it. The heart of Bali. Why not be happy? I was in love—in Bali, and *with* Bali.

Friends from Hawaii were part of our honeymoon vacation, too. Emerald Starr, a neighbor from Door of Faith Road, had built a house in the exotic jungles near a wild river and canyon on the outskirts of Ubud. His other Bali home was near the Kings Water Palace of Tirtagangga. ("Tirta" means holy water or spring; "gangga" is for the River Ganges.) The magic of the water palace grounds with their abundant statuary of Hindu gods and big pools of fresh mountain water delivered through the open mouths of demonic carved gods—protectors of the people, according to Hindu legend—left us eager to return.

Cos had bought land in Legian a year earlier, and we visited his Balinese compound, with its bamboo temple and green mosaic tile pool. We ate at their favorite outdoor dining spots *(warangs)*, walked their favorite beaches, and visited the Monkey Forest, where hundreds of Balinese macaques live together in a small nature preserve on the southern outskirts of Ubud.

Time passes slowly on an island in the South Pacific, but it passes, and, sadly, our last night in Bali came. Late at night we cuddled in bed inside our cloud of gauzy mosquito netting, Charles reading his book beside me while I lay and thought about life ahead. It all seemed so far away.

What differences there were between this man and me. I had committed to his vision and filled the space of his creation beautifully, steadfastly following my heart into this great life. We had made our vision real. Now I faced the reality of returning home and living what I had asked for. We had built ourselves a kick-ass home, written and published a seminal book on Tantra, taught thousands of students who came to learn of the miracle of Tantra and the refined art form of sexual love, and reaped the glory of the seeds we would continue to sow. There were so many reasons to be happy. I felt myself sinking into a melancholy that made no sense to me.

Snuggled close to Charles, I feigned sleep. I wanted to be alone with my underworld. Returning home meant a lot of work lay ahead. What if I stayed in Bali and became an expat? I could say, "I'm sorry, honey. I've had a change of heart. You can have the house. I choose my freedom." What a perverse moment it was, lying in my make-believe cave next to the man and the life I was about to choose for a second or third or millionth time. But the promise of fulfillment, of finding my life's work and experiencing the most love I had ever known, took over my dreams that night. I felt myself surrender to this warm wave sweeping through my heart, carrying me into the unknown. We had a dream. Now we would live it from the home of our dreams. We would bring heaven to earth in our relationship and teach others how to have it, too.

At dawn we dressed in a hurry to catch the cab that would take us to the airport in Denpasar. I barely had time to look over my shoulder and bid goodbye to this treasure of a honeymoon spot. Riding in the back seat of the cab beside Charles, I choked up and began to cry. My resolve of the night before was gone. If it weren't for the life I'd started in Hawaii I might have stayed in this magical place forever, saying yes to every five-dollar massage on the beach or lying in the open mouth of my favorite moss-covered stone demon being cooled by the sacred waters of Mount Agung.

"Beloved queen," said Charles, gently cupping my chin in his hand, "why are you crying? We have had the most wonderful vacation."

"What is wrong with Mamma Queenie?" the cab driver said. "She no like to leave Bali?" Everyone in Bali called me Mamma Queenie. "I'm okay," I sniffled. "Chazzie, it's been the vacation of a lifetime. No one to heal, no lovers in our bed. I don't want to go."

I settled into Charles' arms and he held me close as we watched the land we had come to love pass by our window. We vowed to extend the feeling of a honeymoon vacation into every day of our lives together. That is what I was learning about love, marriage, and belovedness: We can create the honeymoon *and* the vacation in the small or large actions of daily life.

As the airplane climbed high above the clouds, my eagerness to be in our new home began to course through my veins. The vacation had renewed me after all, after the weariness and exhilaration of our big accomplishment. I could imagine stretching out on our huge waterbed with the fluffy down pillows and filling the house with our new Balinese treasures. My favorite Buddha would reside at the foot of the bed, where the Hawaiian sun would rise over its head. Before long we would wake to that sunshine, and Charles, clad in a silk sarong, would prepare a fresh spinach quiche and top our cappuccinos with foam that stood in peaks like Mount Agung, serving me the first sip as always in beloved generosity.

At home again with the front door closed behind us, I was stunned into silence and gratitude: Look what we had accomplished since we first fell in love! We had given birth to a temple by the sea. But not only that, in the center of our bed, welcoming us, was a copy of *Tantra: The Art of Conscious Loving*. Michael had circled it with white hibiscus and a beautiful card of congratulations. We ran to it and squealed as we opened it and read the dedication page: *This book is dedicated to the spirit of the Mother*. Our book would reach the people of the world blessed by the spirit of Goddess Divine Mother. We added a handwritten dedication inside that first copy: "May our love reach every person on the earth." We held the book to our hearts, then kissed each other deeply. "Welcome home, Queenie." "Welcome home, beloved."

The Buddha statue took its place at the foot of the bed right away and a lovely golden Tara took up residence on the headboard. Immediately we placed the book in the arms of our Buddha and made love. As I released my amrita, I affirmed that our book would be a success that weekend at the largest book fair in Europe. In days, we would learn that the book would be published in German, Dutch, Italian, and Portuguese. Soon, it would be in print in nine languages. ("Our book will reach the people of the world…") Our sex magic was working faster all the time.

Sometimes I would stand in one spot in our love temple and turn in a slow circle, taking in every bit of the beauty I was assigned to care for. Trade winds and tropical breezes wafted through the open sliding glass doors that made up the east wall, caressing me with their gentle warmth. To the west, sliding glass doors opened to the backyard and lotus and lily ponds, the deck, hot tub, and outdoor shower with a look at "forever." All of this filled me with enough joy to carry me through the great duality: being in love with my beloved and sharing him with others.

We constantly polished the pearl of our love with the salty irritation of other loves scraping against ours. Blue knew how to ride the waves of an open relationship—she was in her own with Cos—and she helped me through some of the harder times, along with a few other women who understood. They reminded me of Charles' intentions for healing and expanding tantric knowledge and helped me remember his complete devotion for me. It was easy to forget about that when I saw him gazing into another woman's eyes, admiring her body, or recalling the power of her Shakti or the juiciness of her yoni. My friends also helped me remember that I admired these women enough to invite them into our love.

It was true: I was stunned by the awesome beauty of the Feminine. My heart was cracked wide open by it. I was curious about yonis. I wanted to see and touch them, to love them as I had learned to love my own. To do this I had to love the woman, connect heart to heart and honor the divine within her. "Seeing" another's soul is the highest form of tantric practice. From that place sexual loving is integrated into spirit.

The sacrament of intention and prayer was a great ally in my opening with women. With men, even with intention I was more cautious. I rarely had intercourse with them, and even embracing in tantric connection could be a stretch. But with women, I could release my discomfort of sexual intimacy and open to great depth in tantric rituals of love. I felt proud to release any fear of opening and I felt honored to be doing this together, and so did the other women. I was many women's "first" with another woman; they were heterosexual. (I was "universexual.") Sexually loving each other took rewiring in the realms of energy, intention, and consciousness.

In Tantra, loving a woman's yoni with your mouth is called honoring the yoni. Loving a man's lingam in this way is called honoring the lingam. Honoring is one of the art forms of great pleasure, intimacy, and skill. Before Tantra I never had a context of consciousness to go with this part of sex I enjoyed so much. Through Tantra I learned to receive love through my clitoris and yoni by inhaling deeply of the pleasure being given me, while sounding tones or mmmmm's on the exhale. Relaxing the muscles in my pelvis instead of stiffening and trying so hard to reach orgasm enhanced my enjoyment. And hearing my lover's words and seeing the love in his or her eyes expanded my pleasure even more. In honoring another, I learned to focus my mind and breath, at times making eye contact or speaking words of empowerment. Bringing the element of fun to the love exchange lifted it out of seriousness and goal orientation. I grew to appreciate the unique flavor, scent, and taste of women. I realized that no two yonis are alike.

I often enjoyed sharing the pleasure of honoring with my beloved as we took turns loving a dear one. The only times I did not enjoy it were when Charles seemed so deeply involved in giving a woman pleasure I felt a clock ticking in my head. "Isn't it long enough?" I'd think. "Aren't they connecting long enough?" I would lose interest, want to leave and smoke a Clovie or jump in the hot tub, and I would. Once they realized I wasn't returning, the focus on her pleasure usually short-circuited.

Much of what Charles learned about abundant love came from his mother. Charles was the youngest of three, and he was his mama's baby. We scheduled regular weekend seminars in Santa Cruz, Carmel Valley, Marin County, Los Angeles, and San Diego so we could stay with her during the week. Our bedroom at Mama's was Charles' small office, where a futon on the floor made a cozy bed. We shared her bathroom with the creaky pipes, tarnished medicine cabinet, and peeling linoleum. My suitcase of mainland clothes (clothes that actually kept me warm) filled up half her living room. The other half was taken up by furniture, stacks of newspapers, and grocery store coupons. "I know where everything is," Mama liked to say, meaning "Don't move anything." The maple-framed TV console was the centerpiece, with photographs of her family set on lace doilies on top of it. Charles worked in his office during the days while I took treasured daily walks through nearby Del Monte Forest to Lover's Point. We would bring home ingredients and Mama would transform them into a tempting concoction bubbling on the stove. Oh, those steaming plates of Italian love! Her first words when I arrived home were always, "Are you hungry, dear?" In the evenings we cuddled on her couch after dinner to watch her programs with her and give each other foot rubs.

But Mama was growing older and frailer, and eventually began to have difficulty getting around. She hated to leave that drafty little house where she'd lived since Charles had moved his parents out from the Bronx ten years earlier, but she agreed to move in with Rosemarie, Charles' sister, where she would stay until her death in 2008. I helped with the move and visited her whenever I was in the area. She and I would always have a special bond with our November birthdays and our unconditional love for her "Chuckie."

While we were away teaching seminars—over thirty weekends a year at this point—or staying with Mama, back in our little corner of paradise Singie or Jahlia or both together took care of our temple while Michael kept the business running smoothly and Larry handled the groundskeeping. Singie had become our regular housekeeper ("My years as an ashram wife will pay dividends," she chuckled when she offered to take the job), and every week, clad in G-string and sneakers with a bandana tied around her flaming red hair, she spit-shined and polished our temple, washing and folding the towels used by the goddesses who left their amrita as a blessing to all. She swore often at the endless amount of work and questioned our sanity in choosing to live in such a big house by the ocean. But she sang its praises more often than she swore at its demands. Sometimes we'd even come home from teaching trips to find our cars completely detailed. What more could a busy tantric wife ask for? Having Singie to talk and sing with, cook and clean with, and love and adore was an altered state of the highest order.

When we weren't teaching Charles and I luxuriated in long hours of lovemaking alone or with another woman. Our spiritual path of yoga, fasts and cleanses, bodywork, and lots of exercise and swimming kept us in peak condition as lovers.

I became more and more sensitive to energy. My inner vision sharpened with full, deep breathing, and seeing, moving, and reading energy became the focus of sexual play and awakening as our nights of loving lasted into the wee hours. We were both riding a wave of healing so that more pure love could flow into and through us. Eventually, for me, the action of healing became secondary to simply living in a balanced state. But many years elapsed before that choice became my own beloved truth.

As our first year in the house came to a close, the book was selling around the world, and our Tantra seminars were filling up fast in Hawaii and on the mainland. Charles urged me to step out on my own with some of the teachings. "Offer Shakti transmission and sacred spot awakening in an all-women setting", he suggested. "Test out interest with some friends on Maui." Uncertain if this would work, I offered instruction, demonstration, and practice in women healing women to a small group of my friends. Everyone loved the work! My new workshop, "Tantra for Women," was launched.

Singie and Jahlia supported me with Tantra for Women. Either or both were often at my side, traveling to the weekend seminars and speaking to the groups about how Tantra was helping them and describing the shifts in their consciousness about their bodies and sexuality. They offered their music, which always enhanced the group experience, and offered their wisdom and their abundant life force to the two or three dozen women at each weekend training who respectfully trusted me to guide them toward their passion—healing through intimacy practices, massage, sisterhood, and a building of long-forgotten trust of each other. We became the midwives for the worldwide weaving of women.

On a winter day, I went with Singie for a recheck of her PAP test. I was so nervous about it, I barely slept the night before. But the results were good, and we jumped up and down right there in the office, holding onto each other. "You fuckers are healing me, aren't you!" she cried, kissing me on both cheeks.

Maybe we were, emotionally *and* physically. Her life seemed to be on track at last. During Christmas, while house-sitting for us, Singie had met Keith, a handsome welder and good man she had come to truly love. They made love for the first time, she told me, in our bed. Before spring the next year, she moved in with him at his place in Haiku, an easy fifteen-minute drive from our house.

Right away, things began changing between Singie and me. She wasn't comfortable coming over any longer, and I didn't feel drawn to spend time in her new life with Keith. "He doesn't understand this Tantra thing, Queenie," she told me. "I explained it was about healing me, but he's a pretty normal guy. He doesn't get it." Maybe I represented a too radical sexual lifestyle. Whatever it was, it didn't work for her new life. She needed to devote herself to her beloved.

After she and Keith got married, Singie and I stopped seeing each other at all. An era had come to an end. No more arm-in-arm walks on the beaches, breathing in the sea air and talking of everything and nothing. Oh, how I wanted these great loves to go on forever! I couldn't imagine life without Singie in it. One day I would realize her departure gave me my first real insight into the fluidity of love. I would understand that form can be missing but true love is never gone. But for now, I missed her terribly. I had no idea seven years would pass before I would see her again.

Chapter Thrirteen

Mother Love

Change was in the air. That year, just before her seventy-fourth birthday, news came that my mother was in the hospital and that I should come immediately. It might be the last time I would see her. Johnny was on the first flight out of Denver. I threw some jeans, a jacket, and extra sweaters into a small suitcase and Charles drove me to the airport. Holding me close, he pleaded, "Call me every day, my queen. My love is with you."

Before I arrived at the hospital and got more of the news, all I knew was that my mother had been found unconscious on her living room floor. The doctors didn't know how long she had been lying there before the ambulance was called.

It was hard to believe the end could finally be here.

I met Johnny in the hospital lobby and fell into a hug. Worry lines creased his face. "You're here," he sighed, looking down at the floor. That feeling of being the only ones we had came rushing back. But I didn't feel as sure of myself as I had back when we were young and my high school buddies were my armor against this.

At the reception desk we asked for our mother's doctor and we met him on the third floor, where our mother lay in the bed in one of the rooms. His hard eyes narrowed with contempt for us. "Your mother is dying of neglect," he said, looking us up and down. I drew in my breath to center myself and looked directly into his eyes. But there was nothing to say. *How could I have done more?* I wanted to say. He told us about the emergency call from the superintendent at her apartment complex. They had wanted to read the meter inside her utility room and no one had answered the door for several days. The superintendent finally suspected the elderly woman in Unit 104 may have fallen ill.

What the doctor didn't know was that my mother was an eccentric recluse who had refused our help for years. She lived on a trust Nank created for her, so she was financially secure. When she did occasionally tolerate our visits, we took her out to dinner, feeling all the while as if she couldn't wait to get back to her apartment and send us on our way. Now and then she asked Johnny to help with a tax return or another piece of business and later she accused him of stealing from her. These imaginings were real to her.

As a child Johnny was always at our mother's side, adoring her. We called him "mama's boy." For the past few years, every six months Johnny flew from his home in Denver to Kansas City and drove an hour to her apartment to peek in a kitchen window and see if things were okay. If he called ahead Mom might agree to his visit, but when he arrived she'd slam the door in his face. He'd call me, despairing at being treated this way. All I could do was wrap my love around him long-distance in those terrible hours of rejection. Throughout the day he would knock at her door or call a few more times, and then he'd board his plane and go back home. I called her every few weeks, and if she even answered the phone, our conversations were very short. She assured me she was fine and insisted I not call again or worry about her. She was almost immune to the love we offered her, didn't trust it. Modern medicine—and life—had "shocked" any sensitivity right out of her. As time went on, I had less and less desire to go to see her because it hurt too much to feel such lack of connection with my own mother.

When Robin was little my mother joined us for two weeks on our vacation at the Cape. She stayed with Robin a few of the evenings when Arnie and I went into Provincetown, and she seemed to love her role as a needed and wanted grandmother. I felt a hint of fulfillment in completing the motherline link—my mother, me, my daughter. There was so much in my identity I needed to claim as a mother, but when I turned to her to be a role model I found she couldn't teach me. She didn't have what it takes to be constant. When we were home again my mother slipped right back into a depression and lashed out physically or with words. Her sudden personality change upset me even more because of her recent return of attention and availability. I put her on a plane back to Kansas City as fast as I could.

In the hospital that day with Johnny, my mother never recognized us. Johnny arranged for her to be moved to a convalescent hospital once she was stabilized. "Go back to Maui," he told me, despondently. "I'll check on her every few weeks and keep you posted."

Thank God for Johnny.

I visited my mother in the nursing home a few times that summer, meeting up with Johnny there, often even enjoying the hours we visited our mom.

"Would you kids go buy me a red lipstick?" she asked one day. I flew out the door to find a lipstick for Mom. She had actually asked us to do something for her! Later that day I handed her an Estée Lauder Classic Red and watched her apply the lipstick without a mirror like she had done all her life.

As time went on, my mother got weaker. In fall, leaves paved the roads in crimson and gold. This was the Kansas I remembered, mornings spent raking piles of crackling leaves. I always looked forward to November, my birthday month, and to the hours spent riding my bike through those fallen leaves.

Fall looked different now. This would be the last time I would see it in Kansas. My mother was in the hospital again and her nurse didn't think she would make it much longer. My brother and I timed our visit together and met at the hospital. Johnny went into her room first. "I won't be long," he promised, leaving me alone in the waiting room. I sat with a magazine in my lap, trying my best to conjure images of my life on Maui, anything to escape this long-anticipated farewell. I thought about what the doctor had said some months back. Dying of neglect. Should I have tried harder to do something more?

In what seemed like just a few moments, Johnny startled me with a touch on my shoulder. "I'll get the car," he said gravely. He signaled me with a nod to go and take my time with Mom. When he had disappeared around the corner of the long hallway, I took a deep breath and went in.

Mother. Lying in the bed blowing kisses to her heart. Over and over, in rapid succession, she kissed her fingers and placed them on her heart.

I went to her bedside. "Mom," I whispered, half smiling, "what on earth are you doing?"

With her other bony hand, she clutched her silver mesh cigarette case to her chest. She was forbidden the extra-long Virginia Slims it held. Her lungs were closing down and she breathed oxygen through clear tubes in her nostrils.

"Just trying to keep this old heart beating a few more days," she gasped with the same half-smile I used. I watched as she reapplied her red lipstick without the aid of a mirror. "See you next visit, honey, if my heart keeps going." She leaned toward me and I bent down to receive her soft kiss on my cheek. What else was there to do?

"I love you, Mom," I said, turning so she wouldn't see my eyes ready to overflow a lifetime of tears. I headed for the door. A nurse entered as I left the room. "Mary," I heard her say to my mother, "what are you do- ing with those cigarettes? You know you can't smoke with oxygen in the room. Now darlin', come on. It's time for dinner."

I ran down the corridor to the staircase and hurried downstairs and into the shocking cold of a late autumn evening. Johnny waited in the heated car out front. "Got a smoke?" I panted, climbing in. Before he could answer, the dam broke and the tears came flooding out.

Johnny cried with me, and we held each other for a long time. When we recovered, we decided a good Kansas steak and a strong martini would be better than continuing the insanity of the family cigarette habit. The wind howled its agreement, and off we drove into the night. We would dine at an old favorite restaurant and then head to her apartment for a good look around.

When I was very young my mother took me to the ballet, opera, and symphony, and to the Kansas City Museum of Art. These were some of our best times together. I can still taste the triple-layer chocolate cake in the museum café on those precious visits. It was at this museum that I saw my first Monet. I could have looked at those paintings forever, especially after reading Mom's books on the French Impressionists. My favorite of her art books was *The Gold of Their Bodies*, the story of Paul Gauguin and his years in Tahiti. That was my first taste of what it might be to live on a tropical island.

These memories flooded back as Johnny and I explored our mother's self-imposed prison garden apartment, now that we were finally free to enter. The walls were bare. There was a small radio by her bed, no television. Overflowing ashtrays and half-empty packs of Virginia Slims were everywhere. Newspapers and trash littered the floor, furniture, and surfaces, and all we found in the kitchen were empty cans of Folger's instant coffee, a half-filled jar of powdered creamer, and packets of artificial sweetener. There wasn't a single book or magazine, no sign of life anywhere. Outside, the patio was strewn with leaves, and a full can of cigarette butts was the only ornament in sight. Mother still owned a car, and we suspected she threw a coat over her nightgown to drive the block to the nearest fast-food restaurant for a burger and fries, with coffee, of course, for breakfast, lunch, and dinner.

How long had she waited for the end to whisk her off to Never-Never Land? She had lived in a world of dreams and illusions, and she may have found some comfort in them. Now and then she had periods of lucidity and candor, but they were never long enough to sustain the connection with her I craved. Once, many years ago, she had taken me to see the wishing well near my grandfather's old colonial mansion. When we got there, I climbed out of the car to take a closer look. The next thing I knew, my mother was driving off, leaving me to hitchhike back to her place. A crumb of her love would have been enough, but she didn't have that love for herself or anything.

My mother's heart failed the night we said goodbye at the hospital. We got word of it in the morning, changed our flight plans, and began the job of emptying her apartment and making funeral arrangements.

Johnny handled everything and I kept him company, beginning the process of clearing out her private domain—closets, drawers, the essentials of her life. Her world was bland and devoid of color and complexity. No flair, no personality. Mine was filled with brilliance, warmth, color, and love. What an opportunity to experience our vast differences. Now that she was gone, her absence rang louder than all the emptiness that had come before. Now and then, while filling bags with long-outdated newspapers and other things that could finally be thrown out, I wept hard for her lonely and loveless life, for the mother I could never help.

Before her death my mother had chosen a small crypt where her ashes would be stored under the guardian angel stained-glass window at St. Andrews, our family church. At her memorial service, I stood in that vault of crypts lined up under the enormous golden angel window as sunbeams cast radiant light through the glass, illuminating the ethereal golden hues. Heaven on earth was in this room with Johnny and me. No friends of hers came to offer condolences; no other relatives were there. This was how she had lived—alone. I sobbed for her and for everyone who has never known a life filled with love and loved ones. The church organist played softly as Johnny and I stood in silence. Then we left our mother's ashes in this Easter Angel sanctuary.

For years, the perfect mother of my childhood, the one who had nourished me in all ways before her illness took over, was the only mom I could remember. More recently I had come to accept the mom she had become, "a shell of a mom," as I once referred to her. I called my father to ask him for stories about her early years, and he told me something that seemed to hold the key to so much of my mother's sadness. No wonder motherhood had been so hard for her. In 1938, when she was twenty years old, my mother had gotten pregnant while on vacation with her parents on the *Queen Elizabeth*, traveling from New York to Paris. It was a family crisis. Mom had to leave college to live in a home for unwed mothers in upstate New York, where she gave birth to a child that was given up for adoption. Not long after, during his last year of medical school, my mother's older brother jumped out of the sixth-story window of a downtown hotel. The family despaired. My mother's marriage to my father, soon followed by my birth, came as a great relief to all. Here was a chance to be a normal family again. I could see the burden of all that hope weighed heavy on my mother's shoulders. It was too much for her to bear. She broke.

Robin called to offer me condolences when she heard her grandmother had died. She had barely known my mother, but she tried to support me in grieving my loss. I could tell she wanted to care, but the strain was evident. She clearly struggled with her unmet needs for the mother in me, just as I had struggled with the same with my own mother. I may never know how much my mother's departure into mental illness affected my choice to distance myself from Robin when she was so young. I suppose these things unravel over the course of one's life. It is still unraveling in mine as the complexities of the Divine Mother versus the human mother play out their mystery to me.

Johnny called not long after my return to Maui. Mom's Kansas bank had asked him to clear out her safety deposit box there. I can still hear his stunned voice. "You won't believe it," he said, his voice hushed in dismay, "but all that's in there is a seashell."

We had speculated that our mother might have collected cash or jewels or stock certificates over the years, though we knew her primary assets were held in her trust. Bank staff said Mom visited her safety deposit box several times a year, and she always stayed in the little private cubicle for an hour or more. The shell had been used as an ashtray, he said, and charred scars dimmed its pearly luster. Mom had had the last laugh after all.

When I gaze at a worn copy of my mother's favorite book, *Gift from the Sea* by Anne Morrow Lindbergh, which she gave me many years ago, I think of how the poetry from the sea lies in the spiral, the long-lived symbol for continuing life. In this divinely feminine place—the beaches of my sea-sculpted soul—my mother's spirit and I will always connect. In my daily life, I missed her, strange as it seemed since I didn't talk to her or see her much at all. I learned that no matter how old you are when your mother passes or how far away from each other you are in body or spirit, when she leaves the earth, some part of you goes with her. You become whole unto yourself.

A few months later, one of the most meaningful—and unexpected—healings of my life took place. Susan was a lover of Cos and Blue's, a beautiful, curious woman with an open mind and heart and an adventuresome spirit. She struggled in her role as a mother and had left her husband and young son some time ago. We looked with anticipation to what Susan might need from us. I felt Charles intuit with me what kind of healing might be up for her.

It is a special honor to initiate young women, as they can have a more direct channel to their life force than older women have; they've had less time to experience that which closes women down. We also knew it could be a very high-energy evening because naturally vital and beautiful women like Susan tend to carry deep wounds from rarely being appreciated for their vulnerable, tender selves; men usually desire them for their own gratification. Women love being admired and desired as long as it is balanced by their lover's desire to know them to the depths of their soul. With us there would be love without agenda. Susan would be seen for who she was for possibly the first time.

To prepare for the ritual that night I covered the bed with soft sheets reserved for such occasions. On top of this I spread out one of my floral Balinese batik spreads, which added joy to the room. I lit vanilla-scented candles inside hurricane lamps and placed several crystal bowls of gardenias floating in water on the koa wood headboard. Lavender water lilies arched gracefully from tall vases on the table at the foot of the bed, a fire crackled in the fireplace, and the fragrance of sandalwood incense perfumed the air as rain pounded the windows. The mood was dramatic and sensuous, just like in Huelo. In Huelo, a thousand magnificent tropical storms wash through every year, providing a purifying atmosphere for healings. It rained sideways, in circles, and always intensely.

Wearing our ceremonial hand-painted silk robes, Charles and I greeted Susan when she arrived, looking as lovely as I remembered. She followed us into the room prepared for this sacred event. We began by sitting cross-legged on the bed and holding hands for meditation and prayer. Charles invited the presence of the Divine into the session. Then we thanked God and Goddess for their presence with us and for their divine guidance through us. We stated our intentions for the session: to open ourselves to love in its purest form. "We are here to enter into the power that love can provide for healing and awakening," I said, gazing into Susan's eyes. I assured her I was aligned with Charles as his beloved for the intention of offering our consciousness, skills, and love to her. Charles gazed into Susan's eyes, shining out his vast heart of love to her. "Tell us, Susan," he said, "what are you drawn to receive from the session? We want to be clear about your needs."

Susan began by telling us she had never been educated about the mysteries of being a woman, that she had never felt empowered by her family for her beauty and intelligence. She spoke of her husband, from whom she was separated, and of her young son, who had stayed with his father. She had married and given birth when she was too young for the responsibility, and she was confused about how to keep her son and maintain a friendly relationship with his father. She wanted her freedom, and her family disapproved of her actions, especially regarding her sexuality and her child. We held her as she sobbed. After a time, she calmed down and announced she would be ready to begin the healing as soon as she came back from the bathroom.

In our few minutes alone, Charles and I agreed this was going to take several sessions. All that Susan had shared could not be addressed in a single evening. We decided we would focus that night on empowering her with her own ability to unravel her life. We would support her and envision her having her parents' approval of her truest needs.

Just then, Susan returned. "Hey, you guys," she said, smiling proudly from the doorway. "I just got my moon. Is that okay?"

Charles and I looked at each other. I felt butterflies churn in my belly. "Maybe we should do this session another time," I suggested. Charles didn't think we needed to wait. "If you're comfortable going forward, Susan, there's no reason not to."

Susan came forward and lay down naked between Charles and me. I froze. Twenty-five years had passed since I had seen my menstrual blood, the exact age of the woman lying before me. I had missed out on the power of this cycle, this rhythm of nature, for most of my adult life.

When I realized I might touch or smell this woman's blood, I started to panic from a place so deep I didn't recognize myself. And when a whiff of her fresh menstrual blood reached my nostrils, I felt helpless as a giver in union with my beloved when moments earlier I had been powerful in my high priestess self.

"What's going on for you, my beloved?" Charles asked tenderly, when he saw how pale and frozen I had become.

I tried to explain. I told them about the end of my cycle, or my "period," in my twenties. I remembered how my mother had called it "the curse" when I'd started at twelve years old. There was no celebration of having reached this point in my developing womanhood. When I was older I learned that men tended to fear a woman's menstrual cycle, the pungent smell of the blood. Susan gazed deeply into my eyes as I finished my story of the hysterectomy and faced my feelings for the first time about having lost this part of my womanly life.

And then, the unexpected that we always expected happened. Like a warrior goddess or high priestess herself, Susan gently said, "Lie down, Caroline." I didn't understand. "But this evening is for you," I protested. Susan moved to kneel before me, love filling her eyes. "Lie down, my queen. I have something to give you." I felt Charles' wonder and support as I lay back on the bed. He sat beside me cross-legged and watched, stunned by the change of events. *I* would be in the receiver's role! And I had no idea what we were about to do.

Susan bowed a deep, reverential bow honoring the divine within me, her eyes soft with compassion. "Caroline, I offer my new blood to the young girl in you who has held this sorrow for so long. It is your blood. It is my Shakti. I anoint you with it and with all of my love."

I was breathless. What a miraculous event. "We're completely here with you, beloved," Charles assured me. "All is well." Susan put her hand to her yoni and from its deepest folds brought forth some of her fresh menstrual blood. Tenderly, she touched my third eye, or brow center, with it as I began sobbing uncontrollably. I could see the power of the goddess in her as she placed another drop of her blood on my throat. "You will speak highly of the power of this anointing to other women," she said.

By now my tears were flowing so fast I could barely see the radiant being before me. I sobbed harder, grieving the loss of my moon cycle as I had never done before. My only response to losing my menstrual flow so many years ago was a flip, "Hey, great. No more 'curse.' Lucky me!" Now I was awakening to its preciousness, its sacredness, for the first time.

Susan anointed my heart and then touched her finger to my lips, inviting me to taste her sacred blessing. This was so startling that my uncontrollable sobs suddenly stopped; I could breathe again. As I began to calm I felt myself shift into the great aliveness that comes when fear is finally slain. My sobbing became peals of hysterical laughter. I looked at this lovely young girl, so wise for her age, and howled with glee as she anointed my belly and then my yoni with her blood.

"Give me another taste," I said, desiring more of her surprisingly sweet moon flow. I asked her to smear her blood on my face and my breasts and thighs that I might fully claim my return to wholeness.

When it was done, I was emotionally spent but convinced beyond all doubt of the power of ritual in the name of love and healing. And my ability to trust the Feminine was forever changed. Susan had no agenda with me other than to clear the muddy waters of my psyche. I learned of the great power of the goddess when she meets another in safe space.

Charles, too, was astonished by the brilliance of this great healing. He had told me of ancient healing rituals between women in tantric cultures. Over many centuries the cultures were destroyed and little knowledge of the rituals survived. With Susan it seemed we had rediscovered a lost practice—we had spun the tantric weaving, serving the evolution of the power of love as a healing tool.

Given the divinity that dwells within our unleashed spirits, I knew by now of the power that is ours when we allow high magic to spontaneously flow. Once again I understood women's power to transmit their Shakti to one another through sacred rites that are not sexual in nature. We connect with our Shakti energy and then share it through loving touch, eye-gazing, and with the transmission of sound frequencies. We are the midwives for each other, birthing our sexual/spiritual power. We have to trust our intuition. With Mira, and Jahlia and Singie, I had encountered this high magic of the Feminine. But every time it happened it took me by surprise. It's not easy to remember that which has been destroyed by all the many attempts to render the Feminine secondary.

Through subsequent sessions with us, Susan discovered she didn't need sexual healing or awakening, she only needed reassurance of her wholeness. She was already a powerful priestess and she would become more of one as her life unfolded. She could trust herself as a resource of Divine Feminine strength and vision. When she understood that, her confusion unraveled and she returned to her marriage to raise her son in the family she wanted for him.

Susan gave me an incredible gift. I emerged from that first healing session with her feeling more whole as a woman than I had in over twenty years. I had never acknowledged my great sadness over not being able to bear my own child, and I realized that Robin may have borne the brunt of my unfaced sorrow.

I wasn't ready for motherhood when we brought Robin into our lives, although I had tried—for Arnie and for her—to be all I knew a mother to be. I remembered how I had shown up for her and been rejected by her throughout her childhood and teenage years. She relaxed with Rick but tightened up with me when we visited her at Arnie's house when I lived in Ojai. At Christmas, Rick and I drove down and shared dinner and long walks with them in the Hollywood Hills, drove Robin to friends' houses to play, and throughout the year gave Arnie and Nancy needed breaks on many weekends. When Robin wanted to leave private prep school in ninth grade, she called me. I took her and a girlfriend to see Burbank High, where they wanted to enroll. Briefly, I was her ally. But later, when I was married to Ron, she went back to how she had been, and then she went away even further. Robin was distant with Ron. Their lack of chemistry put a lot of strain on me. Her heart was attached to her dad and to Rick and here was Mom forcing another of her husbands on her. She didn't need another of her mother's men in her life. I knew I must have been a very hard mother for a child to have. At the time, I spoke with Arnie about my feelings. He said that Robin rejected him, too. But he didn't take it personally. I did.

As two adults, my daughter and I still struggled. It was hard for us to express our feelings to each other. We were strangers without the key to unlock that mystery of the mother-daughter relationship. Something was unexpressed, unsatisfied, inaccessible. I wondered if she would ever truly like me. And I never stopped doing whatever I knew how to do. When she was very young I had wanted to hold her and invite her to melt into me and allow us to bond, to merge, without separation. She could not do it. Maybe it was her early wounding, having three "mothers" in her first eighteen days (birth mother, foster mother, and me). We just don't know the effect that could have on an infant. I often wonder if I had remained in my marriage to Arnie and done everything "right" as a mom, might Robin have been any more trusting of me? I wonder and wonder … and then I wonder some more.

Robin visited me a number of times in Maui, either with a boyfriend or alone, before she married in 1997. When we were alone, our struggle for warmth and intimacy was right in my face. I would stumble trying to establish connection with her. I would play on the floor with her and the cats or rub her feet. She relaxed with the cats in her arms. I asked questions about school, but her terse answers left me reaching for words I didn't know. I hadn't gone to college. I had no context. I chose the college of *life*. I helped pay for her education so she wouldn't have to work while she was in school. When graduate school finally came, I attempted being parental, suggesting that the tuition be in the form of a college loan, thinking that would be more responsible of me and teach my daughter a value many learn from taking financial responsibility for their choices. It was met with insult after insult, and finally the Trust was happy to pay for her final years in school. I had no idea she could apply to the Trust for assistance. Again, I now looked like the mean or narcissistic mom, a struggle that appears to be never-ending.

Arnie, who had completed college at Fordham University with a degree in psychology, gave her the encouragement to prioritize her education. It really was a team effort. Long, detailed letters came from Arnie describing Robin's endeavors, accomplishments, and future needs. I responded with agreement and enthusiasm to nearly everything she so intelligently wanted for herself. I accepted how different we were, while still longing for a friendship that remained elusive.

There were places and times when Robin and I went beyond separation and into a deeper connection when she visited me in Maui: shopping (even if it was my attempt to buy her love) and the beach. At the beach, we unwound and found our zone of harmony. We were at home in the water and loved the sun-drenched feeling of several hours there. She taught me the value of sun protection, hats, and visors. The sun was like liquid gold to me. I could never get enough.

One spring when she was in college, Robin called and asked to come for a visit. She would be alone. "That's wonderful!" I said. "I'll make sure the sun is shining and put on a pot of your favorite veggie soup." On her visit, as we left the house to climb into my jeep for a trip to the beach one day, Susan stopped by to say hello. A knot tightened in my stomach. Robin seemed threatened by women close to her age that she met at our home in Maui. Susan was scantily dressed in a sarong and the barest of tops (this was Maui, remember). "Aloha, and welcome to Maui!" Susan cried, throwing her arms around Robin to greet her. I watched Robin shut down inside and flatly say hello. I told Susan we had to go.

In the car, the energy was thick. "Who was that?" Robin asked. "Oh, that's Susan," I said, lightly. "She's staying with Cos and Blue and doing some healing work with us." We quickly changed the subject. On the way home that afternoon, Robin startled me with a question. "Is that girl single or married or what?" When I explained that Susan was estranged from her husband and had a young son staying with her parents until she stabilized, Robin seemed to relax.

Robin knew about the tantric healing work. I had no idea how it impacted her because she was closed to communication with me concerning sexual intimacies. She believed her sex life was not something to be discussed with her mother. What a contrast we were! As an initiated goddess of the Tantric healing arts, I was an A student in holding nothing back. I had grown up seeing the danger of holding back and "imploding" (my mother's mental illness). Because of that, I believed emoting could save my life, and I could really scream, kick, pound, emote—or kiss, caress, and surrender to pleasure with abandon. It seemed strange to choose to hide the sounds of joy, love, and pleasure, even with my daughter in the house. These were not angry sounds or demanding words (which in our culture are acceptable in the privacy of the home). These were not the sounds of fucking. These were sounds of laughter, cooing, prayers of gratitude, and an occasional "YES" mixed with many "Oh my Gods!"

During one of her first visits to stay with us in Maui, I was faced with a tough decision. What was a mother supposed to do as an awakening sexual being when her daughter visited and slept only a bedroom away? I suggested to Charles that we not have any tantric practice while Robin was here. "My queen," Charles said, "do you want to teach your daughter by example that you are a sexual woman who loves her pleasure or do you want to teach her you will hide the pleasure we share when she is near?"

I pondered this for several days, trying to decide how I wanted to handle myself with my daughter and her boyfriend sleeping just down the hall from our bedroom, a sanctuary of daily pleasure, frolicking, and multiorgasmic bliss. And then I decided to go for it. From the privacy of my bedroom with my beloved, I offered up a spoonful of my joy-filled "I'm having pleasure" sounds. It was a huge test for me, but I made the decision then to walk my talk even with members of my own family, *especially* with members of my own family. (This included Johnny, on his visits to me in Maui. Charles' Mama and sister always stayed in condos at the beach.) The news was out: Queenie was a highly orgasmic woman and she loved making sounds. They all survived their initiation.

I don't know if I did the "right" thing. All I know is I was tearing down the walls of my cultural upbringing, daring to be authentic. The rebellious pioneer in me wanted to prove I could do it; the nice girl who is considerate of others had a hard time with this much authenticity. Sexual awakening had its challenges right along with all that pleasure.

Because of our teaching schedule in Los Angeles and San Diego, I visited Robin a number of times when she was living in Manhattan Beach and was studying for her master's degree at USC. We would go to the Strand for long walks in the warm southern California ocean air, stopping for bagels and salads and enjoying the colorful crowds who roller-skate and run on that ocean-side promenade. Robin would visit me in Santa Monica when we were teaching at the Sheridan Hotel. I invited her to join in on some of the women's groups and could always feel her discomfort as she sat in the back of the group of fifty or more women. She never wanted to discuss what she heard in those groups about women choosing a journey of healing and awakening, massage of the sacred spot, or simply their respect for how I held the class in the face of very emotional and fearful issues.

While she was studying psychology in college, Robin was willing to join with me in attempting to unravel the difficult energies between us in several sessions with a hypnotherapist I knew in Santa Monica. Even if it didn't resolve everything, it opened some doorways and led us into some of the deeper issues. One day after a session and lunch together, we sat on a park bench looking out over the huge expanse of Pacific Ocean that always inspired my soul. Robin said, "I guess you had a lot of reasons to leave when you did, Mom. I've just had a real hard time trying to understand how you could abandon me to go discover yourself when I was so young." Gulping over the "abandonment" word, I put my arm around her and said the most authentic thing I could. "Honey, I am so sorry. I didn't know how to give you what you needed and give myself what I needed too. Your dad was adamant about keeping you with him, and maybe I was too easy about that. Can you forgive me?"

We walked, talked, ate, and shopped. Only short periods of soulful intimacy were comfortable for Robin, only brief hugs. "Mom, you know I don't like hugging." I, on the other hand, am an intimacy junkie. I more than once invited Robin to take MDMA with me; she flatly refused. Having read extensively about the therapeutic use of MDMA, I had a lot of respect for the drug and believed it could save us a lot of time. MDMA is known for producing a sense of intimacy with others and diminishing feelings of fear and anxiety. Before it was made a controlled substance, MDMA was used to aid in psychotherapy, and it is still being researched as a therapeutic tool in healing post-traumatic stress syndrome.

Every child has a core need for love, along with other core needs such as food, water, shelter, and nurturance. For me, fulfilling my need for love was paramount to my survival, and I tried with all my might to get my core needs met by riding the waves of love, romance, sex, relationship, and marriage. I didn't know that a child needs the same level of emotional passion you would give a lover. Both Robin and I were two little girls needing our mommies, and because of that, we both missed out on a great deal of what was available in the moments we had.

Chapter Fourteen

Lost and Found

Help with my issues with mothering came the way it usually did—as a surprise—with the arrival of two new friends, Maria and Gabriella. Both were mothers, both were in need of healing (a term too loosely used, I admit, but we didn't know what else to call it), and offering healing to them became a healing for me, as well.

Maria Magdalena was around forty when she and I first met at Rio Caliente, both yoga students of Charles'. She was forty-six now. Her smile matched the beauty of her soul, with full, beautiful lips that reminded me of my mother's—she wore red lipstick like it was invented for her. She was petite, with olive skin, dark eyes, a strong body, and very large breasts. She was a swimmer and a body builder, athletic and luscious from head to toe. But like so many hardworking single mothers, she didn't think so, in part because she was so exhausted.

One day, as I sat in our upstairs office with its view toward the Haleakala Crater and the glittering coastline all the way to Hana, Maria called. "I haven't been well," she said. Her voice was small and weak, not at all how I remembered it. She said she had Epstein-Barr Syndrome, a chronic viral infection, and between that and having just finished raising her three children as a single mom, her life force felt depleted and dangerously low. Maria lived in California now, where it was warmer, after giving up her practice as an acupuncturist on the East Coast. She hadn't been sexual for a few years and rarely spent time out of bed. Could we help? Charles and I agreed that night to give Maria a sacred spot massage session the next time we were in California. We both felt the immediacy of love and a desire to be of help.

Maria struggled with the owned and disowned parts of her soul, and we witnessed this as we helped her into integration. At first it was hard for her to believe we wanted to take the time to help her, but she gradually relaxed into our commitment to her return to life. As a child she had escaped Hungary with her family during a revolution and immigrated with them to the United States. She believed she had experienced incest with a relative and had suffered two rapes. She would need a regular practice of sexual healing and consistent, loving friendship to access her wounds and find peace inside herself. There were a lot of emotional demons to confront.

Charles suggested a new approach in the healing work with Maria: He wanted to work alone with her. "I wish you would, sweetheart," I confessed. "The emotional content that you are able to access in Maria is hard for me to assimilate. I see my own mother in her. Oh my God, that's it. I see so much of my mom in Maria." I knew Charles could handle Maria's demons. Over the next few months, Maria spoke with me personally several times, making sure that working with Charles solo was okay with me. I assured her it was; the love from them both melted any of my reluctance, a reluctance that grew from known and unknown fears and insecurities.

I learned so much when I assisted Charles in wrestling with a woman's rage during sexual healing sessions, and yet I disliked what it also made me feel inside myself. I remembered that emotions are always temporary, even though they may feel consuming. I learned not to fear rage in myself and others, and I saw how close rage is to pleasure. They are the flip sides of one another. I have experienced my own rage turn into huge orgasmic pleasure, almost in the same moment. It requires trust of oneself and of one's healer, and that is exactly what was happening for Maria with Charles. Once her healing was under way, orgasmic waves rocked Maria. She was reborn. I, on the other hand, shriveled, although I hid it well. Sometimes.

Maria went on a deep healing journey to open up to her emerging sexual power, and with the awakened state of Shakti moving through her, she became the persona of the Divine Mother. Besides being a tremendously talented healer and doctor of acupuncture, Maria was one of the most sexually powerful women I have known.

Still, I struggled with sharing Charles with her. The more alive and whole she became, the more I felt threatened by her presence as a primary lover in our life, even though Charles encouraged her to have other lovers so he was not the only one, which could lead to attachments forming. When Gabriella came to us for some healing and Tantra practice, I jumped at the invitation.

Gabriella was strikingly beautiful—tall and slender with long silky hair that hung down her strong suntanned back. She had come to the United States from Switzerland at eighteen and had lived on Maui for several years. Her husky voice and accent, her flashing green eyes, and her year-old son, Nalu, melted our hearts.

Gabriella and Nalu's Brazilian father had studied Tantra with us before Gabriella became pregnant. A year after her son was born, she left the relationship, because surfing, it turned out, was more interesting for her beloved than parenting. (Not uncommon on Maui and in all fairness, Nalu has a great relationship with his dad.) Gabriella had lost her sexual desire when Nalu was born, and she wanted it back. She wanted to awaken her Shakti through tantric healing and was only comfortable with Charles and me together for it.

Experiences with Gabriella were sweet, gentle, and easy. She did not have the same kind of need as Maria, and the healing sessions brought us all to new heights. They were fun, almost too fun to be called healing. That's when I began to realize, yet fighting it all the way, that "healing" can be fun, pleasurable, and easy.

Gabriella shared herself generously, as a woman and a mother. One night, when Nalu slept, she asked us to nurse on her full breasts. We both tasted and drank deeply of the pure nectar of her mother's milk as we gazed across her silky skin into each other's eyes. Here I was, nearly fifty years young, having an extraordinary healing of sorts around something so natural for many children. This experience, and lying with Gabriella as she nursed and comforted her young son, taught me about the needs of a child to be held in the rapture of intimacy with the mother. I had never had this much intimacy with my mother. I wished I had understood this when Robin was an infant, giving us both what we longed for.

Before long, the boundaries between healer and lover began to melt for me, and I began thinking of Gabriella as our lover. I wanted to be "monogamous" with her, to have only her as our lover. Simplifying like this seemed it could give me the ease I craved. But Charles believed that what I suggested would create a kind of attachment that is detrimental to this work. He wanted to continue to love other women for our own good as well as for theirs. Again, I sifted through my confusion about this beloved truth. "We certainly wouldn't give up Maria," he reminded me. I pondered all of this, continually trying to find balance with a life I had only imagined I could navigate.

Early that summer, trouble came knocking at my door again. It was time for my annual visit to my father and his newest wife, Anne, in Florida. On my first night there, he announced that he had "the big C"—no warning, no "I have some bad news," no hand on my shoulder, just, "So, you know, I have the big C. I start chemo next month."

I stared at him, numb.

"You don't have to do anything. Anne'll take care of me. But it'll be hell. It's bad."

"I'm so sorry," was all I could think of to say. Mom had died just a few months earlier; now it looked like Dad would die too, within the year.

He leaned toward me. "Hey, wanna sneak a cigarette? I'm saving butts. Don't tell Anne. I know just where to go."

To this day I can hear the phlegm gurgling up after his deep, ecstatic inhale. It's insane, I thought, smashing out my smoke and swearing it would be the last one ever. But smoking gave us time together, and there wasn't much of it left.

The rest of the visit was a blur. I wanted to get home, away from this too-big-to-handle news. I had no desire to be part of the last months of his life.

It seemed urgent that I clean my father out of my psyche. How long would he take up space there if I didn't clear him out? The root of my inner turmoil, I knew, probably had something to do with him. Maybe if I cleared it out I could feel whole at last, finally live a satisfied life with my beloved, sharing him without crippling feelings of abandonment and insufficiency.

I had always known something was "off" with my dad—the wet kisses all my life, the sexual references about women in general or about me, the glazed look when he stared at my breasts or hips. Over the years he had showed many generous expressions of parental love for me. But there was also something unspoken and uncomfortable between us. My dad was preparing to leave his body and I was preparing to have him leave *my* body.

Hypnosis seemed the logical route to start clearing out whatever might be buried in my subconscious. I began work with Dr. Fineberg, a respected female hypnotherapist on Maui. It was terrifying to look more deeply into my hidden realms, but I knew it was exactly what I needed.

Charles supported me completely in opening this Pandora's box. He had suspected sexual abuse was in my childhood since the early days of our relationship. In Dr. Fineberg's office, hypnosis in a therapeutic setting was like parting a curtain to reveal the action on a stage in my mind's eye. In the first session I saw my dad's penis coming toward my face, toward my mouth, in fact. There was that familiar warmth, the scent, the taste and size of my father. Agitated and shaken, I shook myself out of the hypnotic trance and insisted this was simply my imagination. She didn't think so.

I began describing a vivid memory from my childhood.

"Minnie was the live-in housekeeper for my grandparents. Black and soft and round, Minnie lived in a small maids' room off Nanny's big country kitchen." Lying very still in the reclining chair, I continued to see while telling Dr. Fineberg as if it were happening at that very moment. "Minnie's fixings—savory roasts and legs of lamb and "smashed" potatoes—filled the big colonial house with tantalizing aromas. She baked trays of Toll House cookies and let me eat big fingers full of the sticky dough. In summer we sat on the cool linoleum in the kitchen with our corn on the cob and watermelon on newspapers so we could drip all over, saving Minnie hours of ironing good linens." Softly chuckling in remembrance of me at that tender age of seven, I continued.

"I liked to slide about the kitchen floor on my back trying to see up Minnie's white uniform and find out if she really was black all over. She was."

This curiosity with what lay beneath veils may have been fueled by my subconscious, where my father's secret would be buried for forty years.

Growing up, I knew something was out of sync with my dad, but I never knew exactly what it was or why I felt so uneasy with him. On Sundays he took me to his dry-cleaning plant when the shop was closed for business. My job was to clean out pockets for any treasures left there. I dreaded those days in the back of the plant. The only sound was his adding machine calculating receipts, and the room was airless and stuffy. Sometimes he would leave his cubicle and stand and stare at me playing in the rows of hanging pressed clothing—not smiling, just staring. I don't remember what took place in that hot room, but to this day I gag at the smell of dry-cleaning fluid.

Long into my adult life Dad behaved strangely with me. He would wet his lips and plant a big one on my mouth. I can still feel the back of my hand wiping away his spit. How dare he! But I never said a word. No one did, not even when he walked around the house naked, his big "thing" dancing before him. He showed it off every chance he got. It scared the heck out of me. When my best friend, Nash, came to visit, it scared the heck out of her, too. I know Mom was embarrassed, but he was boss.

Dad roared out of the driveway every morning in his latest sporty car, making sure no one missed his departure for work with those loud mufflers. At night he was the life of any party, entertaining his friends with dirty jokes and looking women (and me) up and down, as if drawing some conclusion I never understood.

But there was much more than that. Throughout my childhood I was wary of my dad's "down there" and what he might be thinking of doing next. In Dr. Fineberg's office, I began to remember Dad pressing his erect penis into my mouth. I was three years old the first time it happened; Mom was pregnant with Johnny. I had a vague fascination with that warm throbbing thing, and I probably had fun playing with it. I know I liked the attention and the extra TV time I got before bed if I sat on Dad's shoulders and rubbed his wrinkled neck while he drank Scotch and played with himself down there, probably thinking no one noticed. But in the morning I saw shame in his eyes, and I felt his distance. Somehow, I knew I was somewhere in the mix of that shame, even though I had no words for it. Our little secret was repeated over and over whenever he drank too much and Mommy was nowhere in sight.

Dad and I spent every August alone together in our rented cabin in Estes Park, partly to get me away from home during ragweed and hay fever season. He would come into my bedroom and lie next to me at night, pressing his stiffness into my buttocks before finally passing out. How it terrified me! This is when I learned to "fly," to travel a million miles across the star-filled sky. It was early training for later, during sex, or whenever things felt out of control.

Meanwhile, when Mom was ill and unavailable, Dad held the family together at home with the help of a housekeeper named Rose. He was my tormentor, hampering my sprouting self-worth, but he also could be a lot of fun. On weekends, he took us to the movies and to Jimmy's Drive-In for fries and banana splits, drove us around town in his convertible, and mixed me drinks although I was under age. We even got to ride sometimes on those shiny extended fenders he was so proud of. Now and then he would drop me and some friends at the movies and take us out for burgers and fries afterward. He would comment on whether my friends wore bras yet and gaze at my new breasts with a glazed look. "Your nipples are showing," he liked to say. I would turn away without a word.

From my mother I learned to be obedient and act refined, to wear a smile while my inner world sobbed its heart out. If I could help it, no one would suspect anything was wrong with our typical Midwestern family.

Over the next few months, Dr. Fineberg helped me accept this piece of the puzzle. The same pictures returned, and I was repulsed and anxious to "forget" them again. No wonder I'd been uncomfortable around my dad for most of my life. I also understood my intense addiction to cigarettes. They had been a sense of protection as a young teenager. I had even used one as defense against that poor cop in New York so long ago.

Those cigarettes represented the moments of deepest connection with my parents and especially my dad. The click of the Zippo, his hand cupping the flame against any wind, while I inhaled deeply of what seemed like love.

Charles was eager to hear about my hypnosis sessions. He held me lovingly as I recounted the events and told him of the memories I was stunned to see. But even with his boundless support, I felt a withdrawal into myself, and this concerned Charles, as he had never experienced such withdrawal in me. He continued coming toward me with his amazing enthusiasm to love me and work his magic as my sexual healer, and I was shutting down sexually. I didn't want to connect sexually or tantrically—or at all—as we had done every day for six years.

I admitted my dismay to Dr. Fineberg. It wasn't unusual to pull back from sexual connection when recalling sexual violation. Gradually, though, as memories of the tense and embarrassing moments I'd had with my father since the age of three swirled in my consciousness, it became harder to access the tantric queen Charles and I had grown to know and love.

"Let yourself be the age you were when you were too young to be sexual," Dr. Fineberg suggested. "Get to know the Carolyn of your childhood who needs the adult Caroline to love and protect her inner child."

I loved what she said and did as she suggested, hugging the soft pink "Yoni Bear" I'd bought for this occasion. As I uncovered more and more about my long-felt confusion with my father, all I wanted to do was stay home, buried in my comfort zones, reading books on sexual abuse recovery, and simply being a little girl. I realized those pictures in my mind's eye and that feeling in my heart from Dad's overstepping boundaries formed the basis for a lifetime of mistrust and discomfort with men, with my sexuality, and even with women. Mom had not saved me from him and had therefore betrayed me, too.

While my dad wasted away to cancer thousands of miles from me, I rebirthed myself not only with my beloved's patience and love, but also in healing sessions with Maria and Gabriella. The Divine Mother in both of those women poured into my heart, my psyche, and my yoni during sacred spot massage sessions in California and Maui. Imagine lying before these women, opening myself to trust their love entering me through their eyes, their hands, and the vast sincerity of their hearts.

"Surrender, Caroline. Let love in," said Charles, with the others taking their cue from him.

Charles worked overtime mastering his extraordinary skills, but it was a tender, difficult time to open sexually to my beloved, no matter how supportive he was of me. I felt protective, and my therapist believed I needed to be protective, of my three-year-old self right now. She suggested I consider not being sexual while recovering the abuse memories. When I told Charles of this, he said he wanted nothing to do with it. A year of abstinence! The idea was preposterous, counter to everything he believed about sexual healing. Charles believed that the love and tenderness of a beloved was the best medicine.

My own response wasn't easy to express. I felt they both were right. My deepest truth was that I wanted the freedom to spend this time reclaiming my identity as a pure and innocent three-year-old. But I had committed to a path of Tantra and sexual healing through Tantra, and I could not take a break for very long before I had to admit I was not "walking my talk."

After long and hard consideration, I decided to stop seeing my therapist. Trading Dr. Fineberg for prying open more of my heart to the love being offered seemed the path of least resistance. I am not sorry for the choice I made. How clear it seemed that I needed to open to more love to heal these newly discovered wounds. I allowed Charles to work with me in the ways we were used to doing, pushing past my resistance to uncover and unleash long-buried pain.

When I was at the onset of a urinary tract infection, which I had had almost monthly for a very long time, Charles would lovingly enter me with a gentle finger, barely moving as he held his movements very still. I would feel the rage and fear rise inside as he gently pressed on the tenderness of my emotional body. "You fucking son-of-a-bitch! I hate you!" I would scream, while he patiently replied, "This is your pain I am contacting, my beloved queen. I banish anyone who has been irreverent toward your sacred temple. Take my love into this place." I howled for as long as I needed to, until the pain was gone and my breath came more slowly. "We've chased Jack out of your sweet yoni temple," Charles would say then. "Only love and pleasure are here to stay."

I made my last trip to Florida to see my father just a month before he left his body. Charles came with me, ever the optimist, thinking he could speak the truth and my father would hear it. He rubbed my dad's feet and attempted to create connection between us. "Jack, you would be so proud of your daughter," he said, smiling into my father's expressionless face. "Our students love her. And she's the best wife a man could ever hope for." My dad may have grunted, or maybe he didn't do anything at all. Charles wasn't swayed. "Look into your daughter's eyes, Jack, and let her look into yours. Let the love between you touch your heart."

Dad was too far gone to care.

On the morning of my last visit, Charles waited outside while I went in to say goodbye. From across the living room I watched Anne tend to Dad in the hospital bed they had rented, now taking up most of the enclosed lanai. Dad was barely conscious. The sheet slipped, suddenly, revealing his large, flaccid penis. Suddenly everything fell into place. In the twenty seconds I was not seen across the room, with that view of my father's "cock," I said farewell to the story, farewell to the man who would never understand, farewell to the unresolved love. Our past would die with him. I would move on. I promised Anne I would call soon and raced to the airport with Charles to fly home to my extraordinary life.

When I was informed of Dad's death, I opted to forgo the funeral. I wanted to stay home where I felt safe and loved. I indulged myself in the time to grieve, to look through old photographs, to let my deepest and truest love for my father surface and nourish me. I recommitted to Charles my desire to love and be loved by all of the wonderful people who came into our lives with their hearts wide open. I dove into tantric sexual healing more than ever. I would learn to let myself be loved. Daily, I practiced forgiveness of my dad, to put my heart at peace. I would allow the process of healing to work its magic on me. And I kept a little photograph of him in an oval frame above our bed for a few months so he could "see" from wherever heaven was what conscious sexual loving looked like.

Maria, in the meantime, was flying high. Her Shakti fire breathed passion in her every breath, and her radiance stunned everyone who had known her those last few years before she reached out to Charles and me for help. We rejoiced with her regularly and were thrilled when she started practicing Tantra with a man named Shinzo whom she met at a seminar we gave in Santa Cruz.

Shinzo came to the United States from Japan at twenty years old. He barely spoke English, but he worked hard to save enough money to buy a small home in California. Nearly eighteen years later, he had a nice home and lot of work experience but very little experience with women. He and Maria were doing tantric healing together and trading Shiatsu massage and acupuncture. Maria assured me they were not meant to be lovers; they were dedicated students of Tantra and friends and healers for each other.

For some time, Maria and Charles had said they wanted me to receive the same quality of love and healing I gave to others and they thought Shinzo was perfect for me. "Queenie, you'll feel safe with Shinzo, I'm sure of it," Maria said. But nothing could make me resistant faster than feeling pressured. And I still wasn't comfortable with the thought of opening my sexuality to another man. The few tantric sexual connections I'd had with Cos and Moon, a lover of Blue's from Bali, had never been entirely comfortable for me.

Still, Shinzo was intriguing. His genuine beauty and presence interested me, and Maria was deeply impressed by his skills as a healer. I chose to accept a Shiatsu massage from him and see how it felt to surrender my body to his touch.

Ascending the Heights

Every February we celebrated our wedding anniversary with our intermediate Tantra students, and this year we celebrated our fifth wedding anniversary at the Mana Kai Hotel on Maui. The group of thirty students gave us a bouquet of five dozen red roses to honor the occasion, and we dressed in our ceremonial silks. After the seminar we expanded our celebration with invitations to our chosen lovers and friends to join us in tantric loving. Shinzo came that week, with Maria, and I accepted his invitation for a massage later in his room.

It was hard at first being alone with a man I barely knew, but Shinzo put me at ease with his genuine gentleness and supreme grace. I had never felt so honored before as teacher. In Japanese culture, teachers are sacred; their teachings are seen as bringing wholeness to the individual. Shinzo respected me with this same depth.

As I lay on the massage table listening to the surf break on the shore below, I breathed deeply into my desire to relax and surrender. But as soon as he put his hands on me, Shinzo's healing touch and loving compassion opened a well of grief inside me. I wept as Shinzo tenderly caressed my face and touched my heart center. "Car-o-line, everything going to be okay. I never take anything from you. I only here to be friend, to give you healing massage and give you place to feel safe."

By the end of that session, I trusted Shinzo with my heart. Here was a man who didn't want my sexuality; he only wanted to give me love and respect, and I felt that sincerely. The grief I had released made room for more love to fill my being, and I calmed, relaxing into his masterful Shiatsu massage. His shining face and smiling eyes matched the skill in his hands, and I felt renewed.

By the end of the weeklong seminar I felt the courage to plan my first sacred spot healing session with Shinzo, as long as Charles and Maria would be present. They promised to be there. I also wanted Jahlia there, to sing. She sang during the seminar and in mini-concerts throughout the week, and her music always soothed my soul.

I was determined to maintain a sense of openness to this opportunity to receive love and healing from a male healer, but I worried. What if I loved the quality of Shinzo's love too much? Was there really room in my marriage, in my heart, for another man's love? I was extremely vulnerable when my Shakti opened to a man.

We left the hotel in Kihei the morning after the closing night puja, returning home to the other side of Maui. Our good friends Ricky and Susea had attended the seminar that week, and I invited them to come to Huelo to witness my healing, along with Charles, Maria, and Jahlia.

Late on a rainy night in Huelo we all met at our temple for the tantric healing ritual. We made up the futon by the fireplace with colorful soft sheets and placed a stack of fluffy towels by the futon to collect any amrita that might flow. Charles started a fire, I lit candles, and Maria placed vases of fragrant night-blooming jasmine around the futon. We burned white sage in the main living room to clear the energy and then sat in a circle around the futon, holding hands, stating our intentions, and saying thanks. I looked into everyone's adoring faces and said, "I want to honor my beloved, Charles, for supporting me in this healing ritual. Beloved, I trust you and your vision of sexual healing. I love you eternally. Maria, I feel safe with you. I trust you enough to surrender to your healing friend, Shinzo. You are claiming your radiance and sexual power, and I am very impressed." I caught Jahlia's eyes and felt my voice break as the tears welled up. "Jahlia, you and I have come through a lot of joy and a lot of doubt to get to this evening. Thank you from the bottom of my heart for your unconditional love and understanding of me as a woman and sister. Ricky and Susea, I honor your twenty-five years of marriage and yet you are willing to learn how to trust in the ritual of sexual healing. Your friendship touches me deeply. I offer my Shakti and this healing to all women, who, like Susea and me, carry fear and mistrust of sexual power, which holds us back from greater love. Here's to you, Sister Susea." Jahlia offered sacred chants and songs of opening to love as we then prepared for "the queen" to receive.

I sat on the bed cross-legged, facing Shinzo and gazing deeply into his kind eyes. I felt some fear and slight resistance but I opened myself to the moment so beautifully prepared by these loving friends. Shinzo seemed so fully available. "Shinzo," I said, "your massage is masterful. You are so present with me. Thank you for wanting to give me this experience." Shinzo bowed in Namaste. "I am honored, Caroline, to be chosen by you and Charles as your healer. It is with the greatest respect to my teachers that I offer you my love."

With that, Shinzo artfully laid my body down and began touching me, stretching out my arms and legs as he moved gracefully around my body. Charles was on one side of me, holding and kissing my hand, while Maria held my other hand, petted my hair, and assured me all was well. Every time I opened my eyes there were eyes of love looking back at me.

Shinzo's loose black pants left his strong and youthful body free to move as he adjusted my sarong to cover my yoni, moving around my body, touching, massaging, stroking. The candles flickered, the fire crackled, and my kitties Tai and Chi purred beside me, comforting me as Shinzo massaged my sacrum, my pubic bone, and my groin. I watched his every move, felt the mastery in his hands. Before long I felt warm and relaxed. This man was impeccable in every way—gentle in how he looked at me, tender in his touch, precious in all ways. When he looked into my eyes and said, "May I enter your sacred temple, Caroline?" I eagerly granted permission.

Shinzo's fingers danced lightly into my labia—agonizingly slow, never rushed. With a face full of smiles and eyes filled with sparkling stars, I knew Shinzo loved his work.

What I experienced next was nothing short of amazing. Almost immediately I was releasing amrita in orgasmic waves that rocked me for the next half-hour or more. We never measured the quantity of my amrita, but judging by the soaked layer of four towels and the futon wet through to the other side, I would have to guess at least a liter or more of ejaculate poured out of me. I laughed and howled in ecstatic pleasure for what seemed like hours.

Shinzo's touch was a perfect combination of yin and yang—slow and gentle alternating with fast and deep. He knew just when to slow down and when to speed up his strokes. The love pouring from his eyes touched me even more deeply than the physical touch to my body. Even with his fingers completely still, my yoni contracted so strongly the amrita continued to pulse from the deep well within.

Joy and excitement filled the room as all of our sounds joined in celebration of the release of my life force. Maria and Charles were like a cheerleading team celebrating my opening and surrender. Ricky and Susea waltzed about the living room, sounding and singing, and Jahlia, goddess of song, accompanied with lyre, voice, guitar, and piano. Even the cats sat up in full attention at this glorious event.

The evening ended when we all decided it was late and we needed rest. Maria and Shinzo stayed in the upstairs guestroom for a few days to practice and play with us, and Ricky and Susea stayed in the downstairs guestroom. Jahlia always found a sleeping nest on one of my soft couches or left in the night as silently as she had arrived. When she did stay overnight, she was always there to serve us pots of English tea and cappuccinos in the morning when we woke. I found fresh towels washed and folded in the laundry room, the kitchen spotless, and the temple vacuumed and clean. Love and thoughtfulness abounded.

In Japanese, "shinzo" means "heart," or "the heart that loves." The heart that loves had arrived to take me into higher realms. And I was ready to go. Shinzo had chosen to study Tantra with us because he wanted to learn about his sexuality. I marveled at his skill. He was knowing, sensitive, beautiful, completely balanced in his masculine and feminine qualities. I was entranced. I would need to tread lightly upon this communion with a being so beautiful he almost seemed unreal. Everything about him was different from Charles, yet complementary in many lovely ways. Shinzo was a master in Shiatsu, and he had a black belt in Aikido, but in Tantra, he considered himself a student. His erotic innocence opened me in a new way. I had never been seen or touched by anyone so filled with innocence.

There were several more sacred spot and massage sessions before Shinzo returned to California, and before he left we arranged to meet in Santa Cruz the next month. Maria would join us for a night at a quaint inn, and we would continue our practice. Charles celebrated my willingness to continue tantrically connecting with Shinzo. He would stay at Mama's, an hour south of Santa Cruz, and await my call the following morning.

The anticipation of an entire night with Shinzo sometimes made it hard to sleep as our special weekend approached. Cuddled in the arms of my beloved, I would dream of Shinzo, feeling him hover close to me as my body would arch in orgasmic quivers. I was learning how deeply my sexual body is connected to my emotional body.

When the night in California finally came, I arrived at the inn feeling nervous. I could tell there could be a significant breakthrough in healing my discomfort over sharing Charles with the women in our life. By the end of the weekend, that healing would indeed occur, but not at all in the way I originally imagined.

The weekend began with Shinzo and Maria's arrival at the inn, and we visited for a while, then bathed and rolled back the sheets on the bed where our night would take place. Maria sensed my tension and she held me, gave me an acupuncture treatment to help calm me, and assured me she would be right there with me in my willingness to open to the healing love of another man.

Then it was time for the loving to begin. Shinzo's touch was like angel's kisses, and my passion was aroused from the depth of my being as minutes turned to hours and hours went long into the night. I received Shinzo's loving touch, healing massage, sweet kisses, and respectful adoration while Maria was genuinely happy to simply be there holding space for me to open and surrender. Like a Divine Mother, Maria selflessly and willingly supported my opening to Shinzo's love and passion. She assured me Charles wanted this for me, and we invoked his presence many times during the night.

I had been shy about even looking at Shinzo's lingam, let alone pleasuring him or inviting him inside of me. But at last, after many sacred spot sessions and the flowing of much amrita, I asked Shinzo if he would enter me with his lingam. It seemed strange to be with another man besides Charles in this way, and I was doubtful of the intelligence of this connection, but I wasn't sure if my doubt came from conditioning or because of what I knew I was capable of feeling. Here was my opportunity to allow deep surrender to this healing man if I wanted it; here was the possibility of the breakthrough I knew I needed.

Shinzo accepted my invitation. Tenderly, he entered me with his lingam, gazing deep into my eyes and giving me a sense of being completely loved all the while. I felt his energy permeate my sacred domain as he elegantly moved inside me, generating energy through his wand and moving that energy around in circles. I relaxed into the pleasure of the subtle power in his lovemaking. How completely different this was from my lovemaking with Charles! His lingam was smaller than Charles' but he used his wand creatively, moving in and around me like a dancer might fill the dance floor with the aliveness of his body. I couldn't contain my squeals of delight.

Certain I was comfortable and in good hands, after some time Maria slipped quietly away to rest on the sofa in another part of the room, leaving me to explore this connection. For the entire night I received the tireless energy of this lover man from another planet. Never had I encountered this quality of yin, not from a woman or a man. It was as though a feather was moving about and around my body, knowing exactly where to go at every moment. He knew how to kiss me, how to touch me, how to waltz me under his lithe body, how to carry me effortlessly into ecstatic responses. We loved until dawn, when it was finally time for us to sleep. Shinzo sweetly thanked me over and over for allowing him this opportunity to love me and practice Tantra with me. He bowed before my yoni and then delicately tasted my nectar with unmatched refinement. He pressed his heart to mine as he melted into my eyes with respect and honor, and we wrapped our arms around each other and slept peacefully until sometime in the mid-morning.

When we awoke, opening our eyes at the same instant, we kissed softly to begin the new day, transformed by what had transpired in the night. Maria had crept into bed while we were sleeping, and she cuddled with us, sharing the bond of deep friendship. After showering, we breakfasted in the patio, surrounded by fragrant vines of climbing yellow roses. We sipped steaming green tea and filled our plates with fruit, scrambled eggs, bacon, and warmed croissants. At the end of our meal, Shinzo said, "I so sorry, Caroline and Maria, but I must go to work. I am very happy and very grateful for your love."

Shinzo had eight massages to give that day. He bowed and, with a soft kiss goodbye to each of us, slipped away into the morning sun as delicately as he had slipped into my heart and soul the night before.

What a night! I hoped I would never again question the connection between my sexuality, my heart, and a man's lingam. I understood at last that the quality of energy that emanates from a man's lingam, not the size of it, has the power to transform me. It's the consciousness, love, and magic the lingam transmits that affects me so much.

I was in an altered state. I wanted only to sit in the sun and day-dream about my delicious night while Maria listened to the few words I could utter. After some time, she gently reminded me to call Charles.

"Oh my God!" I cried. "I almost forgot!"

Charles' voice on the other end of the line was enthusiastic. "It's you, my beloved. How did it go?"

"I think I'm in love," I said.

Charles didn't miss a beat. "You mean the healing went well?"

"Yes, I suppose you could say the healing went well."

Charles could handle anything. He could stay centered, grounded, and true to his belief that to love is good no matter where I went or what I said. I felt I was in deep water with a life raft at my side.

And so, Shinzo and I became lovers. With Shinzo in my heart, Charles could have the space to heal and enjoy every woman in the world if he so desired. And through it all, he proved how in balance he was about sharing me with a good and worthy brother. Charles wanted his beloved to be loved, as simple as that. The men showed tremendous respect for each other and offered each other great honor in loving me, and I easily found room enough in my heart to love them both.

The test for me in this dance of more love was in maintaining balance. I couldn't shake the presence of this man in every breath I took. I lost myself in writing poetry and long letters to Shinzo, expressing my love for him. We spoke most evenings on the phone as I ran from whatever I was doing to answer the ring that I knew must be him calling. And whenever Charles and I were in the Bay area of California, we rented two suites at the Highlands Inn in Carmel so Maria could spend those nights with Charles and I was free to soar into the heights with my samurai warrior of love. In Carmel, after hugs and hellos, Shinzo and I would go to our suite and Charles and Maria would stay together for their night of healing and love. Charles was thoroughly entertained by his time with her, but demons still came from Maria, rage at the atrocities that had happened in her childhood, and part of it was work. My time with Shinzo was all pleasure. When Charles would check in by phone from his room down the hall and request a visit, I sometimes refused, finding it hard to adjust to the sudden shift in energy. Sometimes they came anyway, to cuddle with us or sit on the bed. I would occasionally connect sexually with Charles with Shinzo present, but I was always glad to see them leave so I could be alone with my lover. When we four were together, Charles and Shinzo never made love to one another, but they shared their love in beautiful and respectful ways. Shinzo bowed before Charles as his teacher, vowing to always uphold the integrity of Charles' marriage to me.

I had learned the tantric dance of love with Charles. Shinzo had learned the dance in our classrooms, watching us simulate tantric lovemaking with positions, breathing techniques, eye-gazing, the art of sensual touch, the beauty of connection. And now he was taking me to new heights, filling the air with poetry in the way his body moved, in the dance of light pouring from his eyes. Meaningful conversation is a great aphrodisiac and essential to my Shakti awakening, and we delighted in this. We also enjoyed giving and receiving massage before, during, and after sexual connection. We followed our energies, tasted the flavors, experimented with our bodies' movements in variations of creative flexibility, bathed one another, played as children might play. Tantric love is a rhythmic dance, with fast steps followed by slow glides and focus on the art of kissing and deep heart connection, while our genitals rested and then pulsed their passion back into action. Equal in value to movement are the periods of quiet breathing together as I sat astride his lap in shared meditation.

Shinzo and I spent a full night together every month, practicing Tantra and sharing our love. Until I saw him again the following month, his beautiful energy danced through me everywhere I went. I never wanted those nights to end. This man had come on angel wings and found a home on the altar of my heart.

As my love for Shinzo grew, so did my friendship with Maria, and I wanted her closer to me. She considered my request for a few days, then called to say yes, she would accept my invitation to move to Maui to be nearer. We gave her a room at our office—the three-bedroom beach house—while she looked for a home of her own. This way we could see each other daily and still have our autonomy.

Right away, Maui made a new woman of Maria. She grew her hair long and sun-bleached it, had a breast reduction that made her more comfortable in her petite frame, and had her almond-shaped eyes cosmetically changed to look even more almond-shaped. She took up Indian and Indonesian dance and lived the way she'd dreamed of living for so long. When Mary Anne, her twenty-year-old daughter, visited and saw how Maui's magic was working on her mother, she decided to move to the island, too. She was guarded with us at first, but she knew of her mother's love for us, and before long she relaxed and became a dear friend. Mary Anne often joined her mother on visits to our home, and holidays at our house always included the two of them. Our extended family had expanded in new and beautiful ways.

One day, Maria and her daughter asked me to do a sacred spot session with Mary Anne. I was honored they would trust me to imprint Mary Anne with massage to her sacred spot to arouse and awaken her sleeping life force. A virgin except for a brief and disappointing boyfriend in high school, Mary Anne was frightened of her passion. We scheduled the session for Easter Sunday, which was coming up. Charles would be with his mother in California and the three of us would have my home to ourselves.

On Easter morning, I greeted them in ceremonial silks, after turning our bedroom into even more of a temple with vases of white lilies circling the bed and laying out my colorful Balinese bedcover. We bathed in the spa, relaxing into the warmth and comfort of our energy, and then toweled dry and went inside. After prayers and invocations to spirit, Mary Anne invited me to begin the ritual.

Maria lay at her daughter's side, where she could stroke her hair and gaze at her with all the love a mother can offer. I sat between Mary Anne's legs, massaging her for a long enough time so she could become comfortable with my touch and my energy. I coached her breathing as I placed one hand gently over her mound of Venus and my other hand gently on her heart center. This caused Mary Anne to vibrate as her Shakti began to awaken. After a long period of massage, breathing and sounding, with her permission I very slowly entered her yoni and placed my touch tenderly upon the core of her second chakra, her sacred spot. A surge of her life force almost rocked her off the bed. Maria held her daughter close to her body, assuring her this was natural, this was the power of Shakti moving through her. We told Mary Anne she could claim this birthright; she just needed to breathe deeply and allow sounds to escape from her throat, the sounds of birthing herself. Mary Anne did as she was asked, and soon her sexual energy flowed freely throughout her. Joy replaced fear in her face as she claimed her sexual/ spiritual power for the first time. She maintained eye contact with us the entire time, unless we suggested she close her eyes and look inward for the energy running from her sacred spot into her brain. She said, "I see a golden light flowing through me. Is that it?"

After a time, we rested quietly, holding the sacred space and breathing in what had happened. Then Mary Anne spoke. "Mom," she whispered, "does your body rock and roll when you're running your energy?"

"Yes, Mary Anne," her mother said. "This is the power of the goddess within you. This is your life force. Own it, my darling daughter.

Never give it away to anyone who is not deserving of it."

What transpired next was nothing short of miraculous. Mary Anne said, "Would it be all right if my mother touches my sacred spot? I want her to initiate me, too."

I looked to Maria, who met my gaze and nodded. The deep knowing in her eyes told me she had expected this request. With the grace of an empress, Maria took my place between her daughter's legs. I lay beside Mary Anne and held her in my embrace as Maria touched her reverently, assuring Mary Anne of her beauty, purity, and passion. With permission, integrity, and love, a divine mother entered her daughter's yoni slowly with the two middle fingers of her right hand, her left hand resting on her daughter's heart center. She then spoke words of empowerment. "Awaken," she said, as she touched Mary Anne's goddess spot. "Claim your power."

Profound only begins to describe my feelings for this ritual of tantric awakening. Shining this much love into the forbidden and the fearful between women, I believe, cures centuries of separation. I held Mary Anne in my arms and gazed into her eyes throughout the sacred event, held on Easter, a holy day for so many. In years to come I would witness other mothers and daughters enter into this ritual of awakening together in my groups of women healing women. The power of this exchange ripples out into the ocean of the Feminine and heals wounds in the snake pit there can be between mothers and daughters.

It is never a good idea to "over-amp" someone. When we felt Mary Anne had run enough of her Shakti for the first day, we ended the session by gently stopping all movement and massage and meditating together on the energy flowing through and among the three of us. This sexual healing practice releases huge amounts of stored energy, and it is best to proceed in increments rather than attempting to fully awaken someone in one session. They may not be able to integrate that much energy all at once.

Mary Anne was grateful for her newly found identity as a sexual woman. She understood how to let the Shakti energy run through her, and she knew the value of breathing deeply and vocalizing. We cuddled and talked for a long time and then rested again in the warmth of the outdoor hot tub. Together we cooked up a celebratory meal with a fresh green salad, grilled island fish, and glasses of chilled Champagne.

When they left mid-afternoon, I lay down in my bedroom to integrate the day. I hadn't thought it possible that my belief in the power of Tantra and the power of love could deepen, but it had; another miracle I placed in my ever-filling cup of life-changing experiences. I realized the tremendous honor of working with young people who knew that an experience like this was essential to their unfolding consciousness.

Later that year Maria's son came to Maui to see what all the joy was about. Maria asked me to offer Bobby a tantric experience, and I agreed to do it. She would not be part of this ritual as she had been with her daughter, but she wanted her son, too, to understand the sacred art of loving.

Bobby's eyes were wide and round when he walked through my door for his evening with me. We talked for some time, to get comfortable together, and then I asked him if he would like to receive a session like I had given his sister. He was excited and nervous as I led him to my celestial bed and proceeded to massage his strong young body. Sitting between his legs, I massaged his entire genital region, frequently contacting his heart center and teaching him that the power he felt in his lingam must be equally felt in his heart. I taught him the necessity of deep breathing and sounding and maintaining eye contact. He kept shaking his head and laughing, exclaiming, "I can't believe this is what my mother wanted for me."

Bobby was transformed by the experience. He said he would never be the same now that he was a conscious lover. To this day he is grateful for what he learned about himself as a man and for what he learned about loving women.

Maria had come into my life an ailing healer. She brought her hope, faith, and willingness as she opened and tapped into the life force still inside her. I had learned much from my student, as all good teachers do. I had learned about the possibilities for healing into passionate release and abandon, I had witnessed profound sharing of the most sacred passages between mother and daughter, I had seen a young man be loved into wholeness in ways most sons never are. Maria's steady support and loving friendship had led me into the heartful, artful arms of the first man other than Charles that I loved in my core. With her friendship I would travel halfway around the world and back, finally, to myself.

Chapter Sixteen

The World Turns Upside-Down

Five years had passed since our vacation-honeymoon in Bali and the edges of burnout were coming closer. We needed a vacation. In bed one afternoon with my beloved, I conceived the idea of a group vacation, a time for us to celebrate love with our "bouquet of lovers," and Bali was the perfect place. I had received some money from my mother's estate, and celebrating love with our lovers seemed a beautiful offering to my mother, who had chosen so little love in her life. Maria, Gabriella and her son, Nalu, and Jahlia would come, along with Shinzo, who had been my lover now for nearly a full year. Emerald Starr had asked us for years to stay at his place in Bali near the Kings Water Palace at Tirrtiganga. He had access to a number of rooms there as well as to a Balinese house adjacent to his. His cook would prepare our meals, and we could stay as long as we wanted.

That day, I called and invited everyone. They were thrilled. We would leave in early December, as soon as our seminars were done for the year. The rainy season would have started by then in Bali, but we didn't care. It was a magic carpet ride gifted to us by my mother, and we all felt blessed by the opportunity.

And then, as it can do, from out of nowhere, tragedy struck. Michael, our devoted and essential business assistant and friend, broke his neck in a swimming accident three days before our departure for Bali. We dropped everything and took off for Queens Hospital in Honolulu, where Michael was in intensive care, his head braced in a clamp. In an instant, Michael flew from the background to the foreground of our priorities.

Michael was someone you could count on. He managed everything, from office affairs to car repairs. And he was like a brother, Midwestern to his core. We were a team: Michael took care of Charles in running the Tantra business; I took care of Charles in living the Tantra business.

Charles and I sat with Michael at the hospital, holding his hands and trying to adjust to the staggering news that he would likely be paralyzed from his neck to his toes for the rest of his life. Sitting with him just twenty-four hours after his accident, we wondered if we should cancel our trip. Was he in good enough hands without us? We had been delirious with excitement for this trip. Almost imperceptibly, Michael mouthed, "Go. Friends and nurses and doctors will help."

We agreed that we really needed this vacation. The Tantra business would go on hold for a month, Charles would have rest and time to plan how to proceed without Michael, while Michael received the care he needed. When we returned we would decide what to do to help our dear friend. We left the hospital with tremendously heavy hearts.

Bali was everything I remembered and all I dreamed of. We arrived a few days before our friends, giving us time to visit Cos and Blue in their house here, and Moon, a friend and lover in our extended family of friends, was also there to welcome us to Bali.

We languished in love and laughter, swam in the clear blue waters, and held each other close under the glittering stars. Nibbles of LSD were one of the many pleasures that added color to the temperate Balinese nights. From the start, our vacation was an altered reality, a thrill-a-minute adventure for this pioneering queen from Prairie Village, Kansas.

Three days later, we packed a taxi van with our luggage for the two-hour drive to the Water Palace, where, that night, those just meeting each other would get acquainted over dinner. I looked forward to greeting these friends coming in from the States, but Shinzo was the one I was most thrilled to see. This vacation would add more excitement to my life than ever, with my passion for him at an all-time high. Every day Charles teased, "How many more hours until Shinzo arrives, my queen?" or "How many more minutes until you see him getting out of the cab from the airport?" "Why don't you take a cab to meet him at the airport, my queen? Then you'll have a whole hour more with your lover." Could this be real? His eyes were filled with love for me. I could touch the love, feel the sweetness of such a good life. Everything was perfect, except for Michael. The contrast of this much light and this much darkness mirrored the constant dynamic struggle between the forces of dark and light in Bali. Balinese spiritual tradition respected the forces of darkness, often depicting demons in their art to protect the gods and goddesses.

When it was finally time to meet our friends at the airport in Denpasar, I tried to calm myself. I knew there wouldn't be instant gratification for me after their long flight. Everyone would need to get a good night's sleep to acclimate to this culture on the other side of the globe. But when they got off the plane, that spinning wheel of love picked me up and took me for another unexpected turn.

Gabriella and Shinzo had met, and their passion outshined the stunning beauty of this Indonesian island. They had recognized the beloved in each other right away.

I was reeling. Was it true? Shinzo wouldn't be my lover in this paradise? Would he ever be my lover again? Charles was sad for me and disappointed not to make love with Gabriella in Bali, and Jahlia and Maria comforted us both, offering support, while Nalu gave us some perspective with his pleasure at all the love around him. Charles and I were grateful to at least have each other, but when we left the Water Palace to lease a three-story bamboo house in Legian, a block from the beach, shops, and restaurants, I found my heart heavy as I daily said goodbye to the ecstasy of loving with Shinzo. He was blinded by his connection with Gabriella, although he gallantly continued his respectful friendship with me. One morning, when I saw Gabriella's face after having been loved all night, I felt rage burn inside me, physical, vengeful anger that didn't at all fit with the person I felt I'd become. Maria helped, with acupuncture healings and the steady support of her love, and Jahlia, as always, was a gentling presence. She showed me how to make the most out of these weeks in Bali, reminding me that shopping can be a best friend when the going gets tough. "Hit the pavement, girlfriend," she told me. And hit the pavement I did. Daily, colorful plastic bags covered the bamboo bed and chairs in our rented house as I did my best to chase away rejection and disappointment. I felt "over the hill," in denial of what I needed to remember but wasn't ready to know: the beloved was within me, *not* in another.

There we were, in Bali, while Michael lay in the hospital in Honolulu in pain and shock and possibly paralyzed for the rest of his life. What irony was this? What really mattered compared to Michael's situation?

Traveling home through Singapore three weeks—and what felt a lifetime—later, Charles and I stopped for an exotic feast at the Raffles Hotel. We sat holding hands, feeling humbled, our egos slain. Charles reminded me that we were in tantric relationships to awaken, heal, and prepare our loved ones for their own beloved. All of our friends and lovers wanted what we had—they wanted their soul mate and beloved to enter their lives. Sipping Singapore Slings and gazing into each other's eyes across the table at this grand old hotel halfway around the world, we fell in love again. We would ride this raft of our loving friendship through all of the ups and downs. Belovedness was teaching me lessons all the time.

For three years, Shinzo and Gabriella would be beloveds, until their love affair ended as suddenly as it had begun. Gabriella would call me one night, asking if I would consider accepting Shinzo again as a lover, but I didn't feel the safety and trust I needed to become lovers again. I had forgiven Gabriella for her part in turning Shinzo's attention from me, but I had lost the spark for re-igniting my passion for Shinzo. There would no doubt be eventual recapitulation within my Tantric marriage.

When we saw Michael again, a month after the accident, he was paralyzed—a quadriplegic—and propped up in a wheelchair. What would his life be like? Would he ever walk again? Ever make love again? Would he be able to teach anyone all he knew about running our business? The fragility of life was with us in every breath, in every moment.

We jumped into action. Michael would stay at our office/house and we would assemble a group of caregivers for him. We had no idea how long it would be for, and we didn't care. Kyle and Jade had been the two friends who pulled Michael out of the surf at Little Beach the day his head hit the sand bar. Now Kyle and Jade came through again, as they built wheelchair ramps and installed a hospital bed with a special crane to lift Michael in and out of the bed. Everything that could be different suddenly needed to be.

I loved Michael, and I was committed to being one of his primary caregivers. This freed Charles to get his business on its feet. For the next eight years I would spend at least one day every week or so with Michael. I would clean for him, tend to personal needs such as exercising his legs or changing his catheter, open his mail, answer letters, make his bank deposits, purchase stamps, exchange videos at the video store, and do a myriad of other things he could no longer do for himself. There were meals each day to be prepared, medications to administer. Visiting nurses and aides handled his bowel program and the early morning hours of getting him ready for his day.

I couldn't imagine living under these conditions. "Michael," I asked him one day, "wouldn't you rather have died in the water than live like this?"

"Oh, Caroline," he smiled, "and never get to look into your beautiful blue eyes again?"

Michael's sense of humor was unfailing, and his support team was huge. Maria offered her love and her acupuncture treatments; Mary Anne helped however she could; a physical therapist gave Michael his daily range-of-motion exercises; Jade and Kyle came forward with regular help; Miriam worked day in and out with Michael running the office; Marbie, Michael's former sweetheart and forever friend, was always a presence. These were part of a long list of friends who assisted Michael in learning how to live as a quadriplegic. Our Maui *ohana* (family) rose to the occasion like nothing I had ever witnessed.

Michael's daily care regimen took many hours, but we managed because there were so many of us to help. We took shifts, we bartered shifts, we double-shifted, and we consistently came with joy and laughter into Michael's room for the intensely responsible time we spent with him.

Michael loved hearing of the escapades of my life. I kept him entertained with stories of lost loves and gained lovers and cried over my frustrations while he laughed over my freedom.

Daily cards, letters, and donations for Michael's care poured into the office. Tantra students from far and wide who had met Michael in Maui and remembered his warm and friendly ways sent their support. Their donations turned the tide for Michael. With them he was able to purchase top-of-the-line wheelchairs instead of having to settle for insurance-covered models. His six-foot-six-inch frame just didn't fit into a compact, cost-effective chair. Eventually, Michael made it back to work, although everything took a long time for him to do since he had to use a voice-activated computer.

Charles envisioned Tantric sexual healings for Michael, and he came up with ways for us to have them. He suggested that Maria and I use our amrita to help with our intention to heal his neck and spine. We managed to do this, to Michael's great glee. We held his limp hands against our yonis and ejaculated down his arms. We crawled along his body while releasing our amrita on his throat, neck, chest, belly, and genitals. We held his numb feet to our warm hearts and yonis, shining our love into his eyes.

Michael was game for just about anything and he knew that anything was possible. We are a family that believes in miracles, and especially in the miracle of love. For a special occasion, we arranged for Michael to be driven down to our temple during an advanced teaching week for dakinis. In a special ritual we carried him from his chair and laid him on the carpeted floor, which we'd covered with waterproof sheets. Then, seven high-powered Shakti women adored him with our eyes, breasts, hands, lips, and amrita. We swear his toes wiggled during this event, although Michael has yet to rise to his full stature and walk again. But his temperature rose from this adventure, so we decided to back off and not take a chance on over-amping our fragile giant.

Everyone came to the annual black-tie fundraisers, or balls, that Michael organized at the Maui Country Club. They were the talk of the island. Michael was there to greet everyone in his tux and his Mercedes-quality wheelchair, a score of beautiful females surrounding him, as he was the only man with nowhere else to go. He could be fully present with you, which became much of his appeal.

In time, Michael would regain use of the few muscle groups still available in his arms and shoulders with the help of our friend Paul, a personal trainer, who worked with Michael for months, finding unique ways for him to develop what muscles he still could. He would learn to sign his name, move objects with his fingers, hug a friend, feed himself, and even learn how to drive a fully appointed van for the disabled. Michael—the unsung hero of my life and my heart—is a Maui miracle.

Chapter Seventeen

✦

Goddess of the Moon

After losing Shinzo, more than ever I wanted to withdraw from expanded loving for a time and focus on "just the two of us." But Charles saw it as a call to get back on the horse. Here was an opportunity for me to keep my heart open and cultivate more love. He suggested that we each be free to spend twenty-four hours apart in any way we desired, two nights a month. These would be what we called our "sovereignty nights."

I longed for a solution, and so I agreed, unaware that I could be quite desolate if Charles had someone to spend these nights with and I did not. And the chances of my having someone special to share these nights with was small since I could only share with someone who made my heart soar, and that didn't happen often. I could always round up some willing tantric lovers, but to be satisfied I needed to be in love.

And so it was, on sovereignty nights, with Charles having a variety of friends and lovers to choose from, that I deepened at home alone, doing ecstatic dance, yoga, and self-pleasuring into divine love with myself. After that, I lay in bed wondering all night what Charles was doing with his lovers and friends. I tried a few lovers, but nothing made my heart sing and I preferred to be alone.

Then I met Innana, a respected shamanic therapist on Maui, and I drove to her office to find out if her help was what I needed.

From the moment we met, I had the feeling that Innana could lead me to the kind of transformation I wanted. Every week I drove to her cozy upstairs office at her jungle home and poured my heart out. Sitting on bright colored cushions, I described my dad's death, my retrieved memories, and my choice to heal myself through Tantra and sexual healing. There was so much to explain, and talking about it took me further into my confusion about exactly what I believed in.

Charles was the source and center of my life, the beloved who was loving me into wholeness through the practices of Tantra. I told Innana of my choice to enter into tantric marriage with him, even though at the time I didn't fully understand what that meant or how it would feel in practice. We talked about the ecstasy of loving in a tantric way, about the multiorgasmic hours of bliss that matched the exchange of lover and beloved adoring one another. I described the many experiences with others we'd had during our years together, and the miraculous healings I'd witnessed and participated in. I praised my beloved for his skills as a tantric healer and conscious lover, best friend and companion, co-teacher, and husband, and for his consistent and tender love for me. And I expressed my confusion. "How come I'm not happy!?"

Innana was love in balance, the steady ground I could walk on and feel completely safe. She felt my feelings with me; she held me like the mother I longed for; she joined me step by step in excavating the layers covering my tender core. My trust in Innana gave me the strength to trust in myself. Somehow I would need to learn to shift my center of emotional gravity to my own self, away from my beloved Charles alone.

I was still shaken by the realization of my father's sexual desire for me, the drunken pressure of his penis to my mouth when I was a little girl, his frequent stalking about the house with a huge erection. For forty-five years I'd fought believing this was the truth. Now, a year after his death, I had come to terms with these truths and could focus on the buried hurts from the past nine years with Charles. Doing breathwork, shamanic journeys, and many other modalities with Innana let free my festering rage. In the safety of Innana's intelligent love and skillful therapies, I recalled comments Charles had made, like, "Oh, Blue, your ass is so exciting," or to Maria, "I can make you come all the way from the kitchen into the living room," and a range of other comments that seemed outside the teachings of a conscious tantric healer. Was this my beloved? Was it my dad? I knew Charles never meant to say or do anything to hurt me, but his New York "guy" talk pushed my buttons.

Innana listened without allowing me to judge Charles and without judging him herself. As much as I tried to make him wrong, she kept bringing the work back to me, to my choices and my unresolved needs. I agonized over the expanded tantric practice within my marriage and the choice I'd made to live this life with my beloved mate. I described how Charles loved me and the life we lived as Tantra teachers. We were adored by so many we had helped and taught. I explored my need for love as I regaled her with tales of the orgasmic bliss I knew in this relationship with Charles. I told her of my love for Shinzo and of my heartbreak with him.

With Innana's wise and compassionate counseling, the knot of confusion and tension in my heart slowly began to unwind. My biggest fear was that I would go crazy, like my mother, and be institutionalized. Charles sometimes called me crazy in his frustration with my conflicted feelings, which only worried me more. Innana assured me I was far from crazy. Her reassurance was exactly what I needed.

During the early months of work with Innana I shared my progress with Charles, assuring him that Innana did not prescribe celibacy while I experienced the feelings of my childhood recollections. I wanted him to know about how I was evolving, and I longed for him to join me with Innana. He did come with me from time to time, but just to support me; he didn't feel he needed any more clarity than he had.

For a year, in weekly hour-long sessions, I continued to uncover more about my childhood experiences with my father and mother and heal them. We discussed my marital issues, and I became able to recognize what ran my emotional life. We did several all-night shamanic healing journeys. As each knot unloosed and my authentic self revealed itself more clearly to us both, there was Innana, grounded and unconditionally loving, to help me sort out who I was becoming. She wrestled me to the floor and helped my arms pound and my legs kick. We exhausted my pent-up rage until I could think with my heart and my mind in the clear vision of their union. Whatever it took, Innana said, we were in it together.

Innana's respect for me grew as I shared session after session about the courage it took to love my beloved this much. She eventually sent us clients of hers who were working on sexual issues, and we shared our wisdom with them. Innana was interested in the effects this had on her clients, and she was interested in my life in general. Finally, I decided the best way for her to truly understand my life was to become a part of it.

Before talking with Innana about this, I asked Charles to open his heart to include my therapist in our tantric healing excursions with others. He accepted, knowing her importance to me. Next, I encouraged Innana to work with Charles and receive his sexual healing and awakening skills. She considered this. She had a new love, she told me, a man she had met on a trip she'd made to Ecuador. After weeks of joining their spirits and hearts, Robert had asked Innana if she practiced the tantric ways of loving back home, "in real life." Innana did not practice Tantra in her seventeen-year marriage, and she had been thinking deeply about how she could include Robert in her marriage without abandoning her husband.

The moment Innana agreed to practice Tantra with me and partake intimately in my life with Charles, our client/therapist relationship ended and our friendship began. We trusted each other. We had what was necessary for each other's lives to unfold, and we entered into sacred sisterhood as we planned Innana's first visit to our home and the beginning of her sexual awakening. The sisterhood is the key to weaving Feminine power and love into a safety net for expanded healing and awakening experiences, and without question, Innana and I were sisters in spirit.

The next week, Innana and her husband, Sash, came to our home for the evening. Charles and Maria took Sash to another part of the house to talk and I prepared to work with Innana. We started with massage as she lay on a futon by the fireplace. I touched this dear friend with my hands and a heart filled with love. Here was a woman who had pulled me through some very transformative therapeutic sessions with total dedication. My eyes shone their love into Innana and she received me with a heart softening into her trust of my love. When I asked if I could enter her yoni and contact her sacred spot, she invited me into her precious body as if I were the first ever to enter her with conscious love. Maybe I was.

Innana's tears flowed freely as I contacted her sacred spot. I gently invited her Shakti to awaken in her warm and sleeping yoni as she told the story of her sexual longing. She wanted the quality of love she felt with Robert. Before him, she had never experienced anything like it. My empathy ran high for her and for all women who long to be deeply loved. We don't always know this is what we need until the moment we receive it.

Giving to Innana was an unexpected joy. My heart filled with love for this petite woman who stood so tall. Innana was a warrior of the heart, dedicated to helping human souls evolve. I hadn't seen her as particularly sensual or sexy, but by the light of the flickering fire I saw a woman of great magnitude and powerful Shakti. Seeing her in her vulnerability from this place of my power gave new balance to our friendship. Innana is practical and grounded, and she is also a free spirit who lives outside the box. Her heart is as big as her mind, and that is huge.

After some time by the fire Innana and I went outdoors to dance under the full moon in the humid Maui night air. Our bond deepened as we held each other, seeing the possibilities ahead. We forged a promise that night to show up fully with and for each other for the rest of our lives. We dropped to our knees in prayer as the face of the goddess shone upon us in the radiant light of the moon. We vowed to serve her, as we felt our blood flow through one body. We would never again be just Innana or Caroline—we were sisters of the goddess in service to all women with our work, our devotion, and our love.

Innana continued to come to my home for tantric healing nights with our other friends and lovers and, with my blessings, received Charles' love and skills until ejaculatory, multiorgasmic pleasure became natural for her. I felt safe knowing she stopped at nothing to understand what made me tick. She observed my life from the inside out and assured me my confusion would eventually smooth into the clarity I longed to have.

Innana and Charles were great friends. They enjoyed each other's minds and shared a passion for healing, Maui, and me. Innana listened to what Charles had to say about sexual sharing with more than one person. And I knew that when Charles was with Innana I was interpreted in ways that helped him understand me. What more could I want?

Eventually, Robert moved to Maui to live with Innana and her husband on their jungle farm. Innana tried to heal the lost union with her husband through Tantra, but it didn't work, and after a year, they filed for divorce, Sash moved on, and Robert and Innana celebrated discovery of the beloved in each other.

I asked Innana to become part of the Tantra for Women workshops I was leading twice a year, in Maui and in Mexico, and she accepted the invitation, certain we would be a powerful pair. We changed the name of the women's work to "The Divine Feminine." Women coming for this work would receive my understanding of Tantra and have the added benefit of Innana's skill at handling the emotional arena. No demon is too much for Innana. And when women enter into sexual healing and awakening work, anything is possible as they clear their past and make room for more love.

Evolution is essential to the spiral of life. I found Innana when I needed her as a healer and then as a friend; she found me and Robert when she needed to expand in new ways. My relationship with Charles, on the other hand, was not evolving. While Innana and Robert explored the heights of their belovedness, I continued to struggle with my beloved over sovereignty nights, which pleased him but left me more despairing than before we started them.

And then I met Eric Wonderful.

Chapter Eighteen

All in the Family

Dave and Nancy gave new meaning to the concept of a Midwestern family. They had studied Tantra with Charles in Rio Caliente before we became a couple, and they came back to study more Tantra, having met and loved the Kansas girl in me. Dave was a physician and he was curious about amrita. He had never heard of female ejaculation, and he was skeptical yet fascinated.

I liked these two from the start. Dave was handsome, with friendly eyes and a generous smile. He radiated charm. Nancy seemed centered in herself—ready for whatever came her way. They represented the ideal couple from the Midwest, overturning convention while still fitting in. It was easy to say yes when they asked for a private session with Charles and me so they could learn about sacred spot massage and see about amrita for themselves.

We met in our room after a day of teaching classes and relaxing during breaks in the warm Mexican sun, and we invited them to take a seat on our bed, make themselves comfortable, and position themselves so they could see exactly what Charles was doing with his fingers inside of me. As they watched in honoring silence, I lay in Charles' arms and received this sacred massage. My amrita flowed before their eyes, splashing droplets of this nectar on their faces as they gazed in wonder as if a child were being born between my thighs. We all were moved by the intimacy of our experience. This intimate sharing bonded the four of us for many years to come, as with great respect they honored us as their teachers.

Our paths would cross many times, as Dave and Nancy lived in Colorado and we taught in Colorado Springs and Boulder. But I never would have guessed about the paths our lives would take or how much I would learn from their entire family.

Nancy called my home in Maui one day after that private sacred spot session. She had had a guidance dream and believed she could heal her jealousy about women desiring her beautiful husband if she "sent" him to women she loved and trusted. The women she chose were me and Marbie, my dear friend and the dakini in our Tantra workshops.

Marbie and I were touched in a profound way to receive this request from a sister and woman we admired as much as we did Nancy. And we adored Dave. He was intelligent, kind, gentle, present, devoted to his wife and two children, and he wanted to learn the ways of conscious loving, which we admired and were eager to support. We assured Nancy her beloved would be in good hands.

A few weeks later Dave arrived on Maui to fulfill his wife's dream of sending him to the goddess for tantric healing and awakening. Charles and I greeted our dear friend, making him welcome in our home. Charles planned to go out for a sovereignty night of Tantra exploration and as I began to prepare for the evening with Dave, they sat together by the lily pond sharing intimacies of the heart woven with their intelligence and consciousness. They embraced, without fear of any misunderstanding. Their friendship was filled with love and respect and brotherhood. I knew I had Charles' blessings to love Dave.

Marbie had gotten to know Dave and Nancy when they attended more than one "Tantra for Couples" weeks in Maui. She was Michael's sweetheart during the years they worked with us. Marbie was an excellent massage therapist with a myriad of healing modalities at her fingertips. She was our resident dakini as well, meaning that couples who needed help or teachings in the privacy of their rooms could hire Marbie for massage and dakini work. To the amazement of so many couples, Marbie fulfilled a very safe role for them as confidante and teacher. She expressed and adhered to clear boundaries while transmitting Tantra to mainstream folks who were in our classes. This was the first time Marbie and I had been asked to work together with a man, especially a best girlfriend's husband! We felt so trusted by Nancy, raising the bar on how sisterhood actually could express itself.

To begin this ceremony, Marbie, Dave, and I sat in meditation together after thirty minutes of yoga solo practice. We breathed, centered, prayed, and spoke our intentions for this experience of expanded loving. Invoking Nancy as the source for this experience, we called her on the phone in Colorado to bring her into the moment.

With all energies balanced, Dave lay on my bed and we began to massage him. Four hands can feel even more wonderful than two! We know how hard Dave worked as a surgeon and we acknowledged him for his skills as well as for his beautiful family and his dedication to both. We took turns sitting before him as he lay upon the bed, coaching him to breathe deeply, make sounds on the exhale, stay connected to us with his eyes, and take in our love. We caressed his genitals equally to caressing his heart, shoulders, neck, face, legs, and feet. Moaning in delight, Dave took in a lot of love.

His erection came and went. We explained to him that we would not arouse him to an ejaculatory orgasm, we would not insert him inside of either one of us, but we would simply love him tenderly and passionately as we were asked by his beloved wife to do. He agreed this was already more than he ever could have anticipated and smiled deeply, thanking his beloved Nancy with soft words of praise.

We sandwiched Dave between us, naked bodies warmed by the tropical night. We both invited Dave to offer his healing hands to our yonis, massaging us with his skilled touch both inside and out. My sacred spot area was a fertile landscape of pleasure, as I easily contracted in orgasm after orgasm, releasing my divine nectar, my amrita, over him and soaking through four thick towels. Marbie cheered us on as she and all of my girlfriends had learned to do, taking great pleasure in absorbing and celebrating each other's offering of abundance.

I transmitted my Shakti, my life force, consciously through my eyes, my sounds, my hands, my yoni, and all that I was willing to share. This was more than enough for all of us. It was easy to feel and see how we played on the edges of full-on sexuality, but it would not have been appropriate to the powerful Divine Feminine that was responsible for the integrity of this sacred play together. This was healing that was completely fun within the confines of agreements and comfort with our primary relationships.

We walked out into the starlight to soak in the hot tub, thanking Nancy verbally over and over again for this gift of sharing her beloved husband with us before returning to the house, where we set up a bed in front of the little fireplace in the living room. Here, in the light of a quietly burning fire, we both gave Dave a full body massage, including his genitals, male sacred spot, and prostate while loosening up the tight muscles of his buttocks and thighs. With each erection we coached Dave to breathe, work with his internal muscles, and choose to not ejaculate as he practiced working toward mastery.

Marbie and I worked hard, played hard, and laughed our way through this gifting from our sister-goddess-girlfriend to fill her beautiful man with love. By the look on his face as we finished this portion of the evening, we could tell that inside he was purring like a giant cat. By now it was well past midnight and we all felt the pull to rest, integrating our experience in the privacy of our own rooms. I lay in my bed finally, tired yet content, sending love to my beloved Charles for empowering me to give my love to his friend and brother, Dave. I knew that we had fulfilled Nancy's wish for her man.

By the next afternoon, having said goodbye to Marbie in the morning and welcoming Charles home a little later, the three of us sat down to a meal. Dave looked deeply into my eyes, choosing his words carefully as he said softly, "When my kids are old enough, Queenie, would you teach my son and daughter the art of conscious loving? It would mean so much to me and Nancy." I was stunned by the gravity of this invitation. Dave was from Iowa, and he thought my Midwestern innocence and awakened Tantric goddess would be a perfect fit for his kids. I was honored that he would even ask. I promised I would do it when they were old enough and the time was right. He proceeded to thank Charles, his words spoken slowly and filled with the grandeur of his heart. "Brother, you are a fine man. How can I ever thank you for opening up your home for your beloved Caroline and Marbie to love me in such a fine way? I trust you with my life, with educating my precious children about the ways of love, and for helping Nancy open more of her passion with me. I love you, brother," cried Dave, choking back his tears, as he and Charles embraced.

Three years later, while driving along a well-traveled highway just before dawn to meet his family for an Easter vacation, Dave was killed in a head-on collision. Our dear and glorious friend was gone. Sorrow rocked our world. For months we knew Nancy was in her retreat of deepest grief, silent with her children as they held one another through this darkest time of their lives. From afar, so many of their friends, including those of us on Maui who adored this family, helped them hold the grief they needed to feel.

The following January, Charles and I were teaching at Esalen Institute in Big Sur, California, when, surprised and overjoyed, we bumped into Nancy and her twenty-year-old son, who were taking another workshop there. I embraced her and then met Eric, a striking young man with chiseled Nordic features who stood well over six feet six inches tall; his face reflected the sadness and loss he was drowning in. "Join us for dinner," Charles said graciously, taking Nancy's hand as I steered Eric to our table. I fell into the moment as I reverently acknowledged both the presence and the absence of Dave.

As we sat in the dining room overlooking the steep, rugged coastline of this stunningly beautiful part of California, I remembered the promise I'd made to Dave about expanding the realm of conscious loving to include his two children when they were old enough. This was the moment for me to step into being the priestess of love and the tantric arts that I was trained to be. I could never bring his beloved father back, but I had a feeling I could do something about the grief in that boy's eyes.

After dinner and much somber conversation about life for Nancy since Dave's accident and death, I asked Nancy what she thought about my inviting Eric into Tantra with me. She hesitated, her dark, deep eyes glancing away into the void, then smiled and said, "It seems a little crazy, but I can't think of anything better, Queenie. Dave was Eric's best friend. If anything can bring Eric back to wholeness it would probably be your love."

At their workshop's end, they drove back to Santa Cruz where they stayed with Nancy's sister-in-law. I asked Eric if he would like to come back down the coast two days later to spend the night with me, as I had the five-day workshop to finish. His face lit up. "I would love to, Caroline," he said in the same deep, resonant voice he had inherited from his father. Then he winked as he curled his mouth into a half smile. "I'll do it for my dad." I was crazy about Eric from that moment on.

I made arrangements to stay another night at Esalen with Eric as soon as our workshop ended. Charles agreed to stay in Monterey with his Mama while I spent the night initiating Eric, a young man greatly in need of a jolt out of despair and into the life he so loved. Charles was thrilled for Eric and for me, as was the nature of his soul. Healing love and pleasure would surely change the course of both of our lives.

Eric arrived right on time for our rendezvous, as eager and excited as I was. I met him in the lobby and we walked to the private stone house where we would spend the night.

Eric was as tall and tender and gentle as I remembered his father being. He built a roaring fire in the big stone fireplace, and we sat by it while he told me about life without his dad. It was unbearable. "I lost my best friend," he shared through the sorrow of his sobs, the weight of missing Dave shuddering through his strong young body. His father had not even lived to see him turn twenty years of age, and they had planned for a lifetime of friendship and adventure. Sure, he adored his mother and sister, but a big chunk of his heart had collapsed when his father died.

Eric had read our book and he knew of Tantra from conversations with his parents, but tonight would be his first time practicing it. The room was warm as we spread a blanket before the fire, and our tenderness bound us in a comfortable intimacy. I put soft music on the stereo and we took off our clothes, as clothing was a barrier to the intimacy we wished to share. We massaged each other to familiarize ourselves with each other's skin and presence, and then I sat astride him in tantric embrace, and we gazed into one another's eyes, losing all sense of time. Rocking gently to the sounds of flute and keyboard, we breathed into one another, one inhaling as the other exhaled. There was an easy openness in our hearts; limitless love was our home. Eventually, our lips began to explore the irresistible force of attraction, and our tongues probed each other's depths. Our mouths made love for what seemed like hours. Without needing to question where the night was headed, we both knew that explicit sexuality was not the feast for this early experience of discovery. As tantric lovers by nature, we knew we were already there, so in fact there was nowhere to go.

Sometime in the middle of the night, we went outside to bathe in the natural hot mineral baths on the cliffs overlooking the churning sea, luxuriating in the rejuvenating waters and returning just before dawn to cuddle and sleep.

At breakfast in the dining room we spoke of our night together. We had felt Dave's presence smiling on us with joy, and we felt the same presence of Charles as well as of Eric's mother and sister, with whom I was bonded in sacred sisterhood. We agreed we wanted another opportunity to experience Tantra together and further merge into this state of oneness we felt. Eric helped me carry my bags to my car and we said goodbye, both feeling something "forever" had begun.

Driving up the coast highway to meet Charles in Monterey, I felt as young and desirable as a sixteen-year-old chosen by the most popular guy to be his date at the senior prom. Even as captain of the cheerleading team, I hadn't ever felt desired by the cutest or most popular boys in school. They had chosen the more petite and pretty girls, and I soon realized I was not one of them.

Eric saw me beyond where I had been seen and, in that seeing, a healing I hadn't known I needed began to take place.

I thought about Eric's lovely body and savored the memory of it and of his vulnerability and trust, as well as his taste, sounds, and open heart. In Monterey I phoned Nancy to thank her for trusting me with her son. Eric had already called her, she said, expressing the same gratitude and delight. She could tell his depression was already lifting.

Eric called the night I arrived home in Maui, enchanting me with his deep, fluid voice. He and his father spoke as though their words began in the deepest chamber of their hearts. "Caroline," he purred, "look at the moon. It's full and radiant tonight." "I see it," I told him. "I'm right here with you."

In early spring Eric and I met again, this time at a seaside inn north of San Francisco. Charles and I flew to the mainland together, and he went south to Monterey to see his Mama and his son, Orion, while I spent the night in San Francisco and made the drive the next morning across the Golden Gate Bridge to meet Eric. I luxuriated in an evening alone in the city, buying a negligée and slippers and bathing in a tub fragrant with sea salts before sleeping. I spent the next morning in silence, meditating and practicing yoga. I felt as if I were reuniting with my first love. Only the deep breathing of my yoga practice kept the butterflies at rest in my belly. When my body felt stretched and open and my mind calm and clear, I called for my car. Driving north along Highway One I felt as though my car was a magic carpet flying six feet off the ground.

Eric was waiting in the lobby of the Pelican Inn when I arrived, the light in his eyes matching his beauty this time instead of the sorrow that had previously consumed him. He wrapped me in the warm cocoon of his embrace. "It's so good to see you, Caroline," he softly whispered against my hair. I inhaled his scent, then stepped back to look into his eyes and melt into them with our shared excitement. "Come on. I'll show you our room," he said, reaching for my hand.

A spray of white lilies filled a porcelain vase and sunlight streamed in through lace curtains in this room that would be ours for an entire, delicious night. Eric's overnight bag sat unopened by a chair near the bed. He sat in the chair, smiling with his big arms folded across his chest, as he watched me unpack a small goddess statue, my ceremonial hand-painted silk robe, and the new sheer negligée and slippers. I set lubricants on the nightstand along with vanilla-scented candles. "How about a walk on the beach?" I suggested, something to ease our way into connection. Eric jumped up and confidently held out his hand for mine. "Let's go."

We walked along the shore holding hands, and Eric talked of his father, telling me of the things that haunted him as well as the most precious moments. Once, he recalled, when he was sixteen, his dad had invited him into the operating room to watch an open heart surgery. Dressed in mask and gown, Eric stood by his father as he opened his patient's chest. When the heart was exposed, his father reached in and carefully lifted the beating heart. "I'll never forget the look in his eyes, over that mask," Eric said, his eyes still seeing that awesome moment. "My dad was asking me to hold a human heart with him. I knew we connected our love for all time through the heart of another human being."

I told him about my experiences with his dad, about the time Dave was "sent" to Marbie and me. Dave had told Eric about that night of Tantra we had shared, and he smiled a deep, knowing smile. We talked, we walked, we stopped to embrace, breathing in harmony with the breeze, and we walked some more.

Back at the inn, nestled into a cozy corner table in the restaurant for dinner by candlelight, Eric never took his eyes off mine. "You look beautiful in that color blue, Caroline," he said with words and with his gaze in a voice that could melt butter. I tried not to swoon too obviously but truth be known, I was a mountain of female desire.

As we moved toward the hidden stairs that would take us up to our room at the inn, the maitre d' commented with lusty eyes, "It looks like the knight has found himself a queen for the night." We had no wish to hide our desire for union.

Upstairs, standing before our imagined celestial throne, in tantric ritual we invited our loved ones to be present for our loving. We undressed one another, touching and kissing and gazing with appreciation at the beauty of one another's bodies. We bathed, kissing as we inhaled and tasted each other's freshness. Once we lay on our throne made for loving, we ceremoniously invited Shiva to enter Shakti in an offering to the god and the goddess within. Surely heaven and the angels sang.

With conscious loving and full presence, we danced the dance of love with our eyes and hearts as well as the rhythm of his light-wand moving in perfect harmony with my temple of delights. Seagulls soared over sand and sea outside our window. It was as if we were the only lovers who ever existed. The stars belonged to us. We paused at times to stand at the window and gaze at them as we watched the moonlight dance on the sea.

Are there limits to ecstasy? This was so much more than a passionate affair with a beautiful young man. It was a connection to my spiritual lineage through Eric's mother and my sisterhood with her, to my belovedness with Charles and the empowerment he gave me to love with my whole being, to the promise I'd made to Eric's father. We felt Dave was orchestrating this grand event for his son in concert with all conscious beings who want their children to be loved.

In the shadow of the redwood trees surrounding the inn the next morning, Eric and I held each other for a long time, neither of us quite ready to say goodbye. My connection to love with Eric was rebirthing him after the loss of his father, and it was also giving the teenager inside of me her first chance to feel the wholeness of my sexual femininity since losing my virginity. "Thank you, beloved," I said silently in my heart to Charles, "for gifting me with one of the most important experiences of my life." Eric held me into the oneness of all that is love, as he breathed these words into sounds, "My love and gratitude for you is beyond measure, Caroline."

On the way back to San Francisco I stopped at Stinson Beach to write a letter of gratitude to Nancy. Months later, she would tell me how she had read the letter sitting with her women's group at the top of a mountain near the Temple of Aphrodite outside Athens, where they had gone to visit the sacred matriarchal temple. Sitting by the fire they'd made to warm up before descending the mountain, Nancy read my letter and then offered it to the goddess with her prayers. We were making herstory, and she bestowed it in ritual and ceremony of the highest order. This describes the true power of the goddess to go beyond convention and into the realms of magic where spirit can define all boundaries.

When I called Charles, he was already planning the next invitation for Eric. "Let's invite Eric to join us in Maui next month for the weeklong Tantra seminar at the Mana Kai Hotel," he exclaimed excitedly. "Maria will be there. She will be a wonderful teacher and lover for Eric as well." This was the first and the last thing I wanted to hear.

I knew I had to share Eric. He wasn't mine to keep. This sharing was important for everyone involved as it supposedly helped keep attachment from forming. But sharing Eric was not what my heart wanted, any more than sharing Charles was. Somewhere deep inside, I knew I love best in devotion to one man, but it would be years before I had the courage to act on this knowledge. Until then I would continue to learn about the practice of expanded loving according to my beloved's beliefs.

When Eric arrived on the island, I picked him up at the airport and whisked him off to a sunset on the beach, where we sat in the yab-yum position of Tantra yoga on the sand (him cross-legged, me seated astride him), breathing through our chakras into one another. It was good to be together again, and everything I wanted. It was dark outside when we climbed back into the car and drove to the hotel where our seminar would start the next morning. Eric greeted Charles and met Maria, who seemed delighted by the opportunity to assist in opening this beautiful young man to his life source. I gave them some time to talk for a bit before I asked Charles privately for a night alone with Eric in the adjoining room. I wasn't ready to share him quite yet.

For the next two weeks, Maria and Eric got to know one another while I taught with Charles and did all I could to avoid becoming possessive of this Viking god who had entered my soul. Time apart didn't soften my feelings for him, and over the next few months, Eric and I had more rendezvous in Maui and California. I introduced him to Robin, who later told me she was shocked that he was even younger than she was.

"Honey, some of this makes no sense to me, either. Love doesn't always make a lot of sense."

She shrugged. "I couldn't do what you do, Mom. But if it makes you happy, who am I to judge?" Moments of understanding like that made me want to cry with relief.

When December came around again, Eric and I got together in California when Charles and I were teaching there. Right away, I knew something had changed. Eric asked Charles—and Maria, who was there with us—to be present when he told me he needed to end our "lingam in yoni connection."

We met in our hotel room, where he told me what he needed. My heart broke. It didn't matter how gently or tenderly he spoke the words. The hurt tore deeper even than it had with Shinzo. But I did what I had to do. I was stoic. I said, "You will find your beloved. You are everything a woman would want."

After he left, I lost it completely. Charles held me and stroked my hair as I cried, reminding me that his love and sexuality were always mine. Eric felt more alive again, and he needed to return with his wholeness to his world of friends and future lovers.

I knew Eric's decision was right for him. I knew that rising in love was better than falling in love, but it didn't matter. I could barely function. I called my doctor-friend, Jesse, hoping she could prescribe something to balance my emotions. She couldn't see me before I left for Maui the next day, and she referred me to a doctor who specialized in treating women in midlife. Even though I'd had surgically induced menopause at twenty-six, in my fifties I was having menopausal symptoms—temperature changes, emotional instability, fluctuations in libido, and a psychological shifting of sexual priorities. I felt I'd experienced enough sexual excitement to last a lifetime and wasn't sure I wanted any more. When this doctor learned I'd been on hormone replacement therapy for almost thirty years, she took me off it immediately and sent me home with newer, safer treatments, including natural hormonal creams. I prayed the treatments would make a difference.

But home again, I cried through the days and couldn't sleep. Worsening things, Eric continued to share sexual love with Maria in California because she didn't have the same attachment I had to him and he wanted that freedom in connection.

"Charles," I pleaded, "can we *please* take a year to be just the two of us? I can't handle any more disappointments." I ached for simplicity.

"You will always have Eric's love and respect, my queen. It's time to look for your next tantric experience. There are so many more people to love."

I couldn't hear it. I visited Michael when Charles was away on sovereignty nights. He was a compassionate and trusted friend who knew Eric and his family and empathized with my struggle. We watched movies and munched popcorn, and I gave him his vitamins and sleep meds and then went home alone to cry some more. Eventually, a psychiatrist prescribed an antidepressant, which helped. I felt more balanced and was able to think about the situation without feeling so despairing. Each time I opened with someone, I realized, I learned so much about myself, about sexuality, and about Tantra. This really was my path, and my path was my teacher.

In time, my sadness over losing Eric as a lover softened. He met and married his beloved and they birthed two beautiful children. On my visits to teach a weekend in Boulder, I stayed with Nancy and always saw the family. Once, having a lovely dinner alone with Eric, I asked him how he would describe our time together now that ten years had passed. He thought a moment, then slowly spoke. "Every breath I breathe is filled with the love you gave me, Caroline. You and Charles taught me so much."

Seven years after her husband's death, Nancy came to us, ready to trust us with her sexuality and eager for help. She had grieved Dave for a long time and was ready to share her sexuality with a man again.

Charles and I created a special night for Nancy in Colorado the next time we were there for a teaching weekend. With my blessings, Nancy invited Charles—the man whom her husband had called his brother—to make love with her. I assisted in the evening with joy, and the celebrating continued the next day with a hike in the Rockies. Lying on the warm earth in the afternoon sun, Nancy and I held hands as we invited Charles to give us sacred spot massage, blessing our lives, our children, and the earth with the flow of our divine nectar. We laughed as we welcomed this into the weaving of our connection. Eric and his wife were happy to hear of Nancy's experience with us, and they wished for Nancy a lifetime of love. A few years later, Eric's sister, Kim, would attend my Tantra for Women weekend and we would get to know each other more intimately as she experienced the women-awakening work.

Dave's request of me was completed. Every member of the family had received lessons in conscious loving. Dave had learned about female ejaculation and I had had the joy of sharing this beautiful truth with him. Eric and I had experienced the healing of his wounds and mine. Kim had discovered the power of female sexuality and learned to claim it as part of her life source. Nancy had shown me that your children can be your best friends.

My commitment to the expansion of love and healing would continue as the next great lesson in love entered my life—Kealani, my heavenly Hawaiian beauty. All I knew was that I wanted to help her open to sexuality in a safe and trusted environment, a woman who needed healing to accept her own beauty and the presence of the goddess within her. As it would turn out, Kealani would lead me to my own discovery of the goddess within me and exactly what it was *this* goddess needed.

Chapter Nineteen

Attachment and Sovereignty

Kealani was enchanting, and it wasn't just her awesome beauty—almond-shaped eyes, long dark hair, full lips, and voluptuous body—and her island ways. At twenty-eight, she still lived with her mother on Oahu, and she came to Maui during the summer to help run a children's summer day camp. She was very childlike in many ways, and after several years of therapy with Innana, she needed a new approach to healing. She had suffered early wounding by a neighbor who had violated her precious sexuality, and she was afraid of men and sex and didn't trust intimate relationships. Innana thought we might be Kealani's best healers, and we agreed right away to meet her and do whatever was needed to help this woman release her early childhood trauma and live a full and loving life.

Our first meeting was at Innana's house. Kealani was nervous and shy, and conversation was almost impossible. The next time we met, Innana brought Kealani over to our house for lunch and a hike, and we began getting to know each other in this more casual environment.

We had no agenda with Kealani other than to offer her our love and our skills, and we invited her to keep checking us out. Finally, after a number of social interactions, always with a group of friends or with Innana, Kealani began to accept invitations to our home for the evening for the possibility of the sexual healing work to begin. She brought pajamas with her—pink baby dolls—and frolicked about in them, getting comfortable seeing me and Charles naked, seeing us in love, seeing us make love, seeing us in the hot tub or shower, or even on the toilet. Our house had no doors between rooms, and we invited her to come and go as she pleased. She liked this type of family intimacy and it helped her build trust in us.

One day, when it felt right, we suggested we begin sexual healing work. Kealani's eyes went wide, and she immediately disappeared from the room. Shortly, she returned wearing her pink baby-dolls. She was too insecure about her body to reveal it to us. "Caroline," she might say, in her twelve-year-old girl's voice, "my butt sticks out so far and jiggles so much." (Other times she might say, "Queenie, the kids always called me 'thunder butt,'" or "Queenie, how can I ever get slender thighs?" Over and over, the stream of self-criticism would pour from those beautiful red lips.) My instincts were to be like a mom to this young woman, gently encouraging her to begin accepting her body as beautiful and deserving of adoration. I would stroke her hair tenderly and say, "You are so beautiful, Kealani." But she couldn't take it in. "No, I'm not. I'm ugly. Look at these big thighs and fat ankles." Like many voluptuous women, she detested her thighs, buttocks, and breasts—her womanliness—although she did like her lips painted with red lipstick and she seemed to enjoy flipping her long hair across her creamy shoulders.

Charles and I found the best way for Kealani to open to love was for us to focus on each other and allow her to be a part in whatever way she chose. She would usually sit beside us on the bed in her pink pajamas, fascinated by the beauty of our love. She'd squeal sometimes with delight watching us connect tantrically, making sacred love as we danced in the magic of our belovedness. Once, when Charles asked her if she would like to look at my yoni and explore me, she hesitantly and then passionately devoured me with her eyes, but that was all. When I asked her if she would like to touch Charles and meet his lingam with a formal introduction, she shook her head, but then moments later, she reached out and gingerly touched it while speaking the words, "Hello, Penis," before fleeing from the room.

Week after week we invited Kealani back simply because we enjoyed the refreshing innocence of our young pearl from heaven. She was always ready for a hike to a jungle waterfall, and she showed us the islands through the wondering eyes of a child, pointing out rare birds and ancient trees as she skipped along the moist trails in bare feet, a red hibiscus tucked behind her ear. Now and then we talked of the neighbor who had abused her and about the one or two boys she'd had sex with. They were a disappointing memory for this Hawaiian beauty who was creeping into the enormous expanse of our hearts.

One night, during a quiet evening at our home, Kealani allowed us to massage her. She lay face down so we could massage her back side. We spoke of her beauty as we stroked her, but as always, she was quick to assure us she was not beautiful. When she finally did turn over and allow us to gaze at her exquisite form she could only stay there a minute before jumping up to put her pink baby dolls back on and return to insisting it was time for Charles to love his queen.

Months of this went by before Kealani finally trusted us to open her to her sexuality. With infinite love we coached her to open her eyes and look into ours as we gently stroked her yoni and Charles tenderly entered her with a finger and contacted her sacred spot, which was peacefully sleeping and numb. Soon, a beautiful smile replaced the fear drawing her lips tight as she felt sexual pleasure for the first time in her life. We encouraged her to caress her clitoris as "homework," along with inserting a finger into her yoni to find her sacred spot. This would be Kealani's chance to get to know herself in a new way.

When we saw her next, Kealani was excited about the success of her homework. The child was transforming into a woman. That night, she asked us both to touch her yoni, her clitoris, and her sacred spot. We all celebrated that she was feeling pleasure and enjoying it so much. We took time to caress her lovely breasts and assure her of their beauty. She was able to accept that because she loved my breasts and ours were a similar size and shape. I knelt between her thighs, opened them wide enough to place my breasts on her yoni, and smiled at her. I said, "Here is my love, Kealani, through my breasts into your precious yoni." Tears rolled down her cheeks as she relaxed her open thighs in an attitude of surrender. She looked at Charles, who lay by her side, encouraging her to receive the queen's love through her yoni. Then, she took his lingam in her hand as her gaze dropped down to his genitals. "Penis," she whispered, "I am seeing you for the first time without fear. I invite you to enter me."

Charles and I exchanged a glance, and then, with joy, I put lubricant on Charles' lingam and gently placed him at the entrance to Kealani's open flower of life. We were all in this moment together as I lay at Kealani's side, holding her and softly stroking her, encouraging her to breathe as Charles slowly and consciously entered her.

Charles' mastery was beautiful to behold, as was the opening of the flower of my new friend, my heavenly pearl of a girl. I hovered close to her with motherly affection as well as with the desire of a lover.

There is a delicate force-field between sexual healing practice with someone and becoming lovers. Becoming lovers can add a sense of violation if it is attempted before a healing is completed. There needs to be clear delineation, along with ritual, if a sexual healing is to become a feast of lovers. This is probably the least understood yet most imperative action for a sexual healer to understand. It has taken me a long time and many mistakes to realize how important this is.

With Kealani, at first healing was our focus and intent. Several months into the healing work, however, it felt like time for the line between sexual healing and lovers to dissolve, and I encouraged Charles to join me in surrendering to our love for her. "Kealani is a woman now," I told him. "She chooses us as her lovers, and I choose her as ours." Charles willingly agreed yet still held reservation about her being our *only* lover. Once again, he and I stood poised at the impasse of our opposing needs. "Our only lover, Charles…please," I insisted.

We met with Kealani weekly for tantric practice, teaching, and family time. Kealani had learned from watching Charles and me make love, and she welcomed and opened to Charles in a way that made me very proud. Throughout their lovemaking she held full presence with Charles, and she often spoke to me during it. "You are my queen forever sharing your beloved with me. Stay close so Charles can love you next. I'm getting him ready for you, my queen."

Kealani treasured the sounds of sexual love and loved the tantric names for genitals. She soaked up our teachings and wanted to become our best student and favorite lover and playmate, which she was. She helped me keep house, do laundry, and make breakfast, dressed in her baby dolls, and in the evenings she liked to model my beautiful night-gowns for us or waltz around the house in them, showing off her beauty for us to appreciate. From her mother's house, she wrote us love letters, and we called her every day when she was there, whether we were at home in Hawaii or teaching somewhere on the mainland. And when we were home, every Friday Kealani was on the commuter plane to spend the weekend with us.

Over time, I found the bed too small to include anyone besides us three. I was captivated by Kealani's exuberance, unable to resist her in any way. For Charles, it was different. He kept his tantric commitments to several other women and regularly took his sovereignty nights with Maria and several others. Sometimes Maria came over to connect with Charles and me, but I backed away from sexually connecting with any-one other than my pure and heavenly Kealani.

Maria had a hard time with our relationship with Kealani. She could feel our intoxication with this lover, and it hurt. In Bali, I had seen how attached she had become to sexual sharing with Charles. He was her only lover, which he did not support. I didn't like it either. I empathized with Maria, but I also believed it was healthier for her to let go of some of her attachment and find a lover besides Charles. Fortunately, while Charles and I were still dizzy with the passion of Kealani, Maria met and fell in love with a man whom she would be with for several years. Once she brought him over to "share" him with me and Kealani, and I entered into one sexual connection with him, but I was not interested in "trades" and we didn't invite him back. After that, Maria gently faded out of our life as a lover, yet remained steadfast as our friend. She struggled with her new lover's sexual couplings with other women and his refusal to end those relationships. Jealous bones that she didn't know she had rattled in her body. I knew too well what this was like. "My dear Queenie," she said to me one day, "I really understand now. I hope you can forgive me." I did forgive Maria, and I also knew there was really nothing to have to forgive.

Meanwhile, Kealani and I would curl up together for talks about how we would like Charles to settle down with just the two of us. But in my heart, I was torn between my desires. As much as I loved Kealani and the sweet ways she loved us, I knew it was important to avoid attachment, and I really didn't want anyone living with us, not even our heavenly pearl of a girlfriend.

With some women I experienced a healing freedom in exploring tantrically. Our loving connection offered a chance to deepen our experience of the divinity and power of the Feminine without the stickiness of attachment. It allowed for deepened bonding with the sisterhood. Women, too, showed me powers of Shakti that I hadn't known existed. Seeing women like Maria smolder with Shakti fire gave me more permission to be that way myself. I had come a long way from the protected child and unsatisfied young woman to discover myself as the lusty, passionate being I am. Here I was, in love with love—with the perfect partner to share that passion with. I could barely keep up with myself, much less with the intensity of opening sexually to a steady stream of beautiful people.

I decided it was time to get some real clarity, to uncover more of my soul's truths and see if I could have more peace in my heart. I turned to Innana for guidance. We were teaching the women's workshops together, occasionally practiced Tantra together, and she referred some of her clients to me. She recommended a counselor named Christine to help me uncover whatever truths still lay protected inside me.

For the next sixteen months, Christine and I sat across from one another on overstuffed chairs, and I followed her guidance in Reichian nonverbal breathing therapy as I went inside to sense any unrest in my body. As I peeled away layers of protection with her gentle encouragement and scanned my interior landscape for answers, I began to experience a more intimate relationship with my soul. And in my soul I discovered the truth: I yearned for what I couldn't have with Charles. I needed someone to be there for me as I stumbled along the tantric trail of more love, attempting to adapt, not only to please my beloved but also to find a comfortable fit for myself. I yearned for a lover who would be available to me on sovereignty nights ... a lover who wanted *me* and me alone.

Kealani liked going with Charles and our small group of local friends on those nights, exploring the parameters of Tantra and multiple sexual partners. Little did I know what treacherous terrain I was entering into, looking for someone to fill the empty compartments of my heart.

Chapter Twenty

The Fall of Camelot

Love awakens on the heels of passion ... or is it passion that awakens on the wings of love? The mystery of what unlocks this life-driving force will always fascinate me. When I looked into the blue velvet waterfall of eyes so innocent yet laced with shame, I knew in that moment over breakfast that I wanted to love the man sitting across from me with all of my being. He had been brought to me through my brother, Johnny.

Johnny lived on Maui now, married to a chef on the island by the name of Mary. Their wedding in their new home two years ago had filled me with joy, as I had not lived close to my brother since the mountains of Colorado nearly thirty years ago. We didn't see each other as often as we thought we would, because of my insistent teaching and travel schedule. Not to mention the never-ending requirements of my marriage, home, and property—tropical island life was anything but a swing-in-a-hammock for me.

One day, Johnny called with an intriguing invitation. His brother-in-law, Paul, had just relocated to Maui from the mainland. Johnny thought Paul was perfect for experiencing sexual healing work. Johnny shared with me that Paul had lost his sex drive years ago, sometime after he came back from Vietnam and his wife left him and their nine-year-old son. His son, now eighteen, had just moved out on his own, freeing his dad to accept the invitation to move to Maui and open a gym. Paul hadn't been with a woman for a long time. He was ready for a new life. Johnny, Mary, Paul, and I met for breakfast a few days later at the Moana Café in Paia. On first glance, there was nothing extraordinary at all about Paul, who rose slowly from his seat to greet me. Like a boy with a fresh new haircut, his eyes stood out from his ruddy complexion—eyes that still seemed to be looking for the enemy behind every bush, eyes that only softened when the coast was clear. He stood an inch taller than I in his loose Hawaiian Aloha shirt and he seemed to stand at an angle. Paul had beautiful lips, full and rosy and inviting. Did he know I was looking at him in this way, I wondered? We were, after all, in the same family! Which, by the way, only made the whole situation seem even safer. I always felt safe near my brother…and Paul was a brother too.

Female logic aside, it wasn't physical attraction or chemistry that made my heart fly open as I attempted to be friendly with a very shy and reserved gentle man. He exuded a tender innocence, like someone who cares for infants or baby animals. His piercing midnight blue eyes penetrated my thoughts and my heart before I could finish my veggie Eggs Benedict.

My knees weakened and my hopes soared at the recognition that I might be able to satisfy my need for a lover on sovereignty nights to counter Charles and his three- or four-at-a-time priority lovers. I was a sexual healer, but I was also a woman in need…a dreadful combination, to be perfectly honest.

It was a desperate move on my part. I knew that being driven by one's own deeply personal needs is a major mistake for a dakini or a sexual healer. And I knew that defeat was certain if I longed so badly to be victorious in what had become an unhealthy competition with my beloved. But Paul had no idea of what drove me, and his ignorance helped me feel free and bold. I told myself I could bring healing to this worthy man and love him with all my heart. I could continue my sexual connection with Kealani, my only other lover besides Charles, and perhaps satisfy all of my needs at last.

On our next sovereignty night Charles left the house wishing me a wonderful time of healing with my new friend Paul, whom I had invited to dinner and seemed eager to get to know. We would talk later by phone, as we always did on our nights apart, to assure each other all was well and wish the beloved a special time. Connecting by phone was important to the weaving of all the energies. If I had a lover for the night, Charles would ask to speak with him to offer his blessings, and I always spoke with the women or woman Charles was with, receiving their gratitude for this night with my beloved while I assured them of my acceptance and reverence for the joining of love and passion. I wore my teachings well.

But this first night with Paul might also include Maria, whom I would call later if he was comfortable with the two of us. This was a big step for all of us, even though Maria and I had had plenty of practice with sexual healing. Maria was in a love relationship yet she also wanted to stay open to joining in love with other men. Paul was not used to intimacy with even one woman, and so I calculated that inviting Maria would remove some of the discomfort of such immediate sexual intimacy. I was arranging chairs on the patio when Paul's truck came up the gravel driveway. "Over here!" I called out. I met him at his truck and received a light kiss on the cheek as he handed me a bouquet of ginger from his backyard. He looked like a guy on a date in his yellow and blue Aloha shirt, cargo shorts, and flip-flops. Easy and casual, that was island living.

"You didn't tell me you lived in paradise," he said, waving a hand at the ocean view, the tropical gardens and lily pond, the Japanese blue tiles of the roof glimmering in the late afternoon sun. I showed him around, and then we took a seat at the outdoor table, sipping fresh coconut water I had collected from coconuts on the property. We were both a little shy at being alone for the first time. I didn't mind: Paul's shyness and uncertainty were his greatest appeal. Paul was a bodybuilder and personal trainer, in the process of opening a small workout gym in Haiku.

I gave him a dinner choice accompanied by my best smile.

"So, what would you like? Grilled ahi...or Ecstasy?"

Paul laughed. "Are you serious? My son said I'd love Ecstasy."

I told him that my experience had shown me that MDMA can be a great ally in moving past the mountain of imagined and real fears we all have, and into a world of more love...that it can create a sense of relaxed surrender and ease with intimacy, which is what we all want and what frightens us most. I told him there were no expectations, which he genuinely seemed to appreciate, and that Maria would join us if he was open to that. Maria had hired him to be her personal trainer so they already knew each other. He liked the idea from the start.

I called Maria and asked her to join us. "Oh, Queenie, this sounds great. I will be there in about twenty minutes," said Maria. I hung up the phone and returned to Paul. We held hands as we set our intentions for the evening. "May we journey into more open-hearted connection, feeling safety in sharing ourselves with each other. I ask that my beloved Charles be honored for his part in gifting me to you, Paul, in the form of a goddess of love. May all that is sacred and divine be with us this night."

I handed Paul a Bali sarong to change into, and then we ingested our sacrament (we swallowed one capsule of MDMA each) and moved to the ocean-side patio to enjoy the fading daylight while drinking in the view of "forever." Paul talked about his life in Arizona. His son had needed him badly after his mother left. Paul had devoted himself to being a dad, and the lover in him had gone to sleep.

Maria slipped in through the front door and joined us on the patio just as the first stars lit the sky. She wore a plum-colored sarong with pale lavender flowers, and her sun-bleached hair and browned skin harmonized sensually. I wore a favorite silk hand-painted sarong filled with the colors of a tropical island at sunset—golds, salmon and fuschia pinks. We sat together on two lounge chairs placed close together. When we needed more comfort, we would move indoors to the bed.

Maria snuggled up to Paul, whose glittering eyes and enlarged pupils showed he was beginning to feel the effects of the sacrament. I could see his awareness expanding as he sat, smiling with ease and wonder as he received this new experience of two beautiful women seated at either side of him, gazing into his eyes and caressing his face, chest, and shoulders. At one point, he closed his eyes and retreated inside and we invited him to open them, assuring him we wouldn't do anything that wasn't his choice and ours. A soft Maui rain began to fall as he turned his face to receive first a kiss from me and then a kiss from Maria, a kiss from me, another kiss from Maria. He may have been out of practice, but with such full and luscious lips, Paul would soon regain his expertise. Again, we asked him to keep his eyes open and to breathe deeply and fully. His erection rose to life under the sarong, and Maria and I placed a hand on his potent offering and complimented what was indeed a beautiful lingam.

Tears ran down his cheeks. "I haven't even had a sexual erection in years," he whispered. "What's happening with you two?"

Maria and I smiled knowingly and continued our gentle kisses.

"The Ecstasy feels wonderful. This is the greatest moment of my life." He grinned from ear to ear.

The time felt right for Maria and I to take Paul's hands and invite him inside to lie down on my bed. I had prepared the room with candles and overflowing bowls of fragrant gardenias. We disrobed and slipped naked onto the ceremonial silk sheet, holding Paul between us. Paul was still and quiet as we continued to caress his body, roaming over rippled muscles and soft skin. We kissed him lovingly, oiling and massaging him everywhere, including his erect offering. We spoke words of empowerment and assurance as he again said how much he felt he could trust us. My heart was opening easily to this gentle soul whom I would come to call "St. Paul" as I got to know him. I assured him I had no intention to take him to ejaculation. The goddess of love in me would never take a man's seed. I suggested he squeeze and relax the muscles deep inside of his genitals, breathe deeply, and join me and Maria in awakening his sleeping Shakti rather than putting it back to sleep, at least temporarily, by ejaculating.

As tantric dakinis we knew that a man benefits greatly from the awakening of his energy. When he ejaculates, he often goes to sleep or at least recedes into a recharging of his energy. We wanted Paul to feel his full aliveness. This event, as in all ideal Tantric endeavors, had nothing to do with sleeping together; it was meant to awaken together and that is exactly what it did.

I noticed how Paul's lingam curved in a perfect arc toward his heart. "Maria, look! He points directly toward his heart center." Paul smiled. He seemed to know that his connection to his sexuality was very much one with his heart. This understanding of his inspired me to gracefully climb astride him.

I wrapped my legs around Paul and we connected soulfully, with long minutes of eye contact, just being present with one another. We breathed deeply in rhythm with one another. Maria was coming onto her half-dose of the sacrament, and in this magical realm we slowed down to feel the harmony of our energies. We continued taking turns kissing Paul and then closed our eyes for a period of meditation. Few words were spoken. The most obvious sound was that of our breathing and sighs on exhales of pleasure.

After a long period of this I asked about the need for a condom for Paul's safety or mine, and he chuckled, remembering how long it had been since he had last made love. We agreed that a condom was not needed. (In retrospect, I never should have done this. Sexual safety always requires a condom.) I asked his permission to receive him inside my yoni, my garden of delight and pleasure. He had never been asked for permission before to merge with a woman, and he hesitated. Then he said, "I would be honored, Caroline, for you to receive my love through my lingam." "Lingam" is not a sexy word that rolls easily off the tongue unless you are quite used to saying it, but I appreciated his trying it out.

My yoni is a messenger of great wisdom when I listen. From the moment I felt Paul inside me, I knew he would be an important friend and lover. I gently awakened my Shakti on the offering of the wand of light belonging to this shy and uncertain man with a limp as Maria assisted with lubricant, sips of water, gentle touch, and words of love for us both. She maintained total focus on the lovers as I danced the dance of the goddess in a continuation of divine play. Holding his gaze and breathing with him, I moved slowly, speaking words to affirm that he would become a conscious lover, one who is fully present with no agenda other than to give and receive love. I made sure he was breathing and meditating with me, not in a hurry to get somewhere. Maria encouraged him to let my love in as she massaged his heart, placing kisses there as well.

That evening, Paul opened his heart to me and to Maria. He told us that his knee injury had won him a Purple Heart in Vietnam. He had an artificial knee, the cause of his limp. At eighteen, he had been part of the 1968 Tet offensive. Tears streamed down his face as his story poured out, and we listened, giving him all the time he needed to speak. He admitted to killing people and ravaging small towns and villages as he robotically fought to defend his country. Once someone gave him a hit of LSD. After that his eyes were opened, and he hoped for an injury that would send him home. One did. He almost lost his leg. Paul had never spoken of these things before. He was purging his past as fast as he was letting in our love.

After a short break for the bathroom, nose blowing, and wiping of tears, we returned to the bed. Maria suggested an acupuncture treatment to help Paul realign his fragile emotional body with his gorgeous physical body in this time of catharsis. Afterward, I lay at his side and nodded to Maria that she might sit upon this beautiful man and love him with all of her magnitude.

Maria's beauty as a goddess of love was never more apparent. When she climbed gracefully astride him and asked permission to insert him into her sacred domain, he looked like the cat that had caught the mouse. I assisted them as Maria had assisted us, kneeling so that my face was next to hers and so Paul could see us both at the same time.

As the evening progressed, Paul looked younger and younger. His brow softened, the years of struggle seemed to melt away, laughter came easier to him. He began to access his inner and outer lover, and he appeared to like the man he found there. He complimented us over and over, exclaiming, "You women are beyond belief. Is this really happening to me?"

Finally, four hours into the journey and not even midnight, I said, "I am feeling exhausted. I need to end the evening early." I felt my own emotional and physical body closing down. Paul was disappointed. "Aren't we just getting started?"

I smiled. "This is enough for me for this first night together." I explained that this was never meant to be a sexual romp—that expanding into conscious love had a delicate, emotional side to it. And both Maria and I knew we had done our job and done it well.

Paul nodded respectfully and got dressed, thanking us for the most incredible evening of his life. When the door closed behind him, Maria and I melted into a sense of completion … as well as the wonder and magic of the man who had trusted us so easily. I needed to integrate how far and how deeply I had opened to Paul in this first evening. Maria was ready to return home and get some rest.

For the remainder of the night I savored being alone, writing, dancing, doing yoga, relaxing in the hot tub under the stars. I called Charles, who was with several of our tantric lovers at a hotel in Wailea, on the other side of the island. We cooed our love to one another, wished each other sweet dreams, and I turned out the bedside light, ready for some needed sleep. I did not want to admit that once Paul's attention turned completely toward Maria, my energy system totally shut down. I was not ready to let myself see that—I did not want to know just how normal and old-fashioned (dare I say, monogamous) I really was. Knowing this on a core level would change everything.

Part of the beauty of healing work is that it's never one-way. And then there are the unknown factors that can take a person by surprise when you open to love as I had just done. When the quality of love is fully present, as it must be to be Tantric, the chakras potentially open in a profound way and the bonding connection is deep. The bonding that takes place between the chakras happens to a lesser degree in ordinary sex, but it does happen, and it happened that night.

When I telephoned Paul the next day to check in, he sounded cheerful. "I didn't sleep much last night," he said, "but I didn't care. I still can't wipe this grin off my face."

Maria and I were two of his first clients in his new gym. There was an electric camaraderie when we worked out together, as Paul trained his two lovers who just happened to adore him. There is no faster way to get in shape, I discovered, than to fall in love with your trainer! And Paul was highly disciplined in the gym. There was no hanky-panky at all. I was on a fast track to lose all unnecessary body fat, pounds, and excess anything! My diet changed overnight from pastas to priorities. I had to get in shape or die. At my pivotal age of fifty-something, this opportunity to become the body I never had proved irresistible. Maria was already honed into shape from dance and swimming. I had all the inspiration I needed now to re-define myself from the inside out.

I didn't know if Paul would make a return visit without Maria. I both hoped and feared that, knowing that alone with Paul I would unleash all of my love. He assured me that he was considering my offer of being with me on sovereignty nights, with or without Maria's availability. I had never worked so hard to achieve what I wanted.

Paul knew this was more of a journey of the heart than the simple complexities of sex, and he had a lot of healing to do around his journey with love. After two weeks, he called to say he would like to join me again.

"Oh, good! I am delighted," I squealed. "However, Maria will be on the mainland. Are you willing to be alone with me?" I asked, holding my breath while waiting for his answer.

"Let me think about that, Caroline. I am a little afraid of being alone with a woman, especially you. You are married."

Did this mean he really *really* liked me? Was being afraid of me akin to loving me too much? My mind worked overtime while my heart came into full bloom. I would forget to call Charles as part of my daily routine. I was losing weight so fast we both hardly recognized the slimmer, stronger me. Being in love is the best diet pill I know, and being in love with my body-coach was extremely good medicine. Charles even joined the gym, inviting Paul to whip him into shape as well.

On the next sovereignty night, Paul came to the house, a little earlier this time. My inner dialogue all day had included what I would wear when he arrived at the door, but when I heard his truck pull into the gravel driveway, I was still unexpectedly in cut-off jean shorts and a tank top that held my lovely breasts like a kid glove, having been outside working for hours on the property. I excused myself for a quick shower while Paul purred and petted with Tai and Chi. Grabbing a colorful silk flowing sarong, I tied it island-style low on my hips while pouring my tanned body into a halter of iridescent hues. My closets were mostly filled with yoga and exercise tops, bathing suits, halters, camisoles, and sarongs, befitting an island monarch on a gentlewoman's estate.

We walked out to the grand lawn and sat on the wide expanse of cool green grass, gazing out to sea while the sun lowered in the sky behind us. We talked about the purpose and meaning of these excursions into sexual love and Tantra. He questioned my marriage with Charles and where that fit into the obvious energy between us. "All of this experience and love grows out of the sacredness of my marriage to Charles. We are lover and beloved, now and forevermore," I shared from a deep well of belief.

"I can't be 'just the two of us' with Charles. I can't even be that with you," I said. "The tantric assignment is to share you. And yet I long for simplicity. I long for no girlfriends, except for Kealani, and perhaps Maria occasionally to work and play with, I suppose. Just wait until you meet Kealani, Paul. She wants to love you, too."

We talked of how it felt for him to make love with Maria. His words stunned me. "I like her attention—she is a very beautiful woman, but I don't really need more than one woman. And I don't even know if I'll ever be ready for that. I'm not sure I'm up for your friend Kealani, Caroline. This is all so new for me."

I told him of my need for a strong male lover-friend in the midst of all the female energy of the lovers around me.

He sighed. "You don't have to live this way if it isn't true for you, Caroline."

I rested my head on his shoulder and we held hands, sitting quietly for some time.

"I can be your friend," Paul said. "I can be there for you."

"You're already doing so much," I said. "It feels like you're saving my life, Paul. Are you sure you want to do this?"

He nodded. "You've already given me back my heart and my sexuality. I didn't think anyone could get behind the walls around my heart."

It was at that moment, in the complexity of these emotions, that I made a wrong turn. Instead of realizing I simply wanted a life with Charles, my beloved and husband, who would choose only me, I latched onto the hope that it was Paul who would do this for me.

We walked back into the house and made out on the couch like teenagers. I hadn't felt this kind of youthfulness in too long. I hoped Maria would arrive and break the intensity of this intimacy and the attachment I already felt. And then I remembered Maria would not be arriving—she was with her kids on the mainland. I surrendered to passion and love that night in a new way. I wanted to be transformed. I wanted to emerge closer to the truth.

That weekend I told Kealani, "I've met someone. I've met someone I can deeply love, Kealani. Of course I will share him with you." I believed that wholeheartedly. She wasn't happy to hear I had feelings for someone new. Her eyes looked down, and her shoulders drooped as she pouted and struggled with the same jealousies I had about sharing, although she knew it wasn't healthy to want Charles and me for herself alone. I encouraged her to meet Paul and see for herself.

"I can't love anyone like I love you and Charles, my queen," she cried. There we were, neither of us really wanting what we were about to go ahead and do. I was in a love orbit with a man I wanted to be alone with, and the very next thing I did was offer to share him with Kealani.

Coincidentally, two women friends from Los Angeles were coming to spend a portion of the holidays with us, and Kealani would have to share Charles and me with them. Mare and Corinna were tantric and single, looking for healing, awakening, and expanded love with their tantra teachers. Kealani had her hands full now as she deepened into the abundance of what our lifestyle provided.

Originally, Charles had invited Mare and Corinna to stay in our home for three weeks that December. "Not on your life!" I had cried. "I cannot handle everyone here for the holidays!" Charles had to fly to his sister's in California the day after Christmas; I would be on my own with everyone until he returned December 31st. I suggested they stay on the Kihei side of the island and be near the beaches for the first two weeks, then stay with us closer to New Year's Eve. To please me, Charles made those arrangements.

That year, Robin was visiting her fiancée's family for the holidays. I was grateful not to have to tell her much about my holidays. Some things just can't be explained.

Mare and Corinna arrived on schedule and started their holiday in a Maui condo for two weeks. When Charles left after Christmas, I entertained them by inviting Paul over. This way, they could focus their healing attention on him without the distraction of Charles in the house. It was hard for me to share Paul with our two visitors, but I thought that encouraging his freedom was the best way to show him love, and even though he was shy with these women, he trusted me by allowing them to give him love and pleasure. With eyes wide open, it's pretty hard to avoid the awesome power of the Feminine offered by these skilled dakinis, trained by Charles and Caroline! He wept uncontrollably as we all held him, knowing that the miracle of love was healing this sweet man of his wounds of war.

It was harder for me with Kealani, who lifted her wings into more love with Paul. I tried to be present for it, but oh, how my gut clenched as I watched her make love with Paul in my bed one evening, while I sat alone in the big living room. My heart felt as heavy as stone as I praised Kealani for opening to more love while all I wanted to do was to lie in my own bed with Paul, containing my turmoil in the dark. Later, when they emerged, Paul came into the kitchen to say goodnight and I joined Kealani in walking him to the door. Afterward, I attempted to remain the tantric goddess of love while Kealani romped about in her pajamas telling me how fabulous Paul had felt to her. The effect on me was all too confusing. I was so glad I had an appointment to see my therapist, Christine, the next day.

Describing my life to Christine may have been entertaining to her—she lived quietly in Haiku—but I felt her compassion for my difficulties. From a very solid and grounded place, that morning she said, "You don't have to agree to live like this, Caroline. It really isn't working for you, is it?"

I didn't want to admit she was right. Driving back down the country roads to my temple by the sea, my addiction to excitement was reaching a head, especially with Paul acting as a buffer for my heart. Keeping myself dizzy in a state of in-love-ness spurred me to get through the holidays, which were a tsunami about to devour the well-meaning lovers of love.

Charles wanted his version of Tantra to prevail—for all to love each other, but I was not open to anyone besides Paul. Maria wanted to join in, too, but even she found it difficult to be one of three lovers all wanting to be with Charles. Jahlia may have come over for eggnog and song, but she was not interested in expanding with this many new people. Cos and his new beloved had their own friends visiting from Bali.

When Charles called from California where he was spending Christmas week with Mama and his sister, Rosemarie, we spoke on the phone daily about the tantric connections taking place among our visitors and lovers. It wasn't easy for him knowing that Paul was being sweetened by the candy canes of Shakti who waited to welcome him back on New Year's Eve. But when that day came, with great enthusiasm he heard my offer for him to be loved by Corinna, Mare, and Kealani. I had offered him a welcome home reward of lying in the back of my SUV while someone made love to him all the way home. I had thought it would be me in the back with him while one of the others drove. But as it turned out, none of the women felt familiar enough driving my car on the winding road home, so I drove while Charles rode in the back with Corinna and Mare. Their sparks of passion flew fast. When I glanced over my shoulder to check on traffic, my heart turned to stone. Corinna sat astride Charles and was about to insert his erection into her yoni. "Happy New Year, Charles," I said sarcastically through tightly gritting teeth. "Be loved, beloved." Every cell in my body snapped shut as I attempted "bigger love" one more time, my knuckles tense on the steering wheel of my white chariot. In that instant I did not remember all of the fun I had just had during the week Charles was in cold and rainy Monterey entertaining his mom and sister.

And once again, I held out an offer I couldn't stand behind. To say that either of us was wrong is to negate our human nature to want to please, especially the beloved. To say, however, that extending beyond one's own capacity is foolish would be an understatement.

Charles did not see or hear how troubled I was. He believed that everything was wonderful if there was enough love. After all, I had arranged all this with his help. The pleaser in me had hung myself in the misguided universal trap of women who love too much.

That night, the party began. Champagne for all, but not even our friend Mare would join us, as she had a date with my brother who now was separated from his wife. I just wanted Johnny to be loved out of his unhappiness, and so in deepest friendship Mare volunteered to make the night special for my brother in his home. Charles frolicked and played with the others upstairs, while I snuggled downstairs with Paul. Charles came down for a short visit now and then, yet I noticed how closed I felt to him. Holding on to Paul all night, we stayed up to watch sunrise at dawn from the outdoor hammock while the others slept in a peaceful pile upstairs. The New Year had begun.

Paul left early to be with family and friends, while Charles did what gave him and many men a perfect day of rest— he made himself comfortable on the couch in front of the football game while the women went to the beach to enjoy their last day on Maui. I disappeared into my cave, my bathroom, for some quiet. The purple orchids in their pots around the sunken tub waved gently in the tropical breeze.

And that's when I saw it: my jewelry box was open and all of the beautiful rings, pendants, and bracelets Charles had given me over the years of our romantic and gift-filled relationship were gone. Someone had entered our private domain and stolen my jewels, leaving only a few pieces of costume jewelry.

The bathroom was bordered on two sides by sliding glass doors, one side taking in the full view of the Pacific and the other side facing our palm-shaded backyard and hot tub. I lifted the lid of the lacquered jewelry box again to be sure this wasn't some kind of day-after-the-night-before illusion. A few chords of "As Time Goes By" tinkled out of the music box, sending a chill down my spine. I grabbed my emergency stash of clove cigarettes and ran from the house to my hideaway in the rows of panax and coconut palms. This place sheltered me from any activity in the house. I was alone enough to feel everything.

As I crouched upon the piles of composting palm fronds in my secret lair, trembling from the intensity of the theft and loss, I saw the metaphor in the curl of smoke that rose from my kretek. The gems were gone, the gems of this romance, this dream of Camelot, this life dedicated to more love. Squatting in the dried leaves for what seemed an eternity, staring at ants scouring the area for food, I lit cigarette after cigarette, inhaling the intensity of what I knew I had to do. Tell the truth. Simply allow what churned inside to come up and out. The truth was as bitter as the taste in my mouth.

Eventually I left the cool shade and returned to the bathroom to face the beat of my own heart. I forced myself to look in the tarnishing mirror at my morning-after-the-night-before face, now covered with the words I was ready to speak. I brushed my teeth and splashed cool water on my skin, patting it dry with a soft towel. I smoothed papaya cream into my skin for what seemed like an eternity, attempting to smooth out the new wrinkles of truth. In a stroke I smeared raspberry gloss on my lips, and scrunched my curls into place. I had suffered too long, by choice. I had created my own misery. It was up to me to change things. I took a deep breath and headed for the living room, where my beloved lay on the couch in front of the television. There it was, my own forty-yard line to cross.

"Charles," I said, loud enough to be heard over the television. "I need to talk."

"Can it wait until half-time, my queen?" His eyes were glued to the screen. "Lie down with me and watch the game." He scooted over to make room for me, looking up with love in his eyes.

I hated football. In that moment, I vowed to never hear a game in my house again. I wasn't going to lie down with him or even sit beside him for this. "Charles," I said, "I need to become unmarried. And I need you to move out of our home."

There was a moment of stunned silence. Then Charles propped himself up on an elbow. "Sweetheart, let's talk about this after we take our friends to the airport tomorrow. We'll be alone again and more refreshed."

I froze where I was standing. This was simply not the time *for him*. My jewels were gone. The beautiful gifts of his love were gone. As painful as that was, it was far more painful for my heart to finally open to the truth.

He went on. "You're just having a reaction to the long holiday season and too much company. It will be just the two of us again very soon."

I turned from him and walked back to my room. "The truth shall set you free," I told myself. "The truth shall set you free." I chanted that phrase for the rest of the day.

Chapter Twenty-One

A Sabbatical from Marriage

The new year started with our new arrangement—with modifications. Charles moved into the guest room upstairs. With his bedroom upstairs, we both could get used to the idea things were changing before we did anything radical. I could live with his other sexual relationships as long as they were not in my bed, and I could still practice Tantra with him, as we believed this was essential to our work and teaching and we wanted to keep a strong bond. I didn't see why we should end the deep sharing of our love just because we ended the group sharings, the sexual healings, and anything to do with expanded sexual loving. We were trying on a new paradigm for loving, and we needed to keep the love cups filled and the doors to intimacy open.

I'm not saying it was easy. We cried together many times, when the seriousness of my decision hit us. Our marriage was at the center of the life we had created together. To thousands of people, we were the ideal of a tantric marriage, living expanded loving and remaining each other's beloved. They needed us to succeed. Our Tantra students seemed invested in our staying together like children are in seeing their parents' marriages work; we were a family. Could the study of conscious loving promise that their passion and happiness would endure in their lives as well? I saw the hope in their eyes during those five-minute standing ovations, seminar after seminar. "Will Tantra give us the glow of love it gives the Muirs?" "Yes," we told them, "if you practice."

Few knew about the expanded nature of our marriage (we only spoke of it if we were asked, to preserve our private, personal lives). Most people assumed we lived a monogamous lifestyle. Most people need to believe that monogamy—the prevailing paradigm—is what makes successful relationship and marriage possible. When asked, we would tell students that as teachers of Tantra we felt it was our responsibility to explore human sexuality within the belovedness of our relationship and marriage. It was not the smoothest or easiest path for harmony—in fact, it would bring up everything that needed healing to the surface. We never recommended non-monogamy, but we did tell our students that if they were clear they were not cut out for monogamy, Tantra could be a beautiful guide for the practices of loving multiple partners and being more conscious about sharing love, both sexually and spiritually, whether single or in a couple. Tantra is a path with heart. Most couples didn't want to sign up for that much emotional work. They were not given the assignment that we felt we had been given—to explore the possibilities on the edge of expanded intimacy.

How could we explain to these students that our lives were changing? We didn't want to disappoint them as we managed our own disappointment and heartbreak. Finally, the words came to us: we were taking a sabbatical from marriage. Calling it a sabbatical let us live more comfortably with our choice as we led seminars that February and March, saying little about our personal chaos and giving people a transformative week. As time went on, though, it got harder to conceal our grief as we sat in front of students teaching about love. Our ship was sinking, and we didn't know yet that we would preserve the essence of our love in a lifeboat that would never go down.

When I told Charles it was time to end our marriage, I had expected everything to be easier. I was sure Paul would be my lover, but Paul ended our sexual relationship. Charles and I were too visible for his comfort, and the island grapevine was too ready to gossip the spirit right out of anything we had together. He reminded me that he had only committed to being part of my tantric life through the holidays, and they were past. On top of all this, he had started a relationship with a woman I knew on the island and he wanted to devote himself to what was developing with her. I would have to settle for friendship and appreciate him for being the catalyst that had made the castle walls shake so hard they came down.

I felt devastated. I didn't want a new lover. I wanted to heal from the heartaches of the past few months (or however long, I couldn't tell). Some days I wanted to live alone—I felt ready for it, even craved it. Other days, I was glad Charles was upstairs, his voice in the background so familiar, talking on the phone, making plans, laughing. One day he asked if Kealani could spend the weekend with him. My wires crossed, and sparks flew. "No!" I shouted. "I don't want anyone in my house!"

"She still loves you, my queen," Charles protested.

"I love her too, Charles. I just don't want anybody around me here. Take her somewhere, just go away and leave me alone!"

My commitment to honesty could only be as good as my awareness of my truth, and at that time, I wasn't fully aware. Because I wanted him to have what he wanted, I agreed to their staying upstairs. "I just don't want *company*," I said. "Go to the beach or something."

I was a ticking time bomb. As can happen when you say "yes" when your truth is "no," on another of Kealani's visits my rage caught on fire. It didn't matter that she was the luscious girl-woman I had once adored. In that moment she was every woman who had loved me and Charles, and I didn't want that love, those friendships or loverships, that pleasure, those girlfriends. I struck out at her, slapping and hitting in my mindless jealousy. I wanted to clear and release my pain, wanted her to hate me. I raged at having no lover myself and seeing Charles have his, raged at not knowing my needs and how to set and stick to my own boundaries, raged at having to end this marriage. My anger seemed boundless. Charles helped Kealani hold me back out of fear for her safety before I ran screaming from the room and raced downstairs.

In my bedroom with my door closed, I calmed down some. I had to be braver, that was all. I had to face my fear of being alone and find peace on my own. And Charles had to find his own place and move out, and soon.

In May, Charles moved into an apartment on a friend's property in the macadamia orchards beyond Wailuku town. Our separation was official. I sobbed my way through several days, my grief coming in great waves. And then I did what many women in my position do: I cleaned house as if my life depended on it. With my hair bound in a bandana like Singie used to wear, I scrubbed pantry shelves and patios, emptied closets of clothes I didn't wear any longer, drove bags and boxes to Goodwill. I erased all signs of a life that had been unclear about its boundaries—that had withstood years of emotional chaos riding the rollercoaster of big love. I scrubbed and rinsed away any evidence of the four months of tension, grief, confusion, and fear while we lived through the roar of the fall in separate bedrooms, visiting over meals in the kitchen and pouring our love into Tai and Chi, and with one tantric "connect" every week.

May and June were also party-planning months. Johnny's fiftieth birthday, we decided, would also be my "coming out" party. My grief would go on hold so I could set the coconut wireless straight: I had not left Charles for someone else (Paul, Johnny's brother-in-law), and all was right with the family.

And what a celebration it was. Tables draped in white silk snaked through the living and dining rooms. The tables were lit with tall white candles and dressed up with vases of Peruvian roses. I wore a silvery silk dress that hugged my lean and muscular form, proof that my hours in the gym were paying off. Women wore sheer island-style gowns or colorful sarongs, men wore Aloha shirts with pants or shorts. Shoes are always left outside the entry to homes, and this night was no exception. My front walkway was covered with flip-flops of every description, flanked on either side by the lily pond and hundreds of leap frogs for entertainment. This was Hawaii, after all! Jahlia flew in from Australia to be Mistress of Ceremonies, and she played guitar and electric piano throughout the evening, resplendent in a sparkling beaded sheath dress. Three African drummers and an African dancer performed, and people toasted Johnny on his landmark birthday. I had felt proud to be part of my Maui family and proud to be Johnny's sister. At times I wished that Charles could see what Johnny and I had created, but I knew it was time for me to be just me, not a wife seeking my beloved's approval. Transformation into a more authentic queen was underway.

The summer passed, with silence filling every corner of the house we had built, and I loved every square inch of that silence. I was starved for it. I couldn't get enough of being with just me, free of commitments and all of my magnificent and demanding duties of home and career. Tai and Chi cuddled me to sleep nearly every night in front of a movie, and I would wake and fumble for the remote in the blue TV screen light, then make my way in the dark to my bedroom. I learned how to enjoy a king-sized bed on my own, how to buy groceries for one, how to make a single portion of Eggplant Parmesan, strange as it felt sometimes to make his Mama's sauce or bake spinach pie without Charles there to boil the raviolis or brush butter on the leaves of phyllo dough. Sometimes I'd feed Larry, the handyman, my only other companion on the property besides the noisy, squawking parrots in the ironwood trees and my two purring kitties.

Oh, there were down times, when I couldn't sleep at night or it was hard to greet the day with joy in my heart, as I had done on thousands of mornings with Charles. Sometimes I had to listen extra hard to the guidance I knew would lead me out: *It is time to be unmarried. It is time to be alone.* I had to chant the words like a mantra, remember to believe in them.

Larry was a help—three acres was a lot to care for on top of the three thousand square feet of home to maintain. But things began to change with him, too. I started to notice cases of beer stacked in his rusty pickup as he passed by on his way to the lower property. He had too much time on his hands out there in his dome, and pot and alcohol were catching up with him. Some days I would walk down to his place, the cats at my heels, to find him sleeping in the filthy front seat of his truck before noon, with half a case of warm beer to go and the burned-out butt of a hand-rolled American Spirit organic cigarette in his hand. An architectural disaster was piling up in the back of his mini-pickup. I knew I should let him go, but I didn't want more changes right now. And I needed the help. That tropical jungle would erase all traces of the house within a year if it wasn't cut back on a regular basis. Things go wrong with pumps, valves, and meters, too, in the relentless wind, rain, sun, and salty air, and the water level had to stay up in the 21,000-gallon water tank. Water in the catchment tank came from rainwater and from a hundred-foot-deep well. Larry helped with all of this, and there were those days when the palms were trimmed, the lawn was mowed, and the trash was hauled to the dump before he came to collect his check. I would keep him around a while longer if only to see that familiar missing-toothed smile at the end of the rainbow, when I knew I'd survived.

As delicious as the silence was, I needed a friend nearby, and I could use the income, too, from renting the upstairs room. Patti, a woman I knew from Mill Valley, was getting divorced and moving to Maui, and I offered her the upstairs room for six months or longer. She was thrilled. Patti's artistic touch transformed the house. Every change she made helped chase away another memory of the nights spent there with my beloved, wrapped in each other's arms as we watched movies accompanied by coconut ice cream with hot fudge sundaes, bottles of lube, candles, and a stack of fresh towels (for catching all that amrita). She draped the frame of her canopy bed with romantic veils, filled her bedroom with inexpensive treasures she found in secondhand shops or consignment stores, and draped filmy sheers over the windows and sliding glass doors downstairs, adding a sense of mystery to the evenings and a softness to the sunny days. With time, after ten years of being too busy, and a friend to help me decorate my beautiful home, I was inspired to paint and decorate. I bought real furniture for the first time—Cos's down couch and overstuffed chairs, two hand-painted commodes, and a blue lacquered pedestal table with six chairs from a gallery in Lahaina. Home was humming a new tune.

Cos and Blue had separated soon after Charles and I had, with Blue moving to her property in Kipahulu and Cos staying in the house they'd built together. He was sad for a while until he found a new love right in the neighborhood, a Comet of energy who dazzled us all. This intelligent, beautiful woman quickly became a dear friend to me. Many evenings, we sat together on my lanai with bottles of water and glasses of wine, a pack of Indonesian kreteks, pipe, and *Da kine* (Hawaiian for pot), and we "talked story." Cos and Blue maintained a relationship of lasting love and mutual respect, and Blue and Comet became good friends, proving to be the conscious beings we believed we all were—Cos, Blue, Charles, and myself—as we added his new lover to the family.

At last, life on my own was feeling as I had hoped it would. New friendships filled my heart yet left me lots of room for myself. When I wasn't traveling to teach with Charles, I might spend a long day working in the garden or clearing water lilies from the pond, cutting bouquets for the house, washing the endless windows, and taking care of other jobs my magnificent temple required. I was deeply nourished by an hour of yoga before dancing to Gabrielle Roth's five rhythms, finding release and joy in the chaotic, lyrical, and rhythmic movements. After dancing myself into an orgiastic release, I would lie sweating and spent on the floor of my living room, allowing and inviting the music to work their magic on my cells, my thoughts, and my life force. The huge abundance of energy I possessed was, in essence, my Shakti. And my unleashed Shakti was limitless. I had taught this in Tantra classes for years, and now, surrounded by this limitless life-force in the natural world that surrounded me in the wilds of tropical paradise, more than ever I discovered the many facets of Shakti (sexual/spiritual energy). Physical exertion and absolute stillness were my therapies when I couldn't seem to keep it all in balance or needed nurturance and self-healing.

Patti shared my commitment to exercise, and, with Paul's help, we turned the dining room into a gym and huffed and puffed around the circuit of leg presses and weight benches. Every day we talked over morning toast and coffee on the breezy lanai, and we met there again at the end of the day with a bottle of Merlot. As the frogs awoke and started their evening song, I noticed how much more I appreciated the life I had created here on Maui. What a brilliant move it had been to choose Hawaii and risk it all for love. I was discovering the beauty of life without the distracting, deliciously loving presence of a beloved and lovers. I was falling (or rising) into love with myself at last. I stopped the frenetic pace and took time to feed the goldfish in my lily pond, to walk the perimeter of the property, and to gaze at the horizon, a marker for sanity between heaven and earth. I tuned into my own rhythm, spoke gratitudes every day for everything just the way it was, and met my brother for dinner every week or so, upcountry or at his spacious, lovely home in lower Kula. We wined and dined alone or with friends he invited, as he helped me emerge into my new life as a solo queen. Johnny collected beautiful and unusual art and filled his home with sculptures and paintings by local artists. I loved sinking into his downy couch, graciously accepting gourmet treats served on hand-blown glass.

But bliss like this can't go on forever, and for me, it ended the day Singie called, out of the blue, after seven years. "Darling!" I cried. "How are you!?"

Singie wasn't the type for warnings like "I have some bad news to tell you." She simply said, "I'm dying." Singie had ovarian cancer, and it had spread throughout her body. Her birthday was coming, but she wasn't going to see forty-five. "I would love to visit your house again, Queenie," she whispered.

In minutes I was out the door and driving the short distance to Singie's house in Haiku. There she stood, out front amidst the banana and papaya trees, waiting for me, looking so frail, so small. I jumped out of the car and took her into my arms. It seemed like not even a day had passed since I'd held her.

"Can you believe how skinny I am?" she laughed.

I just held her tighter.

I had always thought that one day Singie and I would have more time together. Was it true my angel of music was really leaving this world?

Singie climbed into the car and I drove to my house, where we sat on the sofa talking for as long as her energy lasted. She spoke of her grief about being unmet in the spirituality of her sexuality for so long. "I think that's what gave me cancer," she said. That, and being separated from her children for so long. I told her about Charles moving out, and about Paul, and Patti. "Everything changes, doesn't it," she shrugged.

Singie was tired; she wanted to stay the night. "Take my bed," I told her, leading her to the place where she had received so much love and healing from me and Charles years before. This was also where she had made love for the first time with the man she married, when she was house-sitting for us. I helped her into bed and made her comfortable, then sat for a long time on the living room couch, too numb to cry, too awake to sleep.

In the morning, Singie and I decided it would be best for her to stay here, where she could receive regular care by her loving friends. Jahlia might be convinced to come again from Australia and stay as long as she was needed, and we both would do everything we could to help. Singie's husband gave his blessing over the phone. He would visit a few evenings every week, and he would bring her children to visit as soon as he could get them to come over from the mainland. When Singie was first diagnosed, she had begged her ex-husband to let her see her children again, and he had finally agreed to send them to her in Maui for a visit. Her son was eleven and her daughter eighteen. It was a painful yet joyful reunion, she said. I couldn't wait to meet them.

Life in the house was very different now. The sense of approaching death lingered heavily throughout the house, and the ocean calmed with its rhythmic constancy at the same time its beauty almost hurt. No one liked seeing Singie navigate her occasional trips to the kitchen, but it was important she get out of bed and walk while she could. Patti stayed more and more often with her boyfriend or stayed upstairs in her room. There were no more evenings sipping Merlot on the lanai together. I hoped she understood I had to drop everything for this chance to take care of my friend.

Jahlia returned from Australia several weeks later to be near her dear friend and to help me attend to Singie's constant needs. She loved the temple into vacuumed carpets and crystal clear windows, and she sang whenever she could. One day, when Jahlia began singing a song they had written, Singie cried out, "No singing! Please. No singing." Jahlia and I looked at each other, feeling the great weight of this. Singie was dying. It was one of the saddest moments of my life. I will also always remember the day I noticed Singie's star ruby and diamond ring in a small bowl on the nightstand. Her fingers had become too thin for her rings. How many times had I watched the sparkling light of that ruby dance on the wood of her twelve-string guitar? I sat down beside her. "May I wear your ring for a while?" I asked softly, taking her hand.

Her eyes rested on the ring in the bowl beside her, and then she nodded. "I bought that ring in India." And then she seemed to drift away, to fifteen years earlier, when she was vital and in love with life. There was so much ahead! I saw it, too, and I couldn't hold back my tears. "Wear it, Queenie," she said. "Never take it off or you'll lose it. And when you are done with it, give the ring to my daughter." Over the next weeks I saw

Singie catch a glimpse of her flashing ring as I fussed about her, adjusting bedcovers, plumping pillows, handing her the cup of ice to wet her parched lips. I wear the ring to this day.

Two months and an eternity after Singie made that phone call to me, this dazzling, shit-kickin' angel gasped her last breath, her eyes wide open, her lips forming a perfect "O" in a look of wonder, as if at any moment a song might fly from them. Jahlia held her, singing her softly into the light, guiding her home to Spirit.

Singie's passing was the most glorious, otherworldly event of my already eventful life. It seemed she had given me the priceless gift of witnessing the rising of her soul in return for my offering her the sanctuary of my home for her passage into death. I thought I was numb inside, but actually I was simply more translucent as well as transformed by this sacred pact. We had shared an ultimate moment.

Singie lay in state for the next three days, in my bed surrounded by hundreds of fragrant gardenias and loved ones who came to kneel at her side in tearful farewell. After her cremation, several of her family and close friends chartered a fishing boat to fulfill her desire to spread her ashes at sea. And it was there out on the water that another extraordinary event occurred. I was offered the privilege of smoking some of Singie's ashes. I hesitated at first when the pipe was passed to me. Inhale her into my being? I had gone to the outer limits of my sexual passion with her. I had tasted her amrita in powerful gushes of Pele's fire. She had slept in my bed for the last two months, cancer devouring her insides, while we gave her enemas, cleaned up her vomit, fed her popsicles, wiped her nose, brushed her teeth, painted her toenails. Could I do it? Damn right I could! We were already bonded forever in spirit. This was a way of joining with her cell to cell. Singie's daughter and Jahlia were by my side, tears running down our cheeks as we shared this moment, Singie's recorded music soaring over the boat's sound system. When we were finished with the pipe, we each took a handful of the ashes and let them fly in the wind, watching these remains of life glitter like diamonds as they touched the surface of the deep blue and disappeared into it.

I am forever grateful to the fierce, fabulous, spirited woman who showed me great Shakti and timeless love. I loved feeling her around the house as I vacuumed, swept, and swore, as she had done, at the effort it took to keep the temple free of dust, salt film, cockroach shells, and salamander parts. I see her in the ruby glow on my finger whether or not the sun is shining, and when Singie's daughter comes to visit now and then, I notice her star ruby pendant, and we smile in recognition of the woman we both loved.

After Singie died, Jahlia returned to her mother's home outside Sydney and darkness settled into my heart. The silence I had grown to like so much left me lonely. I felt adrift in my Hale Makani, or "house of the wind," with no one needing me, with no definition of me (a lover, a healer, a friend) from anyone else. So many dear to me had gone. Some days the breeze that blew through seemed like so many bones rattling. Susea, a beloved friend and the silk artist who had made Charles' and my wedding clothes, died of cancer not long after Singie. Charles was gone and living on his own, and now Patti was moving out to start another chapter of her life.

"I guess living with me wasn't exactly what you signed up for," I said, when she announced she was leaving to move in with her boyfriend.

"It's been hard here, Queenie," she said. "It's not your fault."

I was truly alone at last.

Dusk has always been hard for me. Growing up, dusk was when my dad would come home from work, and I was on guard. Later, he might slip into my bedroom and climb into my bed. My body had always remembered the tension from that, even during the years I didn't know why that fear was there. All that could calm me at dusk was lying in Charles' arms. Now, to calm myself, I smoked. It was a shameful habit. I never smoked in public and I took great care to wash the smell from my lips and hands and hair. But for now, I smoked those Indonesian clove kreteks that so reminded me of the air in Bali, drank red wine, and filled my empty evenings with rented movies, trying to integrate all that had happened in the last few months. What had seemed before like silence now seemed noisy, from the croak of the bullfrogs to the screech of the parrots and the incessant wind, blowing the huge palm leaves into a frenzy of clacking company. I often slept wearing earplugs to dull the sounds of the night.

One evening, as I sat on the lanai smoking and staring into the jungle, I heard Singie's voice as clearly as if she were standing right behind me. "Stop smoking, Queenie," she said. Singie?! I turned and looked behind me, then inhaled again, cautiously this time, and blew out the smoke. *"Stop smoking, Queenie,"* I heard her say again. That night, I drowned my pack of kreteks, although I would drown many more before I finally quit. Still, Singie's loving command would stay with me until I finally succeeded.

As summer turned to fall, Charles' constant love helped soften the edges of the new life I'd chosen. I visited him once a week in his sweet jungle dwelling at the other end of Maui for a fix of his love. After all, I believe in the healing power of pleasure, and Charles was still my beloved. He knew my body as no one ever had. My heartbeat would quicken as I drove to his place for our date night, sometimes with Tai and Chi along for a visit to "Dad." The moment I walked through the door was always a wake-up, when reality would rush me. I had a sixth sense for knowing when a woman's Shakti was in the air, and I would remember why I had asked to live apart. Still, in some ways our love seemed even more alive since I had chosen to live alone and have the freedom to love *my* way. We would sit on his screened-in veranda, catching up on closeness and talking about living alone and what we were coming to love about it, and we would have dinner together, or before-dinner yoga. He seemed to be making similar adjustments as he grieved the loss of all that was familiar and foundational for him and drank in the essence of all that had been so real, glimpsing moments of this new reality as sacred for us both.

These intimate evenings were very different from our time together teaching seminars, when we traveled together, meeting at the Maui airport to fly to the mainland. We had traveled so often over the years that we knew all the baggage handlers. And there we were, the Muirs, looking radiant as always and more in love than ever. No one could have guessed how much sadness was packed into those suitcases as our sabbatical from marriage played itself out. We shared hotel rooms, meals, and hot baths, and we rose into our highest purpose in teaching Tantra as we somersaulted through our inner chaos, uncovering layer after layer of personal truths.

"It could be worse, my queen," Charles would say, gazing into my eyes with love when I felt low. And I could pull him out, too, when his hurts surfaced. We seemed to have infinite patience to hang in there with each other, and no interest in changing the way we were living out this sabbatical from marriage. Tantra gave us the foundation for keeping our love alive, and so did our friendship. All I needed and prayed for was to feel whole in myself.

Chapter Twenty-Two

The Divine Feminine

The holidays were coming and the house felt big and empty. But all that and much more changed when Innana and Robert called. They were in Maui for business, married now, and living in Australia. I hadn't seen them in a year, and there was so much to talk about. "Come stay with me!" I said. "I have lots of room."

Innana and Robert were relationship counselors, teaching communication skills and helping people live in greater harmony. I knew Innana's work and I admired her beyond measure. Robert was still new to me, but I looked forward to getting to know him, sure he was as special as she in his own way. They had bought some land in Byron Bay and wanted to build their life there, but they hadn't been able to secure a work permit and didn't feel settled yet.

As our laughter rang through the house, I realized how much I missed Innana and how good it felt to be with them both. I felt grounded, at ease. As my therapist, Innana had seen me through some extremely challenging times. As my friend, she was the ultimate playmate, someone I could go anywhere with, do anything with, always ready for some special time with me. I had seen her try to integrate her sexual-spiritual awakening into a marriage that was no longer fulfilling and then face the inevitable end of it, to go on to marry Robert and create a new life with him. We both understood that once the beloved is clearly home in your heart, nothing can stand in the way of fulfilling that soul agreement. Hers was the voice of compassion I needed; she understood what a hard choice I had made in asking Charles to move out.

It takes great courage to pioneer change, and I knew it would take something radical if I wanted more with these two. One evening, I took the leap. On their way out, I blurted, "My upstairs room is for rent if you two decide to stay in Maui."

Innana glanced at Robert and then took my hand. "That's tempting, Queenie. But we're not ready."

Robert shook his head. "We have land in Australia."

"Just think about it," I said.

Two days later, Innana called. "We'll bring a check and move in next week, if that works for you."

Innana and Robert moved in upstairs and right away swept me into the bliss of their love, their joy and laughter filling the house. We explored being lovers, with Innana offering Robert to me with or without her presence, but I wasn't interested in expanded loving anymore. The emotional attachments I'd formed in the past had taken their toll on me, and I wanted simplicity now. How simple could life be if living expanded love with my best friend's husband and housemate? I would have to be crazy to think I could pull that off! Besides, I needed to redirect my Shakti for my highest good and keep the faith that I would find out what that was.

But I am flirtatious—it's who I am. I flirt with life and with everyone in it. With these two friends I felt free to live "in-love-ness," or, as we called it, "belovedness," purring through the days and nights enjoying sensual play while honoring my need for boundaries. They knew how to have clear communication about how far we could play and keep the air between us juicy without the emotional complication of sex, and it worked for us all as we settled into our home together, each sharing equally in the caretaking of my home and property. Robert was busy overseeing the gardeners and the enormous job of cutting, trimming, hauling, and manicuring this gentlewoman's estate, and the tenderness he gave every flower and fruit-bearing tree was an act of love, another way this beautiful man could love me as perfectly as he loved Innana.

With Innana and Robert, I became calmer. I had inherited that hot Irish temper, and they knew how to deal with it, never taking it personally when I had an outburst, and I had them. They were infinitely patient and loving, hearing me out, showing me I was cared for. Their emotional wholeness helped calm the frightened, still raging child inside me—and helped her integrate with the woman I had become. My "tantrums" had been hard for Charles. They shook up his usual calm. I began to feel more compassion for him and what he had endured during my flip-flopping between believing with him in "the beloved truth" and wanting him to be monogamous with me. Now that I had finally realized the integral nature of monogamy to me—that overwhelming need to be the *one*—I began to understand that Charles and I had come to have vastly different understandings of married life and sexual commitment. I could no longer bend myself into what he needed, sexually and spiritually. But I could still love him.

Innana and I started each day in the kitchen in a hovering embrace, waiting for the tea kettle to boil so we could pour the family pot of Yerba Mate. After tea, we took a vigorous four-mile walk while Robert enjoyed a quiet morning at his pace. He would often have breakfast ready on our return—steaming plates of fluffy pancakes and tropical fruit compote, bowls of cereal—and we'd sit at the kitchen island, the heart of the home, sharing highlights from our morning talks with him. Many evenings, we sat together in my living room, loving friendship filling our hands with the desire to rub each other's feet or caress the soft beauty of one another like kittens nestled in the soft belly of the mother cat. We talked about things that were important to us, connecting the deeper parts of who we are in a weaving of strength and support. We were continuing life as it was meant to be in this home built for loving, nurturing, healing, and renewal, sharing a deep passion to give back some of the blessings we enjoyed.

Inspired, I quit smoking once and for all, went on a cleanse, and renewed my commitment to daily meditation and yoga. Feeling like a proud mom, I watched my dream evolve into its new incarnation as the whole place raised its pretty little head and began to glow. It had become time for Larry to move on, and over a few months Robert helped him pack up and go. I sold Robert and Innana the property where Larry had lived, and they began plans to build their own home and temple on this magnificent piece of paradise, where they would move after giving me the gift of their presence for a full seven years.

Long ago, after sailing the dark waters between England and Spain, I had raised the sails and trusted love to be my guiding wind. Now I had another assignment. I had to untie the knots and ease the strain that had formed in my years of marriage to Charles. Who better than Maui's premier relationship counselors—Innana and Robert—to be our guides? They had the skills to help us live in truth, which is what we wanted. Willing to try anything that might clear our confusion, Charles agreed to the sessions.

My tension was palpable before each therapeutic session. I felt intensely wound up, tight in my belly, my jaw locked yet trembling with rage, confusion, grief, and love as big as it was the day we discovered the beloved truth sixteen years ago. I felt the chaos of righteousness and disappointment, blame and forgiveness, anger and adoration. Even Tai and Chi were skittish as Charles drove up the gravel driveway.

Innana and Robert created sacred space in my living room under the cedar planks of the high pyramid ceiling in the center of the room, a candle or a single flower at the center of our circle. We sat on the plush carpet, our backs supported by couches and chairs that seemed too formal for such intimate work, a bottle of water at each of our sides.

To begin, we sat in silence, holding hands and centering by breathing together consciously. After this, we would each offer a prayer or affirmation for the session, one of us always calling in the presence of Divine Spirit (God/Goddess/All That Is) as we asked for Charles and Caroline to be assisted into deeper clarity as to how their marriage would unfold. What were the needs and feelings that lurked beneath the surface? After the words, "Thy will be done. Thank you, God," we opened our eyes, glancing around to meet each other's gaze, as difficult as that seemed at times.

Innana or Robert led us then into active listening (reflecting back to the other what we heard them say) and periods of emoting and expressing.

They steered us away from blame, accusation, name-calling, and judgment, skillfully keeping us on task with our intention to maintain the foundation of our marriage, work, and teachings while having compassion for our fragile hearts. Charles was close with Innana, but he didn't know Robert very well, and I thought it a heroic leap of faith by him to be led into the therapeutic realm by the man who now lived in "his" house. Charles tried to maintain his center while he spoke of his disappointment, hurt, confusion, and anger. He had never expected his Tantra goddess to evolve into a woman who could not live with the enormity of his love and passion, who wanted to keep that big love all to herself, to be his only beloved. He rocked forward and back as he sat cross-legged, filled with emotion he would release freely later, when he was alone in his car driving back to his private domain in the jungle. Once home, he would call me with outpourings of love and gratitude for my willingness to go through this struggle to know our own truths. It was no longer "the beloved truth"—we each had come to our own, separate truths. We stayed true to our marriage vows, striving to keep our belovedness intact, with an intimacy deeper than most friendships.

I had to admit that in my truth I was coming full circle, back to the joy in monogamy that had been my first experience of sexual love. The young secretary who had felt so uncomfortable when Arnie ogled other women on the street, which was an accepted male behavior back in those prefeminist days, was still inside me somewhere. She still longed to be loved only for herself. But I also freely admitted that during those many tantric years, as I searched for my true self and happiness, Charles and our other lovers helped me heal the little girl who had been sexually abused by her father. Charles' fountain of belovedness cleansed me and healed me, leading me gently into the circle of universal acceptance of love, for which I would be (and continue to be) forever grateful.

Through the months of counseling with Innana and Robert, I kept my teaching commitments with Charles on the mainland and in Maui. I invited him to stay with me once, and as fraught with tension as that night was at times, it was also good to revisit the life we had created and loved, sleeping under the stars in our bed fit for a king and queen with Tai and Chi purring at our feet. We relaxed in the hot tub and shared the spacious bathroom, Charles smiling in the morning as he said a familiar, "Let's give 'em heaven, my queen," before we headed up the street to teach our students about tantric love. In the future, when Innana and Robert had moved to their own house, Charles would often stay upstairs in the extra room so we could have more autonomy, something we both needed to help untie the knots of our dependency on each other.

Eventually, destiny had its way with me again, and my "sabbatical from marriage" came to its natural end, as Charles had thought it would. It started with a phone call to Charles from one of his lovers, an Australian who was prohibited from returning to the States by the Department of Immigration.

"The only way she can get back into the country, my queen, is if someone marries her," Charles told me, crying on the phone.

"Do you love her enough to marry her?" I asked.

"Yes," he said. "I would marry her."

"Then I suppose it's time to file the divorce papers, my beloved." I had the clarity of one who knows the time has come.

His words about wanting to marry another woman were hard to hear, but I knew it needed to happen. We agreed that the marriage based on our early agreements was over. If we ever wanted to marry one another again, we could, but for now, this was best for us both. Our mediator/lawyer put our divorce papers through, and we settled peaceably on everything. Of course we had our sleepless nights, our raging moments, but those moments felt like failure at true love. That was unacceptable. As we had said years before: *We vow to cultivate harmony in our relationship, realizing that nothing is more important than this, not even being right.* "Happily even after" divorce became our motto, and what we told our students when we shared that we no longer lived together.

Four years after our divorce, romance came into my life again. Unexpectedly I fell in love with a man whose passions lay in the realm of ideas. This wasn't a tantric relationship. Will didn't practice Tantra and I didn't feel a need to with him. He lived in California and I was still in Maui, but the miles between us didn't matter. We inspired each other, shared values and interests—art, literature, music, history. We were monogamous because we both preferred simplicity and ease; we weren't engaged, as neither of us believed marriage would define or solidify what we already had. And the relationship we had led me finally to feel ready to sell my island paradise home and move in with him on the mainland, something I had never imagined I would do. For me, the impact of only sharing sexually with Will was immediate, catapulting us into a kind of depth I hadn't known in a long time. At last I had the intimacy of "just the two of us." There is something indefinable about this. I had thought it was merely cultural, the prevailing paradigm. But I could feel the bond between us deepening because we had no other sexual outlets. I *loved* this feeling. I felt whole and true and devoted and content. Even my teaching thrived, as I not only continued some tantric seminars with Charles but directed my teaching more toward the Divine Feminine, committed to teaching the core practice of sexual healing and awakening in a safe space, using the "Nurturing, Awakening, Healing" approach that I developed.

It is a tremendous privilege to teach about the mysteries of love. I channel its fire into every day and into everything I do. Love has been my teacher, my path to God. Love is ever changing. It can be beautiful, it can be painful. It is the rose with thorns, the water lilies growing in a cloudy pond, the flower growing from a crack in the rock. It is the chinks between the stepping stones, the stuff that holds the roof on. It is that unconditional acceptance between people, through thick and thin, in summer and winter, in sickness and health. It is the interconnectedness between my students and me, the reason they keep coming back for more.

I once had a fairy tale vision of love. Now I choose whom to love, how to love, and when to love. I even choose *not* to love if that is what feels right. This is authenticity, this is the art of loving, this is what I journeyed so long and far to find. May you find the right truth for you, and may your journey be blessed as mine is.